# Violence Against WOMEN

# Violence Against WOMEN

*by*

**Yudhishtar Kahol**

Reference Press

4831/24, Ansari Road
Darya Ganj
New Delhi - 110 002
Phone: 23260807
Fax: 23274173
E-mail: essess@del3.vsnl.net.in

First Published 2003

ISBN: 81-88583-16-2

**Price Rs.675/-**



Published by
**Reference Press**
4831/24,Ansari Road
Darya Ganj
New Delhi - 110 002
Phone: 23260807
Fax: 23274173
E-mail: essess@del3.vsnl.net.in

Printed in India by:
Printline, New Delhi.

# Contents

# Preface

Perhaps, from the very beginning of the world history women have been at the receiving end, cutting across the regional and political barriers. This orthodox section of our society possesses a mindset to accept all the atrocities against them with light hearts. The wrong perception among them is (especially in the Third World) that they are born to be subservient to men and their roles in society. They are confined to the child-bearing and rearing. It cannot be an exaggeration to state that in remote Indian villages, still superstitious and deadly rituals like sati are being observed in our society. Child marriage is still prevalent in many parts of rural India.

It would be sheer nonsense to believe that development and liberalization have brought the equality for women. Instead there has been a growing trend of violence against women more so with hunger and greed for material things. Progressive changes in personal life style, living standards, varied growth, caused by urbanisation and changes in social ethos contribute to violent attitudes and tendencies towards women, which have resulted in an increase in crimes against women. In order to enable the Indian women to attain their rightful share and live in dignity, freedom, peace and be free from crimes and aspersions, the containment of such incidences is necessary through the existing rule of law. The war against the crimes against women should be waged by various sections of society through campaigns and programmes with social support cemented with legal protection, safeguards and reforms in the criminal justice system. All these safeguards apart, Indian women continue to suffer because of unawareness of their rights, illiteracy and oppressive practices and customs, prevalent in society.

Wife abuse is perhaps the most prevalent form of the atrocities in family life. It was during the mid-seventies that social scientists in the West started conducting studies to find out the nature and the extent of violence against wives, while trying to identify the precipitating factors, which led to violent relationship between the marital partners.

The most common form of harassment of a woman in her in-laws' family, unfolds in the form of taunts, abuses and threats, which generally escalate into battering, even abetment to suicide or murder in some cases.

Today, in our society, women are vulnerable to all sorts of exploitation, molestation, violence and even fatal assaults. Of course law is there to protect them, but in most of the cases, they do not approach for a legal support at all.

This modest work is an attempt in opposition of evil forces at work against the better half of our social fabric. If this book succeeds in creating an effective awareness, among those who matter in our system and setup, then the undersigned would feel honoured as an achiever.

**Author**

# One

# Introduction

There has been a growing trend towards violence against women, more so with development and liberalization and the hunger and greed for material things. The global campaign for elimination of violence against women in the recent years indicates the enormity as well as the seriousness of the atrocities committed against women that are being witnessed the world over. Development along with its progressive changes in personal lifestyle, living standards, varied economic growth caused by urbanisation and changes in social ethos contribute to a violent attitude and tendencies towards women which resulted in an increase in crimes against women. The containment of such incidents is a necessity so that the Indian women attain their rightful share and live in dignity, freedom, peace and free from crimes and aspersions. The battle against crime against women has to be waged by the various sections of society through campaigns and various programmes with social support alongwith legal protection, safeguards and reforms in the Criminal Justice System. In spite of all these safeguards, the women in our country continue to suffer due to unawareness of their rights, illiteracy and oppressive practices and customs. The resultant consequences are many viz. a constant fall in the sex ratio, high infant mortality rate, low literacy rate, high dropout rate of girls from education, low wage rates, etc.

The State has enacted various legislative measures to uphold the Constitutional mandate. This intended to ensure equal rights, to counter social discrimination and various forms of violence and atrocities and to provide support services especially to the working women.

## Legal Classification of Crime

Women may be victims of any crime such as murder, robbery, cheating, etc. which are not specifically directed at them, there are crimes identified which are designated as Crime Against Women which are directed specifically against them.

***I. The Crimes Identified under the Indian Penal Code (IPC)***

(i) Rape (Sec. 376 IPC)

(ii) Kidnapping and abduction for different purposes (Sec. 363-373 IPC)

(iii) Homicide for Dowry, Dowry deaths or their attempts (Sec. 302/304-B IPC)

(iv) Torture, both mental and physical (Sec. 498-A IPC)

(v) Molestation (Sec. 354 IPC)

(vi) Sexual Harassment (Eve-Teasing) (Sec. 509 IPC).

(vii) Importation of girls (upto 21 years of age) (Sec. 366-B IPC).

***II. The Crimes Identified under the Special Laws (SLL)***

Although all laws are not gender specific, the provisions of law affecting women significantly have been reviewed periodically and amendments carried out to keep pace with the emerging requirements. Some acts which have special provisions to safeguard women and their interests are:

(i) The Employees State Insurance Act, 1948

(ii) The Plantation Labour Act, 1951

(iii) The Family Courts Act, 1954

(iv) The Special Marriage Act, 1954

(v) The Hindu Marriage Act, 1955

(vi) The Hindu Succession Act, 1956

(vii) Immoral Traffic (Prevention) Act, 1956

(viii) The Maternity Benefit Act, 1961 (Amended in 1995)

(ix) Dowry Prohibition Act, 1961

(x) The Medical Termination of Pregnancy Act, 1971

(xi) The Contract Labour (Regulation and Abolition) Act, 1976

(xii) The Equal Remuneration Act, 1976

(xiii) The Child Marriage Restraint (Amendment) Act, 1979

(xiv) The Criminal Law (Amendment) Act, 1983

(xv) The Factories (Amendment) Act, 1986

(xvi) Indecent Representation of Women (Prohibition) Act, 1986

(xvii) Commission of Sati (Prevention) Act, 1987.

**Incidence of Crimes Against Women — All India (1996-1998)**

The Crime head-wise incidence of reported crimes during 1996 to 1998 along with percentage variation is presented in Table. It is observed that Crimes Against Women in 1998 reported an increase of 8.3 per cent and 4.8 per cent over previous years, 1997 and 1996 respectively. In absolute numbers, an increase of 10,073 cases were reported at all-India level in 1998 over 1997.

**TABLE**

**INCIDENCE OF REPORTED CRIMES AND PERCENTAGE VARIATIONS (1996-1998)**

| *Sl. No.* | *Crime Head* | *Year* | | | *Percentage variation in 1998 over 1997* |
|---|---|---|---|---|---|
| | | *1996* | *1997* | *1998* | |
| 1. | Rape | 14846 | 15330 | 15031 | –2.0 |
| 2. | Kidnapping and Abduction | 14877 | 15617 | 16381 | 4.9 |
| 3. | Dowry Death | 5513 | 6006 | 6917 | 15.2 |
| 4. | Torture | 35246 | 36592 | 41318 | 12.9 |
| 5. | Molestation | 28939 | 30764 | 31046 | 0.9 |
| 6. | Sexual Harassment | 5671 | 5796 | 8123 | 40.1 |
| 7. | Importation of Girls | 182 | 78 | 146 | 87.2 |
| 8. | Sati Prevention Act | 0 | 1 | 0 | -100.0 |
| 9. | Immoral Traffic (P) Act | 7706 | 8323 | 8695 | 4.5 |
| 10. | Indecent Rep. of Women (P) Act | 96 | 73 | 192 | 163.0 |
| 11. | Dowry Prohibition Act | 2647 | 2685 | 3489 | 29.9 |
| | Total | 1,15,723 | 1,21,265 | 1,31,338 | 8.3 |

The proportion of IPC crimes committed against women towards total IPC crimes remained around 6.0 per cent during 1996-1998 as shown in Table.

**TABLE**

**PROPORTION OF CRIME AGAINST WOMEN (IPC) TOWARD TOTAL IPC CRIMES**

| *Sl. No.* | *Year* | *Total IPC Crime* | *Crime Against women (IPC cases)* | *Percentage to total IPC crime* |
|---|---|---|---|---|
| 1. | 1996 | 1709576 | 115723 | 6.8 |
| 2. | 1997 | 1719820 | 110183 | 6.4 |
| 3. | 1998 | 1779111 | 118962 | 6.7 |

The available data indicates an increasing trend during the last three years in all the IPC crime against women except 'Rape', 'Sati (Prevention) Act' and 'Importation of Girls' which reported a declining trend during this period. All crimes against women reported under Special and Local Laws also resulted increasing trends during last three years except 'Incedent Representation of Women (P) Act' which reported a declining trend.

**All India Crime Rate Statistics (States & UTs)**

*(Refer to Annexures 7.1 and 7.2 for Statistics under this head)*

All India Crime rate i.e. no. of crimes per lakh population for crimes against women reported to the police worked out to be 13.5 during 1998. However, when estimated with reference to female population this rate almost doubles to 28.1 per lakh female population. This rate of crime which does not appear alarming at first sight may be viewed with caution, as a sizable number of crimes against women go unreported due to social stigma attached to them.

Uttar Pradesh State reported highest incidence (13.3%) of these crimes followed by Madhya Pradesh (12.1%) and Maharashtra (10.9%). In contrast, Delhi, which accounted for only 1.9 per cent of total crimes and shared only 1.3% of the population in the country reported third highest rate of such crimes at 19.6 after Madhya Pradesh (20.5).

*Rape Cases*

Incidence of rape cases (15,031) reported a decline of 2 per cent during 1998 over 1997. Madhya Pradesh alone reported 22.3 per cent of total rape cases in the country. Delhi, which represented only 2.9 per cent cases reported fourth highest rate at 3.4 after Mizoram (9.3), Madhya Pradesh (4.3) and D & N Haveli (3.9).

*Rape Victims*

According to the following Table at national level there were 15,033 rape victims compared to 15,336 in the previous year representing a decrease of nearly 2 per cent. Of these 8,414 (56%) were in the age group of 16-30 years, 3,433 (22.8%) in the age group of 10-16 years and 626 (4.2%) of age 10 years and below. Similar to decrease (2%) in the number of rape victims over previous year, the child victims (below 10 years) of age also reported decrease of 18.7 per cent and the victims above 30 years of age reported an increase of 10.8 per cent, signifying decrease of incidents relating to rape of Children.

**TABLE**

**VICTIMS OF RAPE BY AGE-GROUPS DURING 1996-1998 AND PERCENTAGE CHANGES DURING 1998 OVER 1997**

| *Sl. No.* | *Year* | *Below years* | *10-16 years* | *16-30 years* | *30 years & above* | *Total of all age-groups* |
|---|---|---|---|---|---|---|
| 1. | 1996 | 608 | 3475 | 8281 | 2485 | 14849 |
| 2. | 1997 | 770 | 3644 | 8612 | 2310 | 15336 |
| 3. | 1998 | 626 | 3433 | 8414 | 2560 | 15033 |
| 4. | Percentage change in 1998 over 1997 | –18.7 | 05.8 | –2.3 | 10.8 | –2.0 |

*Custodial Rapes*

During the year 1998 only four cases of custodial rape (one each from Andhra Pradesh, Gujarat, Maharashtra, and Uttar Pradesh) were reported in the country.

*Kidnapping and Abduction*

Incidence of kidnapping and abduction reported an increase of 4.9 per cent in 1998 over 1997. The States of Uttar Pradesh and Rajasthan each reported more than 15 per cent of these cases at national level while Delhi with share of 6.0% cases reported highest rate at 7.5.

*Dowry Deaths*

Incidence of dowry deaths reported to have a rise of 15.2 per cent over the previous year. 32.2 per cent of these cases at national level were reported by Uttar Pradesh alone followed by Bihar 15.0 per cent.

*Torture (Cruelty by Husband and Relatives)*

Incidence of torture cases in the country increased by 12.9 per cent in 1998 over the previous year. 18.7 per cent of these were reported by Maharashtra while the highest rate in the country at 9.5 reported from Rajasthan compared to 4.3 national average rate.

*Molestation*

Incidence of molestation in the country reported an increase of 0.9 per cent over the previous year. Nearly 23.5 per cent of total such cases were reported from Madhya Pradesh which was also significantly higher rate (9.4) than national average rate (3.2).

*Sexual Harassment (Eve-Teasing)*

The number of sexual harassment cases reported in the country significantly rose by 40.1 per cent over the previous year. More than half (59.7%) of these cases were reported from Andhra Pradesh, Uttar Pradesh and Tamil Nadu. Jammu & Kashmir reported the highest rate at 3.8 compared to 0.8, the national average rate.

*Importation of Girls*

A total of 146 such cases were registered in 1998 compared to 78 cases in the previous year, a sharp increase of 87.2 per cent over 1997. Gujarat, Madhya Pradesh and Haryana reported 57, 26 and 25 cases respectively.

**Crime Trends**

*Sati Prevention Act*

Though the practice of Sati is something unheard of in modern times, there have been few cases now and then. No such case from any of State/UT was reported in the country during 1998.

*Immoral Traffic (Prevention) Act*

Cases under this Act registered an increase of 4.5 per cent during 1998 as compared to 1997. More than half (68.3 %) cases were reported from the State of Tamil Nadu only. This should be construed as an indicator of improved policing efforts by Tamil Nadu police in this area.

*Indecent Representation of Women (Prohibition) Act (Torture)*

A remarkable increase of 163.0 per cent was noticed for cases under this Act as compared to cases reported in the previous year (1997). Nearly 45 per cent cases were collectively reported from Andhra Pradesh and Bihar put together.

*Dowry Prohibition Act cases*

These cases reported an increase of 29.9 per cent in 1998 as compared to 1997. Of these, a sizable proportion (42.6 %) were reported from Bihar.

*Disposal of Crimes Against Women cases*

The collection of detailed information on disposal of all the identified crimes committed against women has commenced from the year 1995. The comparative national level status of disposal of these cases by police and courts is presented in the succeeding paragraphs. However State/UT-wise details are presented in the main chapter on Disposal of crime cases.

*Disposal by Police*

During 1998, at national level, the disposal of IPC cases by police accounted for 76.5 per cent (including 0.4 per cent cases where investigation was refused). The crime-head-wise analysis of crimes against women cases revealed a fairly high disposal* percentage for 'Sexual Harassment' cases (92.2%), 'Molestation' (85.1%), and 'Cruelty by Husband & Relatives' cases (79.3%). On the other hand, while at national level 87.5 per cent cases reported under SLL were disposed of by police (including 0.6 per cent where investigation was refused), the quantum of cases disposed under 'Dowry Prohibition Act' was comparatively low at 75.4 per cent.

The position of cases charge-sheeted to total cases for investigation was quite satisfactory for all the crimes committed against women when compared to national average of 55.2% for total IPC crimes. Only in case of 'Kidnapping & Abduction of Women & Girls' the percentage was lower (35.9%) than the national average.

The percentage of charge-sheeted cases under SLL at national level stood at 84.4. Comparatively, the charge-sheet percentage in cases of Dowry Prohibition Act and Indecent Representation of Women (Prohibition) Act was lower than the national average being 62.4 per cent and 62.1 per cent respectively.

*Disposal by Courts*

As compared to 76.5 per cent disposal* by police in case of IPC crimes at national level and 87.5 per cent in case of SLL crimes, the disposal** of these cases by courts was reported to be very low at 19.0 per cent and 52.1 per cent respectively.

The disposal by courts of heinous crime cases such as 'Rape' and 'Kidnapping and Abduction of Women & Girls' was reported to be nearly17 per cent and 15.3 per cent respectively during 1998. At the end of the year 48,685 'Rape' cases, 39,103 'Kidnapping and Abduction' cases, 18,523 'Dowry Death' cases and 1,07,192 'Torture' cases were pending for trial in different courts of the country. Amongst SLL cases 42.9 per cent cases under 'Immoral Traffic (P) Act' remained pending for trial while pendency percentage was as high as 80.5 per cent and 86.1 per cent for cases registered under 'Dowry Prohibition Act' and 'Indecent Representation of Women (P) Act' respectively. The only case for trial under 'Sati Prevention Act' during 1998, resulted in acquittal. No case remained pending for trial at the end of the year.

*Note:* * Disposal of Police is taken as cases investigated by Police + cases where investigation was refused.

** Disposal by Courts is taken as cases tried + cases compounded & withdrawn.

# Two

# The Weaker Half

Women in India through the ages have been victimised, humiliated, tortured and exploited as long as history can tell. There have been incidents of murder, rape, abduction and torture from time immemorial. In spite of such a dark past, violence against has not been given much attention, more so, no attempt was made on the issue of why such a socially relevant theme has been left neglected and ignored.

Living in a country which is the world's largest democracy, a sovereign, socialist republic with a comprehensive charter of right written into its constitution, a signatory to most treaties for struggle against colonialism, imperialism and racism is a matter of great pride for all of us. However, underneath this impressive veneer and national pride about our three thousand-years-old civilization lies a history of systematic violation of basic civil, democratic, and human rights of large sections of our population, such as women. Ironically in a country where womenhood has been put on a pedestal for worship, incidents of wife battering, molestation of women in various forms like rape, eve-teasing, abduction and bride burning keep on increasing year after year. Women find no security be it home, where they are ill-treated by husbands and in-laws, or the streets and work place where they are vulnerable and fall prey antisocials, moneylenders and men-colleagues, bosses and are subjected to innumerable indignities, perhaps in higher frequency than in most of the civilized societies world over. The general perception today is that the crime against women has increased to such a great extent that women cannot move freely and participate in the community. There is no safe territory left for women not even in their "*mohallas*". Apart from being widely harassed but women are also being assaulted and raped before the eyes of their family members be— they single or married. Significantly, female victims of violence have not been given due attention in the literature on social problems or in that of criminal violence. Nor any attempt was made to explain why both the public and the scientific communities ignored for so long the varied instances where women were being greatly exploited in our society.

This attitude of constant indifference and negligence can be attributed to three factors: (1) a lack of awareness of the seriousness of the problem, (2) the general acceptance of man's superiority over woman because of which violent acts against women were not viewed as violent or deviant, and (3) the denial of violence by women themselves due to their religious values and social attitudes which leaves no recourse.

**The Girl Child**

Victimization of women in India starts from the time of their birth. Boys are preferred to girls. In most of the cases the birth of a girl child does not make happy even the parents of the child, not to speak about other members of the family. On the contrary, the birth of a son is enthusiastically celebrated with blessings showered on the couple by all the members of the family, friends and neighbours alike. If a woman accidentally gives birth to two or three daughters, she is made to hang her head in shame. She is subjected to abuses and all sort of ill-treatment specially by in-laws. Many women have committed suicide being fed up with torture by mother-in-laws and husbands for being unable to give birth to a son for the family.

There are innumerable instances where the parents leave the female babies at the door-steps of some orphanage or hospital or in parks and say goodbye to the child for ever. A couple from village Tatigharia under Bishungarh police station of Hazaribagh fled the hospital after throwing the baby in the bushes closer to the hospital compound wall. In the meantime a sweeper of the hospital found the baby while cleaning the campus. She brought the baby to her house and started looking after her. Later the police arrested the couple and released them only after executing a bond that both the husband and wife would look after the baby properly.

*Dowry Issue*

There are cases where the parents kill their young daughters because of their inability to fulfil the demands of dowry and sometimes young girls commit suicide due to their fathers' meagre income sources to fulfil the demands of dowry.

Leading newspapers of India almost daily publish as banner news, crimes against women in various manifestations, i.e., bride burning, rape, abduction, eve-teasing, wife battering both in rural and urban areas of India. This is a news item which is generally noticed, keenly read, and attracts our attention. The issue of crimes committed against women has been a topic of discussion in various forums of public opinion. Press reports reveal that crime against women has increased manifold. The problem of crime against women is not new. Women in Indian society have been victims of humiliation, torture and exploitation for as long as we have had written records of social organisation and family life. There are many records of episodes like rape, abduction, battering, and so forth of women.

Violence is present everywhere though the incidence of violence by men towards women is not identical in all groups and communities, the type, frequency, intensity and control of crime against women may vary from time to time, community to community, or place to place.

No woman who has escaped at one time or another the harassment, humiliation, exploitation and violence that shadows her sex. A woman's life swings between pleasure at one end and danger at other end. Daily women are being defined by sex and even if not all men are potential rapists, kidnappers, eve-teasers and wife batterers, all women are potential victims.

## Law and Social Legislations for Women

There have been scores of amendments and inclusion of various laws in the statute book to check the victimization of women. The Dowry Prohibition Act 1961 was amended twice to make its provisions more punitive. The Indian Penal Code, the Criminal Procedure Code and the Indian Evidence Act have also been amended simultaneously to deal effectively not only with dowry deaths but also cases of cruelty to married women. Similarly, the law against rape was also modified to remove some of its drawbacks. But all these changes cannot reduce the volume of the crime at all. One reason why crime against women continues to increase being that the laws are not deterrent enough. So, the culprits feel that they can easily get away with anything.

### *Their Implementation*

Women in India are way ahead of from women of elsewhere in the matter of social legislation. But the implementation of laws granting rights to women are inversely related being slow, lopsided and haphazard that socially, economically and politically women are kept far behind the men. Even today, many decades after independence, women are suffering from various kinds of discrimination, exploitation and torture, mental and physical in society and within the four walls of the family. In a male-dominated patriarchal society, women are protected by the family from other men, but may be unsafe in their own families.

Incidents may occur in the family, offices, agricultural fields, industries, and even public places for which women have to pay the price. Indian women thus can be described as the underdogs of a society where theoretically, the law of equality is supposed to practise and women are considered to be on a par with their male counterparts, but in practice the men remain powerful and thrive at the expense of the women.

The issue of crime against women has been graduated from a private issue to public issue. The large scale reporting on incidents of crime against women by the mass media has brought the ugliness of such crime right inside our homes and makes us realize that the existing efforts have been hardly able to create even a dent in the structure responsible for such crimes.

Lately, Indian women have started rising against their victimisation and there is a growing understanding of the pathetic condition of woman in our society. However, something substantial is yet to be done. Crime against women is one such problem that now offers a challenge. The problems faced by Indian women and specially the crime committed against them need to be realized and checkmated at the earliest, so that no more time may be lost before the situation deteriorates. This study is meant to contribute something concretely to this understanding.

Norms of behaviour exist in every society and any deviation attracts censure from those who are authorised to enforce these norms. Where the behaviour is intentional and harms another person or property, it amounts to punishable by law. There are numerous acts which have been declared offences under the various laws by the Central and State Governments from time to time which are applicable both to men and women. In this study we confine ourselves to a discussion of crimes against women.

**Crime against Women: Meaning**

The phrase "crime against women" refers to those the crimes involving violence against female. Defining the term in parts: (i) "Crime", (ii) "against women". The latter terms refers only to those crimes in which the victim is a female. The former term refers to those acts which are legally forbidden, intentionally committed, and punishable by courts.

Human violence includes any aggressive behaviour of a person or persons hurting body or positive regard or both of another person or persons. Further analysis reveals:

(a) Aggressive behaviour means vigorous behaviour or action.

(b) A person means victimiser either a male or a female.

(c) Hurting body means inflicting physical injury.

(d) 'Positive regard' means need to be level or accepted.

(e) Another person means the victim. Keeping in view this definition, certain misconceptions regarding crime against women may be removed.

*Misconceptions*

1. Men alone are involved in crime against women and it is a battle of sexes in the general belief. But crime against women is both an inter-sex and intra-sex problem as the victimiser may be a male or a female or both. In bride burning, the husband alone or with the in-laws, male or female, may be the victimiser. The mother herself discriminates between a male and a female child in rearing practices. In sexual crimes, males are the victimisers. Mostly men are the victimisers. But in many cases of domestic violence, females also play their roles in victimising women.
2. Violent behaviour is misconceived to be only on physical level. It is not so. Crime may be expressed in physical torture like wife battering, killing, it is also expressed on verbal level in the form of abuse, rebuke, threat or teasing and also in its talent or indirect forms like all sorts of deprivations, discriminations and obstructions imposed upon women in achieving their goals. These latent forms of crime psychologically hurt women.
3. Crime always results in physical injury. This is not so, criminal behaviour of the victimiser may results in physical

or psychological injury but both to the victim. When a woman is raped or abducted or battered or burnt, she is not only physically injured, but also psychologically hurt.

*Categories*

Crime against women may be classified into three broad categories viz., (i) Sexual offences, (ii) Offences for gain, and (iii) Customary laws and customs.

Offences of sexual character may be divided further into those which have a predatory element and those which are non-predatory. Predatory element is violence. In an offence in the first category there is a deliberate injury to the victim such as rape or molestation.

The second category includes prostitution, here the victim is a willing participant. The case of rape constituted by sexual intercourse with a girl below the statutory minimum age, stands on a special footing and may not strictly fit in with the above classification. Reverting to the two broad categories contemplated by the dichotomy, it may be mentioned that crimes in the nature of obscenity and bigamy stand midway between them. There is no coercion here and no physical injury and the 'victim' may or may not be a consenting party. The real damage is to the morale of society and such damage is present even though the parties involved in the act give their implied consent. Bigamy where there is full knowledge of both the parties, involve no fraud in contrast to bigamy, where one of the parties may not be aware of the existence of the previous marriage. Crimes indicated by the impersonal desire for gain do not themselves constitute 'crimes against women'. Robbery, burglary, theft (and even some cases of assault), may occur between persons of two sexes but they cut across several lines. Such crimes are intended to enrich the thief and not to express personal hatred or passion towards the victim. Offences under customary laws and customs are generally peculiar to a particular society. As the customary laws and values are intricately woven in our society through which violence is perpetrated against women, there is need for fundamental changes in the patriarchal values. Else such violence is bound to continue in its familiar forms and newer guises.

# Three

# The Vulnerable Lot

There are a variety of social, economic, legal, and psychological forms of victimization against women. We live in a society in which men are in hold of the majority of institutions. Economically, women are discriminated against in the job market. Sex role stereotyping has victimized and "imprisoned" a number of women, often women have been victimized by the institution of marriage, in which, although they are no longer identified as property, they are still repressed by implied and covert socio-cultural practices. In some cases in the course of a marital relationship, women have been exploited physically, emotionally, and sexually by their husbands. Mental as well as physical "injury" has been inflicted on women by the health profession. Until recently women did not have the right to decide whether they could continue a pregnancy or terminate it. Number of women have suffered through months and years of psychotherapy by therapists whose attempts are being objective all too often fall short of that goal, resulting in the perpetuation of a value system that feeds the sexist social structure. The fact that the Equal Rights Amendment remains unratified is perhaps the most apparent indicator of the victimization of women.

## Victimology: A Branch of Criminology

The study of victims has emerged as a recent development in the field of criminology, criminology itself a discipline not more than a century old. Victimology as a branch of criminology developed first in the United Kingdom, West Germany, France, the Scandinavian countries, Canada, Australia, New Zealand, and the United States. Indian scholars are also focusing their attention on the victimology to understand the importance of victim in criminal justice system.

The dynamics of victimology could be useful tools within the criminal system for administration and policy makers.

**Types of Victims**

The term "Victimology" and its parameters of the subject, are not yet well defined. The concept "Victimology" was coined by a French jurist named Benjamin Mendelsohn, who is now a citizen of Israel. He states that victims are of five types:

(a) Completely innocent victims such as children and people who are victims of crime when unconscious;

(b) Victims with minor guilt and victims of ignorance, such as pregnant women who got to quacks for miscarriage;

(c) Voluntary victims, such as the ones who commit suicide or are killed by euthansia;

(d) Victims who are more guilty than the offenders, such as persons who provoke others to commit crime; and

(e) The most guilty type of victims who commit offences against others and get killed by the victim in self-defence (Mendelsohn: 1963).

A more popular categorisation is the triple alliterative pattern, which describes victims as provocative, precipitative and participating. Another recent and fairly authoritative view, as provided by the classification of Abdel Fattah of Canada as follows:

(a) the non-participating,

(b) the latent,

(c) the provocative,

(d) the participating, and

(e) the defiant.

Victimology is basically a study of crime from the point of view of the victim, of persons suffering from injury or destruction by the action of another single person or group of persons. Dadrian (1976:42) has broadly described this field as "the study of the social processes through which individuals and groups are maltreated in such a way that social problems are created." This encompasses two areas of concern: "the social context in which victimization occurs, and the social consequences of such victimization." In this study we will look at the social context of female victimization, its social consequences though organizing a discussion of the social context of female victimization is difficult as the problem has historical, cross-cultural, and inter-disciplinary dimensions. The fact that most men are physically stronger than most women, so that when it comes to fight, women are more often losers is the simplest explanation of male-female maladjustment. To add to this is their vulnerability by their child-bearing function (Chapman and Gates, 1978:10-11).

**Aggressive vs. Non-Aggressive Behaviour**

Aggression and victimization are correlated, be it physical or verbal. Men are socialized to be aggressive and women to be victims. Support for the theory that aggressive behaviour is instinctual comes from:

(1) ethologists such as Desmond Morris, Conrad Lorens and Robert Ardrey;

(2) research on electrical and chemical brain stimulation;

(3) psychoanalytic theory.

The ethologists propose that our animal ancestors were instinctively violent beings and that our violent behaviours are products of these inherited instinctual drives. However, this is not always the case—some research (Binford, 1972) confirms that certain animals are not aggressive at all, and humans do not always pattern themselves on other primates' behaviour because of their more complex nervous system. An intriguing theory is that violence is not an instinctual behaviour but a learned one, resulting from the same matrix whereby we learn to speak, dress, and socialize. The expression of such learned aggression may be varied as the environments in which it is learned. Freud and his contemporaries held that aggression is instinctive. Coldstein (1975:19) viewing aggression as a learned behaviour, proposes that there are long-term and situational factors that facilitate either aggressive or non-aggressive behaviour. Long-term factors include the process of socialization, we undergo as children; for example, the values, norms, attitudes, beliefs and expectations that our parents, teachers, and peers instill the selectively reinforce, situational factors facilitating aggression include familiar environments, the presence of a alcohol, or the presence of relatives or peers with whom aggression is associated.

Situations place even the most violent people as non-aggressive and vice versa. Therefore, the factors that facilitate non-aggression are notable. Goldstein (1975) believes that there are certain environments and individuals that do not elicit or facilitate aggression. Inappropriate locations for aggression include churches or theatres, and inappropriate targets are hypothesized to include children and the aged. Psychological experiments demonstrate that aggressive behaviour is learned or acquired (Kagan and Moss, 1962; Loew, 1967). Interestingly, several of these studies find that males are more prone to aggression than females. Kegan and Moss (1962) found that aggressive behaviour learned in childhood persist through adulthood, especially for males. Loew (1967) and Green and Pigg (1970) found this if parents positively reinforce verbal or nonverbal aggressive responses in their children's behaviour.

*Theoretical Explanations*

Erich Fromm's (1973) analysis of human aggression clearly defines the errors and limitations of both the instinctive and behavioural schools of psychology in explaining the causes and origins of human violence and destruction. Extensive studies of violence as innate and instinctive in origin, as opposed to being learned through the socialization process (nature versus nurture), have ignored the question of observable difference between the levels of male/female human aggression. Regardless of which theory predominates at a given time, it would be logical that the theory hold true for all members of the species, regardless of sex. Fromm specifically includes women in his definition of mankind as it relates to human destructiveness. It will be wrong to assume that the male is innately more violent than the female. There are certain prevailing cultural and psychological conditions which encourage male aggression as its own reward and encourage acceptance of female passivity as its own reward.

There is a little evidence to explain female victimization beyond the shadow of culturally conditioned gender-biases. The major explanations which seem to evidence certain degree of objectivity in their treatment of the subject put the problem of female victimization in a socio-economic, legal and cultural context. Srivastav (1989: 33-37) views female victimization as a product of socio-economic factors including the status, role, right of women in general. The explanations discover the genesis of female victimization in the institutions of marriage and family, in the different sex-role socialization, etc.

*Classifications of Theories*

Various scholars namely, Gelles and Strauss (1979), Steinmetz (1974), Strauss (1974), Wolfgang and Weiner (1982) etc. have given different explanations to violence. After a detailed study of these writings Ahuja (1987: 166-185) identifies fourteen theories for understanding violence committed by an individual. Theories range from intrapsychic theories to macro-sociological theories. He divides these theories on the basis of three (theoretical) levels of analysis:

(1) psychiatric or psycho-pathological analysis;

(2) socio-psychological analysis; and

(3) sociological or socio-cultural analysis.

*The psycho-pathological model*

This focuses on the offender personality characteristics as the chief determinants of criminal violence. This model includes analysis that links mental analysis (i.e., a very small portion of mentally ill persons are violent), alcohol (i.e., what one does under the influence of alcohol and violence).

*The socio-psychological model*

This assumes that criminal violence can best be understood by a careful examination of the external environmental factors that exercise an impact on the individual offender. This model also examines the types of every-day interactions, patterns, etc., which are precursors to violence. Theories such as the Frustration-Aggression Theory, the Perversion Theory, the Self-Attitude Theory and the Motive Attribution Theory approach criminal violence from a socio-psychological level of analysis.

*The sociological or socio-cultural model*

This provides a macro-level analysis of criminal violence. This model examines criminal violence in terms of socially structured inequality and social and cultural attitudes and norms regarding anti-social behaviour and interpersonal relations. Besides the two well-known theories, viz., the structural-functional theory and the theory of sub-culture of violence, the learning theory, the exchange theory, the anomic theory, and the resource theory, etc., also come under a socio-cultural analysis (Ahuja, 1987: 166-167).

Ahuja (1987) examines his own Social Bond Theory to explain crime against women. In view of these theoretical approaches, he calls this a "middle range theoretical proposition" based on the phenomenological approach. This has been borrowed by certain concepts from sociologists and criminologists like Hirschi (1976), Schutz (1964), etc. Social Bond Theory based on adjustment, commitment and attachment and the relative feeling of deprivation is different from the Frustration Aggression Theory in the sense that status frustration as the consequences of interpersonal relations and the functioning of sub-system in the society. Hence, Ahuja (1987) claims his theory has a sociological orientation.

Various explanations have thus been advanced to account for crimes against women discovering the genesis of female victimization in the history, literature and culture of different societies. The dominant view holds that female victimization is a complex phenomenon having deep roots in the male dominated socio-economic, legal and political order. It is an expression of imbalance in the power structure that relegates women to a secondary social position, thereby making them vulnerable to various forms of oppression, exploitation and abuse.

**Forms of Victimization**

Ill-treatment of women takes several forms. Singh (1990:104) categories the oppression of Indian women into three manolateralistic forms. All these three take the form of victimization, namely:

(i) *Patriarchal victimization* (inter-gender: man *v* woman)

Here men are responsible for crimes like sexual harassment, wife beating, rape, dowry murders, and setting in processes like patriarchisation, genderisation (a process of social differentiation based on gender) (Singh, 1989:1)

(ii) *Patriarchally propelled self-victimization* (extra-intra person)

Here the present suicide committed by four girls of Kanpur (three sisters and the other drawing cue from the former) and the suicides committed by brides figure. In the former case it is the patriarchal forces which compelled the three sisters to commit suicide notwithstanding their being educated.

(iii) *Victim-propelled victimization* (intra-gender; women and women)

Here the publicly celebrated rift between mother-in-law/ sister-in-law versus daughter-in-law to discredit women as oppressor of her own sex figures.

Ashish Nandy notes that "...even man's cruelty toward women is not match for the cruelty of women toward women." "Indeed", observes A.R. Wadia that "the greatest enemy and the only one that ultimately counts-of women's 'Emancipation' is women herself'. To Renuka Singh "the worse deprivation of the 'deprived class' takes place when the women vs woman battle begins resulting in the loss of support of women for the cause of their own liberation." K.L. Sharma observes, "it has been observed that it is women who obstruct the path of other women even more than men do; as is the case with mothers-in-l;aw and colleagues at work." And a more shocking aspect is that "women are murdered by women themselves" (Taneja: 1987:4). However, it is unjust to say that behind every crime or injustice against a woman there is a woman.

*Categories of Crime*

Atray (1988:33-34) classifies crime, into three categories. The first category consists of individual acts which stop short of death of the victims like eve-teasing, wife beating, etc. The second category of crimes which is the most common and the least appreciated is the consequences which visit women as a result of enforcement by the society of its own rules and regulations. In the third category would fall cases of outright homicide whether it is intentional murder or forcing a woman to take her own life by committing suicide. In these categories of crimes, the first category of cases are to be treated more as social failing bordering on crime while the second category is out and out criminal. The third category raises certain basic issues concerning the society's own code of conduct and the blame is squarely on the society as a whole.

Mishra and Arora (1982: 5) classify crimes into three broad categories viz., (i) sexual offences, (ii) offences for gain, and (iii) customary laws and customs. Offences of sexual character may be further divided into those which have predatory element, and those which are non-predatory. Predatory element means the element of violence. In an offence is the first category that is a deliberate injury to the victim such as rape or other physical molestation. In an offence in the second category such as prostitution, the 'victim' is a participant who is willing.

Rajan (1981: 84) identifies the following categories of offences against women:

(i) Wolf-whistling, ogling, winking, passing lewd remarks, sometimes openly, and at other times behind the anonymity of the telephone.

(ii) Bottom-pinching and forcing physical intimacy on board public transport, in bus queues, on festivals or on other occasions when large concourses of people together.

(iii) Molestation and rape.

(iv) Harassment at home leading to suicide and murder of young brides.

(v) Immoral trafficking, exploitation of women, and commercialization of sex.

The IPC classifies women related crimes in six categories as follows: Offences against women's bodily interest; offences against women's proprietory interest; offences relating to marriage; offences relating to criminal intimidation, insult and annoyance; suppression of Immoral Traffic in Women and Girls Act; and Dowry Act.

Deshpande (1984:71) classifies crimes against women into three categories which are as follows:

(i) Crime against personal liberty which may be sub-divided into kidnapping and abduction of minors and majors who are mostly women;

(ii) Crime against marriage which includes bigamy, attacks on monogamy, fraud, decoit etc.;

(iii) Crime against persons which includes harm to both body and mind. The two interact on each other and harm done to one affects the other also.

Verma (1990) enumerates crimes against women into categories, namely physical torture and mental cruelties. These are further divided as follows:

*Physical Torture*

Medical termination of pregnancy, abortion of female foetus (if it found that it is a female child, the pregnancy is terminated), malnutrition of female child, female infanticide, eve-teasing, molestation, abduction and kidnapping, wife beating, wrongful confinement, fraudulent marriage, adultry-enticement of married women, cruelties on married women, rape, outraging the modesty of women, defaming young girls, prostitution, indescent representation of women, etc.

*Mental Cruelties*

Discrimination in male and female child, married women debarred of employment in several organizations, female generally having no say in her marriage, no equal remunerations, wife having no title in her husband's or in-laws property or home, the dowry menace, discrimination under law etc.

Two significant conclusions emerge from the above classifications: the *first* is biological. This reflects that violence against women occurs only because women are on average weaker. The implication of this statement is clear that the position of women has been historically structured as hierarchy in which men possessed and controlled women. This become the cause of physical violence against women and is one of the most brutal and explicit expressions of patriarchical domination. The *second* is to consider violence in its social-cultural context. A greater understanding of violence against women will be achieved through a consideration of the social environment in which it occurs.

*Statistics on Crime Against Women*

With the constant rise in dowry deaths, bride burning, rape, molestation, kidnapping and other crimes against women in the country, it has become difficult to determine the extent and nature of crimes against women accurately on the basis of cases reported to the police.

*Reasons for Under Reporting of Cases*

Firstly, due to the social stigma attached to the victim of sexual offences (i.e., rape, molestation, uttering word, making gesture etc.). Secondly, in dowry cases, parents do not want to stress the issue to the extreme for the future of the victim. Thirdly, to shun publicity being given by the media. Fourthly, in certain societies (Tribal) such crimes are not viewed with concern. Another reason may be the inadequate strength of the women police (Misra and Arora: 1982:7).

Crimes against women may not be reported due to the social stigma attached to the crime. A victim of sexual offences like rape, molestation, etc., may have to suffer the severity of social stigma, if it is made public. Besides, the social situations, there have been increasing reports regarding the rate of crime against women, which gives us an impression that such activities are on the rise. Although statistics regarding criminality against women are compiled officially in accordance with the provision of existing status of our country and collected, codified and classified at the national level in crime in India reports, yet there are no officially recognized figures available except their depiction under broad categories in the publication of significance. Taking IPC crime as an index of the situation of crime, the rise in the rate of crime against women has been reported in all types of crimes ranging from eve-teasing to abductions and killings for the period 1977-1979.

Data which reveal an average percentage of crime against women committed during 1977-79 which represent that a little more than 80 per cent crime against women has been reported: for molestation (28.94 per cent); offences under SITA Act (24.67 per cent); Kidnapping and abduction (20.96 per cent); and rape (10.70 per cent). Moreover, these four crimes have gone up further during the 1983 to 1985. Besides these crimes, there is also an increase in eve-teasing and dowry deaths as reflected by the percentage change in 1985 over 1983. It was pointed out that against 2487 cases of rape in 1971, 4300 cases were reported in 1979 averaging 12 rapes a day or about one every two hours. The All India figures of dowry deaths is about 4000 per year. Similarly, 619 cases of bride burning were registered by the police in Delhi in 1982 against a total of 421 cases in 1980. Registered cases have also been going up alarmingly in the past few years though the number of cases reported is much more than the recorded ones.

Reported figures in Delhi for crimes against women reveal that dowry deaths rose from 43 in 1985 to 64 in 1986 and 59 in 1987 to 71 in 1988. The number of such deaths had risen to 132 between January 1989 and February 1990 as disclosed by the then Union Home Minister in Parliament. This apart, Delhi led all union territories in 1987 with 103 registered cases of rape; worse still innocent minors were the victims in more than of these cases.

The total incidence of such crimes are estimated to be in the country with a population of about 700 million are estimated to be 50 times higher because of the inherent hesitation on the part of victims to complain about such matters. These figures do not represent the whole picture except in the case of murder and suicide. This is particularly so in the case of the offences of eve-teasing where the victim, as a rule, tries not to report the matter as they feel that in the absence of any strong provision in the law to deal with this crime, the only consequences of reporting would be necessary harassment to the victim and her witness. The crime of wife-beating goes almost cent per cent unreported for the same reason of the law and also the fact that reporting of such incidents to the police would put an end to all hopes of future reconciliation (Atray: 1988).

**Case Study**

Misra and Arora (1982) conducted a study of six districts, namely, Hissar, Sirsa, Jaunsar Bewar (Tehsil Chakrota in Dehradun), Kanpur, Delhi and Bombay representing respectively the agrarian/smaller towns; tribal areas; and urban/metropolitan cities. Crime against women constitute only a small proportion of the total crime reported to the police. On an average for every 100 cases of crime reported to the police during 1977-79, there were only 0.43 cases of crime against women. In tribal area this ratio was 2.27, in agrarian area the same was 1.68 and in urban area it was 0.42. It also reveals that the ratio of crime against women to the total crime increased in the urban/metropolitan cities and the tribal belt while it declined in the agrarian sector.

The overall ratio of crime against women to total crime has increased from 0.40 in 1977 to 0.43 in 1978 and to 0.47 in 1979. In the urban areas it increased from 0.38 in 1977 to 0.41 in 1978 and further to 0.45 in 1979. In tribal belt, it increased erratically from 0.69 in 1977 to 4.59 in 1978 and declined to 2.04 in 1979. In agrarian area the ratio had declined in 1979 over the year 1977. The ratio in 1977 was 1.63, 1.91 in 1978 and 1.54 in 1979 (*Ibid:* 79-80). The volume of crime against women rose from 12.64 per lakh population in 1977 to 14.18 per lakh population in 1979. In the agrarian areas during the same period, the increase was 10 per cent in 1978 and 11.1 per cent in 1979 over the year 1977. In the tribal area, the percentage increase in 1978 was 400.0 and 100.0 in 1979 over the year 1977. The urban area registered an increase of 0.8 per cent in 1978 and in 1979 by 20.2 per cent over the year 1977. Thus, we see that the crime against women had increased at a much higher rate than the other crimes. Moreover, the ratio of crime against women to the total crime increased in the urban/metropolitan cities and the tribal belt while it declined in the agricultural sector. Out of the total of 6483 cases of crime against women reported, the maximum (37.2 per cent) cases were of Suppression of Immoral Traffic Act, followed by kidnapping/adduction (21.7 per cent), molestation (14.2 per cent), rape (8.6 per cent), chain-snatching (7.2 per cent), murder (5.1 per cent) and enticing or taking away or detaining with criminal intent a married women (3.9 per cent). These offences together constitute above 98 per cent of the total cases of crime against women.

The other offences committed against women were very less in number. These offences in order of reporting were: Eve-teasing (0.8 per cent), dacoity (0.4 per cent), abetment to suicide (0.3 per cent), Dowry Prohibition Act, unnatural offences, importation and selling of minor for prostitution 0.1 per cent each, procuration of minor (0.04 per cent). In the agricultural sector the highest number of cases were of molestation being 46.8 per cent followed by kidnapping/abduction (23.2 per cent), rape (14.9 per cent), abetment to suicide (3.1 per cent). A solitary case of eve-teasing was also reported. In the urban areas the order of reporting was SITA Act (38.9 per cent), followed by kidnapping/abduction (21.7 per cent), molestation (12.7 per cent), rape (8.2 per cent), chain-snatching (7.5 per cent), enticing or taking away with criminal intent a married women (4.1 per cent). The other offences committed against women are very less in number and the trend of these offences were similar to the total cases of crime against women as mentioned above. In the tribal areas, the highest cases (75.0 per cent) were of rape/kidnapping/abduction followed by molestation (25.0 per cent). Thus, the nature and extent of crime against women differ from area to area.

## Statistics on Rape in India

The victimization of the fair sex has been showing an upward inclination and incidence of these crimes is on the rise. Eventhough the available statistics are very high, they don't represent even 25 per cent of the total because it is well-known that in actual practice hardly one fourth of the cases are reported. The reasons for non-reporting are obvious. A critical perusal of statistical data on crimes against women reveals that rape is increasing throughout India. According to *Crime in India Report 1986,* a total of 7,952 cases in rape were registered in 1986 against 7,289 cases in 1985 thereby registering an increase of 9.1 per cent in 1986 over 1985. The highest number of cases among the States was registered by Madhya Pradesh (1,506) followed by Uttar Pradesh (1,292), Maharashtra (804), Bihar (794), West Bengal (612), Rajasthan (598), etc. Thus, about 50 per cent of the total cases in the country are reported in four States of Madhya Pradesh, Uttar Pradesh, Maharashtra, and Bihar together. However, the highest volume of rape cases was reported from the State of Jammu and Kashmir being 2.8, followed by Madhya Pradesh (2.6), and lowest from the State of Punjab (0.3) and Karnataka (0.3) respectively. The volume of rape cases for each population was 1.0 in all the States taken together, in all the union territories taken together as well as in the country as a whole.

Overall the volume of rape cases to per lakh of population had increased critically during the period 1974-86. It increased from 0.5 in 1974 to 1.0 in 1986 exceptionally in 1979, it had declined to 0.66 as compared to the year 1078, which was 0.71. However, in the last one decade, rape cases have just doubled and it would be seen that the percentage victims of rape was the highest in the age-group between 16 to 30 years in all the seven years between 1971 to 1977, the average being 62.5 per cent followed by the age group below 30 years accounted for 14.6 per cent.

**Statistics of Kidnapping and Abduction in India**

The incidence of kidnapping and abduction has also been increasing in our country. The total number of cases recorded in 1971 was 9,647. In 1973, the incidence under this head increased by 8.7 per cent over 1972; in 1976 the incidence increased by 10.0 per cent over 1977; and in 1978 the incidence increased by 11.2 per cent over 1977. The rate of this crime, per one lakh of population is 2.0 in our country. Manipur topped the list among the States with the average per annum volume per lakh of population being 13.33, followed by Jammu and Kashmir (6.85), Rajasthan (4.09), Uttar Pradesh (3.07) and so on. Delhi topped the list among Union territories with the average per annum volume of 5.0. No case was reported from Dadra and Nagar Haveli and Lakshadweep during the period 1977-79.

**Statistics on Molestation in India**

The average annual volume per lakh of population of reported cases of molestation of women and girls were the highest in the State of Madhya Pradesh being 5.56 followed by Jammu and Kashmir (5.36), Manipur (4.72), Tripura (3.48) and so on. The average per annum volume in these States was higher than the average volume (1.82) of all States taken together. No cases of molestation of women and girls were reported from the State of Sikkim and the Union Territory of Lakshadweep Islands.

Among the union territories the average per year volume of this crime was the highest in Andaman and Nicobar Islands, bring 12.27 per lakh of population, followed by Mizoram (6.04), Pondicherry (2.33).The average volume per annum in these Union territories was higher than the all Union territories average 7.87. Statistics reveal that the volume of molestation of women and girls per lakh of population on all-India basis had increased from 1.77 in 1977 to 1.92 in 1978.

**Statistics on SITA in India**

Of the major crimes against women, the volume per lakh of population of cases of SITA taken together were the highest after cases of molestation of women and girls. The highest volume of SITA cases were reported from the State of Tamil Nadu being 10.57 per lakh of population, followed by Karnataka (6.55), Andhra Pradesh (2.37), Maharashtra (1.37) and Uttar Pradesh (0.50). In other States insignificant or negligible cases of SITA were reported. No case was reported during the year 1977-79 in the States of Gujarat, Meghalaya, Nagaland, Sikkim, West Bengal.

Amongst the Union territories, the maximum number of cases of SITA were reported from Delhi with the average volume of (0.77) followed by Pondicherry (0.36). No case of this offence was reported from the other Union territories during 1977-79. In the Union Territory of Delhi, the volume per lakh of population had shown a continuously arising trend.

**Statistics on Dowry Deaths in India**

The number of dowry deaths is on the rise despite the various legislative and other measures taken from time to time to tackle the problem. This has threatened our way of life (Mir, 1982). There were 162 cases of burning of women reported in the capital only between April 1, 1983 and June 30, 1983. Figures reveal that in many States, the reported cases of dowry deaths or deaths by burning or suicide more than doubled within two years. Andhra Pradesh reported 14 cases of dowry deaths in 1983, 27 cases in 1984 and 38 cases in 1985. In Uttar Pradesh the death figures of bride burning or suicide, were 323 in 1985 and 110 in the first four months of 1986. Madhya Pradesh reported 42 cases of dowry deaths in just five months June-October in 1985. In Maharashtra, there were 129 cases of dowry deaths in 1984, the number of such deaths recorded in 1985 was at 211 and it had reached to 247 in the first ten months of 1986. Maharashtra recorded 411 cases of suicide by young married women in 1983, 652 in 1985 and 662 for the first ten months of 1986 (*Indian Express*, 24.5.1987).

Statistics provided by the Home Ministry regarding dowry deaths also helps us to some extent in assessing the prevalence of this phenomenon in our country. The figures show a sharp increase in the incidence, year after year, which could partly be due to the increased awareness about the problem.

Official figures between January 1980-March 1981 show that there were 139 dowry death cases registered with police in various parts of the country. Of these Punjab and Haryana accounted for 231 cases each and 17 cases were from Uttar Pradesh. Whereas by latest figures, the number of dowry deaths for the year 1987 stands at 1649, and Uttar Pradesh on the whole is found to be the leading State in dowry deaths.

According to statistics, the figures of dowry deaths by burning or suicide are only a part of the actual number of deaths caused in this respect, therefore, the reported figures are usually misleading. Sources of information include the special cell in the Delhi Police Headquarters and numerous non-governmental organization which clearly prove the point of gross variability in information in this regard, the figures supplied in the Rajya Sabha could probably be treated as the third source of information. The number of cases of married women in the age-group 16-30 years with third degree burns admitted in the various hospitals of Delhi is yet another source of information. In the capital 736 cases of death due to burns, suicide and poisoning were reported in the year of 1985. The number of such deaths increased to 775 in 1986 and 426 in the first six months of 1987 (Bhatia, 1988). There is no doubt about the fact that crimes against women are increasing in every country, but in India, like other developing countries the proportion of such trend is on higher level.

To sum up, on an all-India basis taking the 3 years (1977-79) average of all the selected offences against women, the highest number of cases were reported under the head 'Molestation' being 11642 (28.94) per cent of the total cases reported. This was followed by the cases under SITA and Girls 9926 (24.67 per cent) cases; kidnapping/ abduction 8432 (20.96 per cent), rape 4305 (10.70 per cent); Enticing or taking away with criminal intent a married women 2736 (6.80 per cent), chain snatching 1298 (3.23 per cent) procuring minor girl 908 (2.26 per cent). Interestingly some of the offences like abetment to suicide and penalty for demanding dowry which are reported in the mass media were comparatively less. The average per year cases reported under abetment to suicide were only 169 (0.42 per cent), demanding dowry-Section 4 were 103 (0.26 per cent).

The vulnerability of women to various forms of oppression, exploitation and abuse should be given its due share while framing of policies and laws so that they can be given their share of respect and status long due to them.

# Four

# Eve-teasing

Eve-teasing has been a serious menace in our society. The commission of this crime is an indicator of extent to which the women folk are insecure in our society. Eve-teasing which involves the verbal and physical harassment of women is the scourge of the urban society. A woman cannot go out in the street without the fear of being harassed by strange men. In busy crowded areas the women get pawed and pressed, jostled, rubbed and squeezed, the miscreants taking advantage of the press of the crowd and indulging in whatever physical intimacy the situation permits. The miscreants hurl indecent remarks. There is no woman who has not suffered this menace of society. In daily life if not all men are potential eve-teasers, all women are potential victims. All women suffer from the fear of being teased, irrespective of her age, health, appearance, mental state etc.

Having largely affected the peace of mind of women and they are not able to move freely and participate in the social life of the community. This is a challenge to our constitution which ensures all citizens the right "to move freely throughout the territory of India". There is no safe territory left for women, not even in their "mohallas". In a cross-section interview, a girl of Patna women's college says "Eve-teasers are everywhere outside our campus, in the markets, in parks and in buses, you have to face their hooliganism". Do we not understand why girls avoided attending classes on the day Saraswati idols were to be immersed? The girl students avoid attending classes much before the closure of the colleges during Holi festival. The boy students of St. Columba's College, Hazaribagh have started celebrating Holi festivals before fifteen days, creating panic among the girl students. Even the girls' common room which was locked to avoid any ugly scene was also attacked. As a result the police already was posted there owing to an earlier incident of damaging a car, escorted the girl students to their houses. Now the girl students are missing their classes and practicals because college authorities are unable to control the hooliganism in the college. Great resentments is prevailing among girls and their guardians. Eve-teasing hinders healthy academic atmosphere and damages the career of girl students. It is an irony that we talk of the 21st century and don't allow girls to enjoy freedom in society.

The culprits are not only those who belong to goonda class but they belong to the so-called educated and cultured and affluent families. Young men include sons of senior government officers have been named in an eve-teasing case off and on. In case of anti-social elements, eve-teasing is a group activity and often assumes violent proportions. On several occasions eve-teasing led to communal disturbances. Three persons including a woman of Bhabhua were injured when members of the two families clashed over the issue of eve-teasing. A man of village Chhata of Siwan district was killed by an angry mob for teasing a girl of the same village. In the case of boys belonging to educated, cultured and affluent families, eve-teasing is individual and a concealed phenomenon.

Being no longer confined to students, unemployed and unmarried youth only, this evil has no boundaries. Some recent news report eve-teasing committed by professionals like lawyers, teachers, and civil servants. Of course, the elite class is a bit sophisticated in nature. They play with their subordinate working women in lighter form and watch the response of the opposite sex in this regard.

**Forms of Eve-teasing**

Eve-teasers are in the age bracket of 15 to 40 and some of them are married too. In a cross section interview a girl student has given an interesting twist to the story more than the young boys, middle aged men with receding hairlines and broken teeth, indulge in eve-teasing.

Their despicable deeds cover the following:

1. Indulging in cat-calls, waving wolf whistling, winking and uttering indecent remarks about female anatomy or singing obscene songs in such a way so as to be heard by women. Songs are deliberately chosen from popular film so that these could appear innocuous if it came to an argument.
2. Brushing past hurriedly, pressing against women, trying to pinch the bottoms or the breasts and disappearing in the crowd is very common for such perverts. If caught

they pretend that rubbing was all accidental. They get a free hand during the breakdown of power. In the process sometimes the aged women are not spared from this kind of menace.

3. Eve-teasers board crowded buses and trains, prefer to stand or sit next to ladies and depending on the situation, the teaser sometimes gets himself sandwiched with her in the crowd and leans on her.
4. In recent years, in some universities these forms of eve-teasing have replaced with brazen acts as *dupatta* snatching, back patting and in some cases even forced kissing.
5. Eve-teasing has also taken the form of telephone a girl and uttering obscene and suggestive words.
6. Mailing anonymous love letters in the most filthy languages.
7. Exhibiting male genitals in front of women and thereby deriving strange perverted sexual pleasure out of it.

Such vulgar acts occur in educational institutions mostly around women's college and girls' schools. The very act gets intensified particularly during festivals when pre-festivals shopping is on or in the puja pandals, which remain crowded with women folk in the evening.

**Socio-legal Aspects of Eve-teasing**

Eve-teasing by itself is not an offence under any law at present. But a close reading of Sections 294 and 354 of the Indian Penal Code would clearly indicate that the substance of the act of eve-teasing would be covered by them. Section 294 states that "whoever to the annoyance of others (a) does any obscene act in any public place, or (b) sings, recites or utters any obscene song, ballads or words in or near any public place is liable to be punished with imprisonment or with fine." The section is very wide in nature and a person can be hauled up even if the acts forming part of the substance of the offence are addressed to the public at large, provided these cause annoyance. Clearly, a girl or a woman who feels annoyed by any obscene song or words can take recourse to the provision of the section and put up a complaint before a police station. The offence is cognizable, i.e., a police officer can arrest the offender without a warrant but it is bailable. A graver form of eve-teasing is accompanied by the use of gesture indicating threat or use of force. In such a case also, action can be taken against the person using it. It would be covered by section 352 of the Indian Penal Code, which provides the punishment in such a case. The substance of the offence is given in section 351 and is known as assault. The making of gesture should be accompanied with preparation so that the person against whom it is directed has the apprehension that criminal force will be used against her. Apart from this, there is a special provision which recognises the gravity of the offence when it is directed against a woman, and has been given in section 354 of the Indian Penal Code. The punishment in such cases is imprisonment for two years or fine or both. The offence is cognizable. The only condition is that the person should have the intention or knowledge that such an action would outrage her modesty. Small cases of eve-teasing, social disgrace and other inconveniences are rarely fought to the notice of courts, fewer still are challenged in the courts and negligible number end in minor convictions and that also after a long lapse when the offenders and his likes continue committing many more such acts.

The provocation coming from the opposite sex like the style of dressing, talking, walking etc. should not be overlooked while condemning eve-teasing. It is not that all women behave in identical provocative manner. Sometimes women consciously or unconsciously invite such hazards. In a cross-section interview eve-teasing was viewed as reaction and not an action. According to some of the male interviews "Eve-teasing took place only when girls provoke. They incite others by their action, dress and manner. It is a form of admiration. Girls dress not for girls but for boys". Then why not let them be aware that they are looked great. But this is a partial statement. Interview to girls gave another point of view. They said they dress themselves in modern way only to show that they have equal status and not to attract boys. Thus it can be said that eve-teasing may result due to wrong impression of girls' image by the boys.

The social malaise of harassing the women is assuming such proportions that one shudders at the shape of things to come. The exercises of passing annoying and embarassing comments from a distance, if unchecked, are found to lead to more serious forms and proportions. Eve-teasing, if not properly checked will end up in entering a house and committing criminal assault or homicide. Every eve-teaser is a potential murderer.

**Suggestions**

1. The need for creating an awareness in society has always been there and as a result the attitude of common people in general and the police may be more sympathetic towards the victims themselves in particular.
2. Girls should be bold and give back to the ruffians in the same coin. They should be taught a lesson. If he gets even a slap from an opponent, he takes to his heels. Training in 'Judo' and 'Karate' to girls is very helpful and for this the government must open training centres.
3. At times fact can be of great help until she is able to sight others who can come to her rescue or get hold of any lethal substance with which she can strike at.
4. It is a must for the case to be reported to police. There should be no leniency exercised on this account.
5. The Parliament should pass stringent laws for the police to enforcing them vigorously. This can be expedited through public pressure.
6. The public have also to help damsels in distress and not behave in an unconcerned and impersonal way. It must encourage the victims to report the incidents to police and help the police and the courts in punishing the offenders by deposing truthfully and by being not won over by the threats or lures of the culprits.
7. There should be a massive boycott by public of eve-teasers and they should make it a point that they do not prevail. The names of eve-teasers may be written on big hoarding to be kept at a public place for days together in every 'Mohalla'. Voluntary women welfare organisations that we have in the country like the All India Women's Conference, Nari Raksha Samiti, Mahila

Dakshta Samiti, etc. could well bring awakening and alertness among eves in this regard.

8. The parents must ensure that their children dress properly without an effort to expose the anatomy unncessarily which invites the attention of the evil minded.
9. Parents should be initiated to talk about basic sexual matters with their children. Failing this they gather dangerous knowledge from footpath publications which are worse than anything else. Talk about sex is taboo in Indian society. Society need to change its attitude towards sex education. In fact, eve-teasing is only a superficial manifestation of the imbalance in the relationship between man and women.

What we need is public consciousness and a serious rethinking about our morals and values and public action can go a long way in acting as a deterrent to eve-teasing.

**Factors Promoting Eve-teasing**

Greater degeneration of the male vis-a-vis eve teasing is a symptom of social, economic and moral disorder. It is a symptomatic of a combination of varied and complicated disorder. First and the foremost is the abandonment of the traditional moral values, the lack of religious education and the absence of the sobering effect of the family and the teacher. Secondly no body is born an eve-teaser. If he is neglected at home, he grows rowdy. Thirdly, there is the pernicious influence of the cinema and the cheap literature in which sex permeates. The current advertisements trying to promote sale of under-garments, towels and bedsheets by incidently exposing the female anatomy also lead to degradation of woman as a commercialised commodity in the mind of man. Fourthly, there is the rush to the urban in search of adventure and employment. Away from the restraining influence of the families, the youngsters look for kicks, excitement and thrills which they seem to get in acts of eve-teasing. Infliction of pain on the eve acts as a stimulant to their sexual desires. Fifthly, there is the lack of fear of punishment or adverse publicity or social disgrace. The police with its insufficient strength and preoccupation with other problems of law and order and the courts with their proverbial delays and intricate legal procedures fail to bring most of the vagrants to book.

# Five

# Roots of Violence

People have always been deeply disturbed about violence against women, but they have never quite understood what makes the sense of pain conveyed by the term violence more painful than any other pain, the sense of fear more awesome and the terror more terrifying than any other. Women suffer and are made to suffer in many ways. In behavioural terms, violence against women ranges from simple suppression to abuse, aggression, exploitation and severe oppression. We know it as female infanticide, the abortion of the female foetus, the neglect and undernourishment of the girl child, denial of education to girls, rape, pre-puberty marriage, wife beating, the harassment of a bride leading to her suicide or murder. Each of these is more awesome than comparable or even greater pain or fear experienced in other contexts. For instance childbirth can be extremely painful, but one never refers to the pain of childbirth as violence, no matter how severe it is. The fear of death in a situation of terminal illness, can be extremely terrifying but one does not refer to it as violence.

In an effort to try and identify the element that makes violence different an attempt has been made here to define violence. A recent Indian report of a study on Women and Violence sponsored in India and in Korea by UNESCO, Bangkok, looked promising in terms of providing a lead. This report, edited by Dr. Krishnaraj, has been prepared by the SNDT University's Research Centre for Women's Studies. It is based on an analysis of violence against women reported in Gujarati, Marathi and English language journals and newspapers and on findings from some case studies specially undertaken for the purpose. It also offers a review of Enactments on Violence against Women made in the decade of the eighties (1980-1990) and discuss women's action groups and the State machinery against women.

**The Definition**

According to the report,

Violence, in general, is a coercive mechanism to impose one's

> will over another, in order to prove or feel a sense of power. It can be perpetuated by those in power against the powerless, or by the powerless in retaliation against coercion by others, to deny their powerlessness. Any hierarchical system of social organization, where there are categories of dominant groups and subordinate groups, is inevitably accompanied by the victimization of the latter through various means — subtle pressure through the power of ideology, through mechanisms of socialization that reward compliance and punish noncompliance and also through open force. Usually, the last form is resorted to when other methods fail. In fact, it is often not even necessary to actually use physical force or inflict severe injury, for the mere threat to do so is enough to subdue the subordinate person or group. Any individual or group facing the threat of coercion or being disciplined to act in a manner serving the interests of another individual or group, is subject to violence. This is not necessarily confined to physical violence but the creation of an atmosphere of terror, a situation of threat and reprisal..... A hierarchical social structure has violence built into it.

Impressive as it is this statement on violence leaves one feeling more inadequate about the understanding of the concept. To start with the very first line, describing "Violence as a coercive mechanism to assert one's will over another to prove a sense of power" leaves one wondering about where one would place punitive action considered socially legitimate. For instance, the State legitimately uses coercive mechanisms to assert its power over deviants. Whether it does so to "prove" its power or to "assert" the power legitimately given to it is a matter of semantics. What matters here is that this coercion and exercise of power are socially accepted as a legitimate means of resolving a problematic situation. One of the core elements of violence seems to be that the coercion involved is neither legitimate nor socially acceptable. The statement does not make this point. On the contrary, by saying that "any individual or group facing the threat of coercion or being disciplined to act in a manner serving the interests of another individual or group is subject to violence", it reduces all coercion, legitimate or otherwise, to violence.

There are other problems with the definition. For instance, the third line talks of "Any hierarchical system of social organization where there are categories of dominant groups and subordinate groups, etc." The "Any" in this sentence suggests that hierarchy is not a universal feature of social systems and that there may be some social systems without hierarchy. This is not true. All societies, even those that are supposed to be egalitarian, have distinctive hierarchies. Not surprisingly the author of the introduction to the report, who makes this statement on violence, seems, herself, to find it too broad to be of any use. She says, "If we accept this very wide definition of violence, it is difficult to know where to draw the line" and decides to go on with her project with a relatively limited definition of violence against women as sexual harassment and sexual violation.

Among other definitions of the term, Collins dictionary defines violence as :

(i) "Behaviour which is meant to hurt or kill people";

(ii) "a great deal of energy used in doing something — usually because you are very angry";

(iii) "words, actions or other forms of expression which are critical or destructive".

The Oxford dictionary defines violence as :

(1) "the quality of being violent";

(2) "violent conduct or treatment, outrage, injury";

(3) "the unlawful exercise of physical force; (3b) "intimidation by the exhibition of this".

The Thesaurus adds a few additional dimensions to the concept offered by the two dictionaries. It indicates that the noun violence connotes vehemence, impetuosity, vigorousness, excess, destructiveness, vandalism, turbulence, turmoil, roughness, severity, brute force, brutality, savagery, mercilessness, exacerbation, explosion. The adjective 'violent' is explained among other terms by the terms aggressive, charging, disorderly, turbulent, stormy, anarchistic, nihilistic, intemperate, immoderate. Thus, at the end of the exercise of consulting the dictionaries and the Thesaurus, the connotation of the term violence comes across as coercive, destructive behaviour, with a great deal of powerful, aggressive energy and force, destroying in a merciless manner what it is directed at and disorderly, anarchist, turbulent, outrageous and unlawful in its functioning.

**T.V. Series on Violence on Women**

This concept is further elucidated in a television series entitled *Maharashtratil Stree Muktichya Paulkhuna* (Footprints of the Movement for Liberation of Women in Maharashtra). Depicting the emergence of new values, a new self-image, self concept and consciousness among the women of Maharashtra during the course of the nineteenth and early twentieth centuries, it depicts how values pertaining to the rights, the status and the situation of women, steadily changed in this part of the country under the influence of Christianity and European Liberalism. History indicates that the change first occurred among Western educated men, who, inspired by these values, were stimulated to social reform. It occurred somewhat later among women. The series also conveys the fact of the gradual change in values very cleverly. It picks characters, events and scenes from novels, plays, biographies and autobiographies from during a century between 1840 and 1940 and uses the dialogues, soliloquies and events from these literary sources to illustrate how awareness perceptions, and values steadily changed in those times. The core element of this change was a gradual transformation in notions of right and wrong. Practices like child marriage and the denial of the right of re-marriage to widows which, were the social norm of yesteryears, came to be considered oppressive. Shaving the heads of widows in particular, a routine practice among Brahmins and other upper caste Maharashtrians, came to be seen as an outrageous violation of the helpless widow. There was something terribly wrong about a situation wherein both the parental family of the woman as well as the family of her husband, responsible for protecting her in her widowed state inflicted such torture on one who was an important member of the family, loved and cared by all. She was disfigured as soon as her husband was gone with no consideration that widows subjected to this practice were often no more that ten or twelve years old did not seem to matter. As change occurred, this fact made the practice seem even more cruel and heinous bringing about protests and movements against such an oppressive custom.

With the unfolding of episodes to reveal how the reactions of the women to some of the traditional practices steadily changed, it was obvious that not only did these practices gradually come to be seen as wrong but the sentiments that they evoked also changed. What was once accepted and respected as religious customs and generated sentiments of pity, sadness and even horror accompanied by a feeling of the inevitability of destiny, a deep sense of awe, and a commitment to surrender to the authority of religion transformed into sense of outrage and injustice, a feeling that what was being done was enormously inhuman and wrong and must be stopped. Initially this was only felt by the reformers. The reaction of the others, including the women subjected to the practices, was that the practices were extremely painful, but virtuous. Steadily this changed. The women themselves started to question these practices and began defying them. In essence, reform thus consisted of a transformation wherein what was earlier acknowledged to be painful but accepted with reverence as something required by religion, now came to be seen as aggressive and inhuman. The religious norms and beliefs that legitimized this aggression were seriously questioned.

**Changes in Values**

Significantly the forces that led to this change came from outside the Hinduism. The change occurred because Christian values and European Liberalism had established their hold, first on the consciousness of the Western educated reformers and then on women. Hindu men and women had acquired a new sense of humanism influenced by these new values. A new notion of the dignity of the self, of the sanctity of personhood and of the obligation to protect the helpless was introduced. Seen from the vantage point of these new values, the earlier practices were a transgression and violation of humanism. What was earlier only seen as painful and sad, now appear to be inhuman and therefore violent. This then seems to be the essence of violence — a feeling of violation, of the transgression of what is considered to be human.

*Corollaries of 'Violence'*

Thus conceived, the concept of violence has several important corollaries. For instance transgression implies a transgressor. Thus violence is something that a transgressor inflicts upon a victim. Violence in a manner is socially unacceptable. This corollary to the concept of violence fits in very well with the definition of the verb "violate" defined in the Oxford dictionary as: (A) "to disregard, fail to comply with (an oath, treaty, law, etc.)" (B) "to treat profanely or with disrespect" (C) "to break in upon: disturb (privacy etc.)" (D) "to assault sexually, rape etc."

Behaviour viewed as violence in one society may not be so in another is another interesting corollary to the concept of violence, defined as violation, transgression or socially unacceptable infliction of pain. This is so because what is unacceptable in one society may be acceptable in another. There are many examples of this. For instance, female circumcision, routinely practised in some African countries, is viewed as violence by those of us who do not belong to the African culture. A related corollary is that practices that are not perceived as violence in a society at one point of time may be considered to be so in the same society due to transformation of values. For example, the fact that practices such as child marriage or the denial of the right of remarriage to widows, which were acceptable within our society only three or four generations ago, are now considered to be violent by all of us is by far the best example. The change in values that occurred with respect to traditional practices governing the lives of women in our society has been highly uneven, thus generating serious turmoil and unrest, this turmoil has often been channelized into constructive movements for social reform and change. Finally, practices and behaviour that may not be considered to be violent by a person at one point of time may be considered violent by the same person as his/her values or awareness change. This can lead to deep personal conflict, anomie and even complete breakdown if the person experiencing the change is unable to contain or manage the fluctuating values.

An example of the last two corollaries is the transformation in the awareness of Black Americans after the Second World War. Discrimination on the basis of colour resented by the Black population of the United States of America had been broadly accepted until the Second World War where the Black soldiers fought shoulder to shoulder with White, with equal courage and patriotism. On their return from the War these soldiers resented the racial discrimination they had earlier subjected to. They saw it as a serious violation of the equality promised by the Constitution of their country. So did many White Americans. Those who had acquired a new awareness of equality suffered deep resentment and personal conflict when they faced racial discrimination. But this new awareness of equality was not evenly shared in our country. And this led to the strong movements against racial discrimination that rocked American society in the decades of the fifties, sixties and seventies. As the change continues to be uneven, the feeling of violation persists. This is a source of continuing personal and social conflict in the USA. There is no denying the fact that the people may undergo deep personal conflicts and upheavals due to this.

Women all over the world have started to resent the discrimination they suffer in different spheres of life. This has been channelled into constructive activism towards the empowerment of women, and towards legal measures and structural reforms aimed at improving their status and situation in life. However, some of it has given way for angry feminism, and resulted in deep personal conflict, even breakdown, among women who have been unable to cope with their resentment against gender discrimination.

In keeping with the trend of Women Empowerment, SNDT University launched a foundation course entitled Women in a Changing India. The objective of this course is to make the students aware of their situation as women, to help them to look critically and analytically at their status in life, to recognize the restrictions that women face because of gender discrimination. The course also aims at enabling students to recognize their strengths and to inform them about the Constitutional provisions ensuring them equality. It attempts to introduce them to the range of new provisions and opportunities now available for their advance.

This course has been enormously well received. The feedback from those who teach the course indicates that students are eager, alert, receptive and full of questions. Many of the students at SNDT University come from very orthodox families. As expected, the feedback reveals that exposed to the course, they have started to question the discipline and the traditional values within their families. They have started, questioning traditional role expectations which they had earlier accepted with ease. Many of them now consider some of these expectations to be a violation of their personal dignity and individual freedom. Some of them are able to cope with this sense of violation and advance towards greater autonomy and independence. But many face deep personal conflicts in striking a balance between what they have been raised to believe and what they now determine on their own. This conflict is part of the process of their empowerment. It is part of their advance towards autonomy, freedom, and the new rights and opportunities available to them. But it is difficult to handle. The challenge for the University committed to the empowerment of its students, is to help them to resolve this conflict and to advance without allowing their new awareness and sense of violation to seriously damage their personalities or destroy their relationships within their families. It may not be easy but surely there will be a way out some day.

### Transition of Indian Society from Traditional to Modern

Two points are sought to be made here :

First, that India has always been the land of contrasts and that a wide spectrum of value systems, from the extremely "traditional" to the extremely "modern" exist side by side.

Second, that Indian society remains firmly rooted in the patriarchal ideology which is premised upon male supremacy and a legitimization of women's oppression. Because this basic ideology remains largely unchallenged and unchanged, violence against women is also perpetuated, sometimes in the old forms and sometimes in different and newer guises.

The concept of tradition and modernity is debatable as indeed the factors for classification are based on tradition and culture which are largely followed in underdeveloped countries. There is the additional need to distinguish between "modernization" and "Westernization". However, we can bypass these complexities by simply employing the term "tradition" to mean age-old customs and "modernity" to mean partly Westernized social practices thus focusing primarily on the multiple forms of violence against women which remain an oppressive reality.

### Prevalence of Patriarchy

Patriarchy as prevalent in India a hundred years ago was premised upon the male predominance authority, power and female subordination and subservience, the woman's wife-mother role as her *raison d'être*, and her status as the legal, economic and sexual property of her husband. This was sacralized through the ancient Hindu socio-legal treatises. The most authoritative of these, the *Manusmriti*, stipulated that a woman had to be under the protection and control of her father in childhood, her husband in youth and her sons in her widowed old age, and furthermore that a woman does not deserve independence. This dictate was translated into practice with ease given the practices of universal and early marriage for women (always before puberty in the upper castes and usually so in other castes and also among other religions), immediate post-pubertal consummation of marriage, early and frequent pregnancies and physical and verbal violence in the marital home. Thus, the traditions were legitimized due to sanctions from treatises.

A woman's life revolved around the extended family which was a small community in itself, finely graded along the triple axes of sex, age and degree of relationship with the head of the family. The extended family spanned several generations and comprised the patriarch and his younger brothers with their families, all the married sons with their families, all the unmarried sons and daughters and sometimes widowed or deserted daughters who returned to the parental home. The source of power was the patriarch who designed the chief economic resource of the family, its immoveable property and ancestral wealth, to be held in common by all the males born into the family, as coparceners: so that the daughters were not entitled to a share in this indivisible property and were therefore compensated at marriage with a smaller share of the moveable property, especially jewellery, clothes and household articles. This bridal portion was intended to be treated strictly as her "woman's wealth" solely under her control but was eventually transmuted into "dowry" to which her husband and marital family laid claim. The economic dependence caused by this loss of assets was considerably aggravated in those regions where women were largely economically inactive. Directly or indirectly man controlled all the wealth and made woman a puppet to their whims and fancies.

*Male Monopoly*

The male monopoly of domestic authority and decision-making powers increased women's dependence on their husbands and grown-up sons through whom alone they could access power. Whereas a son would remain within the family, carry on the family name, care for his parents in their old age, and perform the necessary rituals after their death, a daughter would marry and leave the parental home and was thus in effect "a stranger's wealth" — to be nurtured and trained only to be given away at the great expense of a suitable dowry. The preference for a son and undesirability of daughters stemmed from this situation, as did the mother's possessive love for her son/s as her future protector/s and provider/s. Such values relegated women to a low value premium in the family.

*Mother-in-law Syndrome*

A bride entered her husband's family after marriage according to the practice of patrilocal residence as the junior-most and most vulnerable member. A strong bond between her and her husband was prevented from developing by his mother who wished to monopolize his affections in the interests of her own survival. Thus the institutionalized harassment of the bride or the "mother-in-law" syndrome came into being. Whereas all the brothers grew up and continued to live together in an atmosphere conducive to male bonding, a parallel female bonding was effectively prevented by the fact that all daughters-in-law were unrelated outsiders in competition with each other for a better share in the common resources for themselves and their children and that the mothers-in-law were in competition with their daughters-in-law. Thus patriarchy effectively pitted the women against one another and revealed the divisive potential of the extended family as far as women were concerned. The pattern thus cultivated was a well calculated move and developed through well-motivated ideals.

*Female Undesirability Deprivation*

This normative structure has resulted in the traditional institutionalization of violence where violence against women started almost at birth, its most extreme form being the culturally legitimized femicide through female infanticide. Limited to parts of Rajasthan and Gujarat (and was forbidden by British legislation introduced in 1877 specifically in these areas), a girl was usually made to feel unwelcome and undesirable as well as inferior to her brothers and to all men in general. Physical chastisement, sometimes in quite severe forms, was meted out to her by her mother who was solely entrusted with the task of socializing and disciplining her for her future wifely role — thus sometimes obstructing a warm mother-daughter relationship from developing. Given her burden some share in the household duties, a girl experienced only daughterhood and was deprived of a carefree childhood which was reserved for boys. The denial of education to girls even among the traditionally literate upper castes which provided mandatory education for boys was another discrimination largely aimed at keeping females submissive and ill informed about their rights.

## Value Systems

### *Early Marriage*

Marriage well before the age of puberty, the girl was sent to her husband's house as soon as she came of age, and the marriage was consummated immediately usually with appropriate ceremonies. The early start of married life followed by early motherhood — sometimes in the early teens and always by the midteens — was physically traumatic, debilitating and injurious upto the point of death. Failure on the wife's part to produce a child — and sometimes failure to produce a son — could jeopardize her position in the marital family and could lead to her being deserted by her husband making it even worse for the women.

### *Widowhood*

Widowhood in some parts of India (notably Bengal and Rajasthan) lead to the widow's immolation on the funeral pyre of her husband until stopped by British legislation in 1829. In other regions of India and in the castes which did not practise widow immolation, a widow still suffered a social death. Having outlived her main sexual and reproductive function in life, she was made to live a life of sufferance by renouncing all forms of enjoyment and wear drab clothes. She was sometimes physically disfigured (for example, by shaving off her head as in Maharashtra) considered inauspicious and treated as a household drudge. Upper caste widows were forbidden by religion to remarry, even though they were widowed in childhood and even after the Widow Remarriage Act of 1856 made it legally valid, while widowers were encouraged to remarry at once.

## Forms of Violence

The large bulk of the population living in rural areas has not changed much during the last hundred years and still follows some of the customs outlined above. There are occasional female infanticides in small rural pockets in Tamil Nadu and Rajasthan, frequent early marriages (sometimes below the minimum legal limit), early motherhood, inadequate information about the access to family planning methods. Dowry demands and related harassment, as well as wife-battering are rampant. A few incidents of widow immolation have also been reported in the recent past from rural Rajasthan.

Other forms of violence which are passive include inadequate nutrition and health care for girls and women. Many demographers claim that the unbalanced sex ratio in India, showing a female deficit is due to higher mortality among women caused by health neglect. It is alarming that the general proportion of women in the total population is not only unbalanced but also declining consistently, at the Census of 1901 there were 972 females per 1000 males, while in 1991 there was a further drop to 929 females per 1000 males.

**Indian Society Today**

At the other extreme is a very small progressive segment in urban upper class Westernized areas where the situation has changed radically and where women enjoy the benefits of education, careers, economic independence and occasionally of political power, although true gender equality still remains an elusive dream.

Somewhere in the middle lies the urban, educated, relatively well-off and partly conventional section of society where the value system is less harshly patriarchal than before, but where gender discrimination and oppression still continue. The undesirability of daughters still remains deeply entrenched in the Indian psyche, and a new form of eliminating girl babies through female foeticide is becoming prevalent through the diagnostic technique of amniocentesis — basically designed for detecting foetal abnormalities — to determine the sex of the foetus, followed by the selective abortion of female foetuses. The practice continues despite the recent legislation to prevent sex-determination and sex-preselection — a telling example of misuse of science. Having enjoyed a childhood relatively free from cares or household duties, the girls are psychologically always being made aware that marriage is their primary career and educational achievements or job-oriented careers are of secondary importance. Marriage takes place after (usually soon after) the age of 18, the minimum legal age at marriage for women, and still tends to be universal. Though now with education and awareness, girls do not want to join the bandwagon of lifelong drudgery. They would rather settle for an identity of their own through entering into an occupation of their choice and stand on their own feet.

Dowry demands are on the rise whether due to increase in registration or in reality is a matter to be studied. Torture of the bride for extorting more money and consumer goods resulting sometimes in death (either through suicide or outright murder by burning camouflaged as an accident while cooking), continue on a large scale in spite of relataively stringent legal provisions. The culprits are rarely arrested more so, rarely convicted.

The chief attribute which earns a woman true respect is motherhood. The pressure to produce sons remains unabated. The wife/mother has to submit to the decisions of her husband or mother-in-law rarely having any say. Even when families are planned and limited, the chief responsibility for contraception rests with the woman, and usually takes the form of sterilization through surgical procedure.

The man takes the back seat — not ready to face any inconvenience — all at the woman's expense. A widow can rarely claim her rightful share in her marital property and continues to be economically dependent.

**Sexual Violence**

The ever-present threat of sexual violence, by far the most common type of violence against women, similar in all societies covers a wide range. The least serious is "sexual harassment" or Eve-teasing in India (and the offenders labelled indulgently as "roadside Romeos" and glamorized in Hindi movies) though it remains a very humiliating experience for women. It is encountered in public places and on the streets, in the form of wolf whistles, touching, pushing or pawing. In the workplace it may lead to sexual demands from superiors, in rural areas it is village headmen or other powerful men who exert such pressure. More serious is sexual assault which does not technically amount to rape and does not carry a severe penalty. Rape is legally defined in India as involving penetration of the vagina by the penis, thereby revealing the underlying patriarchal assumption that the offence consists in the violation not of the woman's body and personhood but of another man's sexual property. Another way of holding the man on the helm. A male chauvenistic viewpoint.

Other than the physical trauma, there are several frightening aspects related to sexual assault and rape. The stigma attached to the victim rather than the culprit, even when the cultprit is apprehended (which is well-nigh impossible because of the private nature of the offence and the difficulty of proving lack of consent on the woman's part when her own testimony is not considered sufficient) being one aspect. The second aspect is that the victims are not necessarily adult women of a sexually active age group, but can be small babies or old women, a proof that the crime is directed against the entire sex and stems from a view of women *per se* as sex objects.

If a woman is viewed primarily as her husband's property, an effective way of penalizing him is to snatch away or violate his property, that is, his wife. An increasingly common phenomenon in India today is the large-scale violation of women, with rape used as an instrument of revenge upon men, this has been widely experienced in situations of ethnic violence.

Indian society is a mixture of traditional and modern values. On the one hand, we have the belief that women must get education, employment, better health care and more freedom of choice; we also accept their entry into the professions and positions of power (including the prime ministership, the highest office in the country). On the other hand, the basic view of women as inferior and subordinate remains unchanged. Again, the improvement in their status is usually, though not always, more apparent than real and modern technological knowledge and health facilities are sometimes used to the detriment of women. This is the nature of society — a strange blend of tradition and modernity.

**The Role of Media**

Without changing the basic view of women as inferior, servile, self-sacrificing and as essentially instruments of sexual gratification and reproduction, the problem of violence cannot be resolved. The mass media of entertainment is largely responsible for this image. One powerful influence on public opinion is exerted through movies. In a country which is largely poor and illiterate, movies are inevitably an important source of entertainment; and they provide a skillful combination of the woman's traditional role model as the submissive, self-sacrificing, all-forgiving, nurturing wife-mother and the liberated girl who flaunts her bodily attractions to satisfy the common male fantasies. An additional obnoxious feature of popular movies is the depiction of rape as entertainment.

To resolve the problem of women therefore needs a revolutionary change in values, else the problem will continue in their usual and even newer forms.

Six

# Victims of Violence

The fact that violence against women should have attracted so much attention in recent years may speak for a greater sensitivity to human suffering, a keener sense of the demands of justice in our society. But that such violence should persist, even increase as a backlash as the women's movement gains strength, would indicate that matters are much more complicated. To combat this violence one must first understand it. Here the breakthrough has come with the feminist movement which has been able to conceptualize violence in terms of an inevitable manifestation of the patriarchal system, a system resting on and vesting in the subordination and exploitation of women, a system that is age-old, worldwide and is only beginning to be challenged. One reason why violence against women is so difficult to eradicate is precisely because it is socially sanctioned to some degree. Even today the wife and mother roles are seen as women's primary roles. Thus patriarchy legitimizes women's oppression.

## Types of Violence

How pervasive and how brutal the violence is proves by the fact that 50 per cent of Canadian women have experienced at least one instance of violence since the age of 16. Around three quarters of the women killed annually in Canada are by the very men they are living with. Many of these killings are of an exceptionally brutal nature and are accompanied by sexual assault, also brutal. Six women are burnt every day on an average in Gujarat. Studies of the violence that is prostitution indicate that it has taken on the dimensions of an industry. It is estimated, for instance, that 2 lakh Nepali women are working in Indian brothels, the largest number of them belonging to the age group of 10 to 14 years. There are numerous instances of the extreme brutality to which young wives are routinely subjected, such as being locked up without food, light or air, being made to stand on one foot, being made to stand with a grind-stone on the head.

The vulnerability of children to sexual abuse and violence also co-exists in society. No place is safe, not the home, the campus, the work-place or the street. No age is safe: infants, old women, paraplegics can all be victims of rape. Several of the victims of rape are children. There are instances of child brides who develop a horror of sex, leading to their abandonment by their much older husbands. It is devastating to note that vulnerability of children in flesh trade. Exposed to infection and violence at the pre-natal stage, forced to sleep at night under the cot of the mother who is presented herself with a chain of clients, they are, if girls, soon forced into the trade and are constantly exposed to the danger of rape. Lori Haskell cites figures demonstrating the revictimization of women abused in childhood, while Julie Lee stress the utter isolation of such a girl child, whom no one believes and whom her own mother will not protect. Jaya Sagade points to some of the factors such as superstition that prompt men to rape a child.

Mass violence against the weaker sections of society, whether on the basis of class, caste, race, religion or gender, frequently takes the form of mass rapes and gang rapes of the women of the targeted group. This amply bears out our contention that violence is a means of asserting power. The dishonouring of the women of the other group is a blow directed at the men, a violation of their property and it is noteworthy how the upper castes, the upper classes and the state machinery act in collusion in the mass rapes of lower class and caste women whenever their community struggles for its rights, whether it be the right to own the lands they till, or the state's decision in favour of positive discrimination in their favour in matters of education and employment. Police harassment of the poor is a routine, which in time of stress, leads to the targeting of one particular community. It is important to draw attention to a recent tendency that is particularly dangerous to the women's movement, the tendency of women themselves to become polarized in terms of community, setting up a dichotomy between 'our' women who are sacred and 'their' women who are fit targets for attack.

### The International Scene

Another issue which is of concern is the violence in the form of racial discrimination that is directed against women of colour in Canada along with their men. These women are assigned ill-paid jobs in the unorganized sector which are not commensurate with their qualifications. Women's organizations working with women of colour are reluctant to recommend mandatory arrest for male offenders, since they are keenly aware that the justice system will deal with them much more harshly than with white offenders.

The machinery of the State — the law, the police, the judiciary — has an important role to play in the eradication of violence. There was a mandate given to the Women's Commission recently set up in Maharashtra State to ensure that the Fundamental Rights and Directive Principles of the Indian Constitution which stipulate equality before the law and prohibit discrimination are effectively implemented. The Commission recommends legislation monitors the implementation of existing laws and frames schemes for more effective implementation. It is privileged the authority to investigate complaints and to inspect detention and custodial centres. The Committee has recommended the setting up of vigilance committees and of police cells among other measures.

The Government of Canada has become increasingly conscious of the demands of gender justice, while recent reports revealing the magnitude of violence against women have spurred the consideration of a national action plan aimed at its eradication. Equal opportunity guidelines and policies on affirmative action have already been formulated. The Provincial Government of Ontario has set up the Ontario Women's Directorate under a minister responsible for women's issues. The Directorate has been able to provide funds for support services such as Rape Crisis Centres and a criminalization strategy has been enforced whereby the laying of charges for wife assault becomes mandatory. One goal of the Directorate is the creation of public awareness along with a programme of sensitization of those responsible for law enforcement for which seminars are being organized for crown attorneys and from the judiciary.

The situation in Alberta where a minister for women's issues who totally lacked a feminist perspective went so far as to say that there are no women's issues left and where appointments to commissions are patronage appointments shows clearly the importance of a feminist perspective. Institutionalized power generally perpetuates violence against women, even services such as health and education. And within this general scenario there is marked discrimination against non-whites and lower classes. There have been instances of bitter experience of the reluctance of the government machinery to fund support services.

Disillusionment with regard to the law, the police and the judiciary is widespread among victims and activists. Studies and statistics show how few cases are reported to the police, an activist who studied law in order to be of greater use to women victims, now advises them to avoid going to court. The reasons for this failure of the machinery of redressal are several. In the first place there are lacunae in the law itself. A glaring instance is the rape law in India. In the law, as it stands, a woman has to prove that consent was withheld and the criteria for this are so framed that it becomes virtually impossible for her to prove that her passive submission was not consent. Then again women are ignorant of legal provisions. Hence they do not know that the law offers them protection. Thus, majority of women do not avail themselves of the law regarding maintenance. Nor do they know that certain necessary measures must be taken in time. The medical report required in cases of rape is an instance.

It is reported that the legal system in the case of women represents further victimization, sentences being light and discriminatory, depending on the race of the perpetrator. The system apparently views crimes against property as more serious than crimes against persons, particularly female persons. The humiliation of rape victims in court and the social stigma that is attached to the victim are reasons for the reluctance of girls and women to appeal for justice. There is evidence corroborating the fact that child victims are disbelieved and are humiliated on interrogation. The poor are subjected to persecution by the police which is why they distrust the machinery of the law. The pressure by local bureaucrats and politicians is particularly unchecked in rural areas and small towns and bribes are freely given so that the woman victim ends by finding herself put in the wrong. Similar discriminatory treatment, in this case of non-whites, is observed in Canada.

Several case studies reveal, the reluctance of victims of domestic violence in their dying declarations to implicate their husbands reasons being: The woman often fears retaliation against her children and her parental family in the event of her accusing her husband or in-laws. She also pathetically clings to the notion of a family honour that must be protected. In the absence of such clear evidence it is often difficult to establish that a death by burning is a case of homicide and not a suicide or accident as claimed by the culprits.

The police and judiciary are all the products of the same

patriarchal system that subordinates women. Their attitudes to the victims as well as the perpetrators of violence are shaped by patriarchal beliefs. It is small wonder that there is delay in bringing cases to trial and that the accused get away with light sentences. Activists have therefore come to see the need to liaise with the police, while at the same time striving to bring about a change in their attitudes. An attempt in this direction is being made by the cell run by the Tata Institute of Social Sciences at the police headquarters in Mumbai. Since members of the cell are available to assist victims in registering complaints and obtaining legal aid, victims feel assured of competent advice and a following up of the case. As it is backed with the support of police, the cell in its turn carries more weight. The police have collaborated in rushing emergency aid in crises, in recovering *stridhan* (the wealth given by the parental family to the bride, which is to be treated as her property, not that of her husband) and in obtaining custody of children. Training for police personnel has also been organized in which they are given information regarding the law as well as trained in sympathetic interviewing and investigation. Ultimately it is only a strong women's movement that can galvanize the state machinery into action, change deeply-entrenched social attitudes and provides a safe space and redressal for individual victims. Such a movement gathers strength through organizing study circles to create feminist awareness among women, pressing for changes in legislation, banding women together in mass campaigns imparting awareness in society through pamphlets, posters, songs, street plays and films. The play "A Girl Child is Born", produced by Sharada Sathe's organization, was enacted before large audiences of women all over Maharashtra and sharply brought home to them that the many instances of denial and oppression they had lived through were part of the lot of the girl child in patriarchy.

Research has proved that small determined groups can, in the face of the discouragement and hostility, step by step, build up their services so as to provide a centre for counselling and redressal, a crisis line, access to a safe space. During the worst communal riots in Ahmedabad, it was a women's organization which protested arrests, registered cases, set up night vigilance committees, nursed the injured. In a rare demonstration of courage, a group of women could intervene in a case of rape by accosting the perpetrator. Demonstrations in support of individual victims have been able at least in some cases to press for justice for victims of rape and domestic violence in rural Gujarat and this gives them encouragement. The home for prostitute's children in Pune run by Vijaya Lavate's organization has given these most vulnerable children a chance to have a normal childhood.

Counselling services also provide a great support to victims of violence. All of them stress that a sympathetic hearing brings immense relief to a woman who has hitherto been disbelieved and belittled. Even centres which lack trained workers, such as the student centre at McGill University in Montreal can offer this service, while directing the women to other centres which are staffed by experienced professional counsellors. The stages through which counselling must proceed if it is to lead to resocialization are: in the beginning women learn to identify controlling behaviour and to understand at the impact of violence on themselves and their children. Later they are led to question the patriarchal system itself, which represents a challenge to deeply-embedded cultural and social beliefs. They also undertake the counselling of perpetrators of violence. The object is to make them realize that an act of violence is a conscious choice made by themselves, that they cannot push away the responsibility.

The counselling of children is again skilled task, whether they are themselves victims or are witnesses to violence directed against their mothers.

Activists are acutely aware that without a shelter where women are safe from their persecutors, what they can achieve for these women will always be limited. For want of a shelter there is often no alternative but to work for a compromise and run the risk of sending the woman to her death. There are two major drawbacks of the existing shelters run by government or by charitable organizations lacking a feminist perspective. These will generally not accept children above a certain age and they also confine the women to the premises. Hence many women who can make no alternative arrangement for the children and who must work to support themselves cannot avail themselves of their facilities.

Women in India, however, can draw encouragement from the fact that it was only after a long struggle and much disappointment that these shelters could be established and similarly their own efforts too will, in time, bear fruit. One notes also to what extent can be done even in the absence of a full-time shelter. When the shelter in Kenora (Canada) had to close down for a length of time for lack of funds, members sheltered women in their own homes, accompanied them to the police, the courts and hospitals and operated a crisis line.

Dilemmas and differences of approach do exist even among feminist workers struggling to combat violence. There is a tendency among some to avoid involvement with the police and courts, whereas others take the view that these too serve a purpose. Sharp differences of opinion exist on whether an organization should clearly declare that it is feminist in aims and outlook or should refrain from doing so to avoid alienating some sections of women. For instance, there are several diametrically opposed attitudes to prostitution. Among feminists there are those who see it as a choice of profession by the individual woman which must be respected, while others stress the fact that large numbers of women are not only forced through poverty to turn to prostitution but are literally forced into it, having been sold or abducted. They are then faced with a dilemma: how can they reconcile their support for these women in their struggle for better treatment without condoning prostitution as an institution?

In spite of such differences, their commitment to the cause of women has led women's organizations to network and to fight shoulder to shoulder on issues of common concern. But not all these organizations have a specifically feminist commitment. It is only such a commitment that can take them beyond individual issues and lead them to challenge patriarchy as a system for reaching the desired results.

# Seven

# Coping with Violence

Women are the pillars of our society. They constitute half of the population and play a crucial role in all spheres of life. Creating life, nurturing it, she also guards and strengthens it. Through her role as mother, she plays a vital role for the nation.

Why then has her status been ranked lower as compared to a man's status. She has no identity of her own. Her identity being her relationship with a man — being the mother, wife, daughter and sister of a man.

Women are victimized in many ways through overwork, undernourishment and ill treatment, having no say in any matter. It is for us to investigate into the attitude of indifference prevailing in our society and ensure justice and equitable status for them.

Factors which attribute this indifference are: Lack of awareness of seriousness of the problem, general acceptance of man's superiority over woman being the reason why violence against women was not viewed as violent or deviant, and the denial of violence by women themselves owing to their religious values and socio-cultural attitudes. As the cases of wife-battering, rapes, kidnappings and abductions, intra-familial murders, dowry-deaths, eve-teasing, molestation, etc., have been more frequently reported since the late 1960s and early 1970s, the issue of violence against women has been transformed from a private issue into a public problem.

## The Issue of Violence Against Women

We should focus our study on interpersonal relations and the social context in which violence is committed or atrocities are inflicted on women and in which the victim recovers and adjusts. All these issues have to be examined and assessed with a sociological perspective. The present study presents not only the conceptual perspectives with which to understand the problem but also analyses the socio-cultural and interpersonal determinants of violence, shock, and recovery.

In the West, sociologists have started taking interest in social problems like gender equality and female exploitation ever since they shifted their perspective in order to consolidate their appreciation of social dynamics. Similarly, criminologists, particularly radical crime scientists, have started taking interest in problems such as criminal violence against women ever since they initiated reappraisal of the old assumptions underlying certain crucially socially-problematic behaviour. This has had profound consequences in research and theory building. It has become increasingly difficult to perceive that criminality, specifically male criminality, is a behavioural quality monopolized by a narrow section of the lower class. However, in India, both sociologists and criminologists have yet to develop sustainable interest in this crucial problem of deviant behaviour against women and realize their academic as well as social responsibility; in fact, they have conveniently ignored the evaluation of social and legal norms and the underlying morality of society that criminalizes activities, born out of the contradictions in social values and sub-systems.

It may be true that the incidence of violence by men towards women is not identical in all groups and communities, and that moral and social beliefs and family arrangements differ from group to group, yet instead of looking into these group differences and analyzing the subcultural and socio-ethical beliefs of these groups, we should concentrate on violence against women as perceived in general terms. There is no woman who has not suffered at one time or another the harassment, humiliation, exploitation and violence that shadows her sex. A woman's life swings between pleasure at one end and danger at the other end. In daily life, women are routinely defined by sex, and even if not all men are potential kidnappers, rapists, batterers, molesters and torturers of women, all women are potential victims.

## Status of Women in India

Women in India are way ahead of their counterparts elsewhere in the matter of social legislation. However, in matters of implementation of laws granting rights to women we have been lagging far behind. Women are discriminated against at work and are denied their due in every field. At home, they are ever worse off, being reduced to slavish drudges and maltreated in a hundred different ways. Constantly rebuked and mocked at, frequently bullied, sometimes assaulted, and occasionally burnt to death, they remain victims in every role. Indian women, thus, have been described as the underdogs of society where, in theory the law of equality exists, and women are considered to be on a par with their male counterparts, but in reality, men remain all powerful and thrive at the expense of women. While in the West, women's problem/issue is mostly one of identity, job equality, and sexual roles, in India, the question is simply one of stark survival.

The Constitution of India guarantees equality, freedom, opportunity and protection to women, and various social legislations give them several exclusive rights. Yet, they enjoy an unequal status. This may be due to the social conditions in our society like illiteracy, poverty, social customs, ignorance, and lack of awareness of rights, while others relate it with their personality characteristics like feeling of helplessness, inferiority complex, poor self-image, lack of self-confidence, self-reliance, and resourcefulness. Added to these is their unrecognized output in domestic chores and help to male family members in their economic pursuits.

Recently, incidents of aggressive violence against women are reported to be escalating alarmingly in our country, and this in itself is a sufficient cause for growing concern, and on the other hand, awareness of rights among women has increased, leading to the rise of feminist movement, resulting in a new sensitivity to all forms of subjugation of women by men. Rise in the rate of crimes against women have been reported in all types of crimes—ranging from eve-teasing to abduction and killing. For example, against 2,487 cases of rape in 1971, 5,409 cases were reported in 1981, 9,793 in 1991, 12,351 in 1994, and 13,754 in 1995 (*Crime in India*, 1995: 222). This comes to 38 rapes a day or about three rapes every two hours. Similarly, 28,475 molestations were registered in 1995 against 20,611 in 1991 (*Ibid:* 222). Such trend has been seen in other crimes too. The number of registered cases having spiralled alarmingly in the past few years, the actual number of cases reported is estimated to be many times more than the number registered. In cases like rape, it may be even 15 to 20 times more— large number of rape, assault, and battering cases being marginalized due to social pressures.

**Data on Crime Against Women**

Let us first have a glance at the background material for general issues in some important categories of violence against women.

Strangely, no statistics on crimes against women were collected separately by the Ministry of Home Affairs or the Police Research

Bureau till 1988. It was only in 1989 that data relating to crimes against women began to be collected. These data relate to: (a) incidence of crimes committed, (b) number of persons arrested, (c) cases disposed of by the police/courts, and (d) social background of victims.

**Classification of Crime under Law**

Crimes against women are broadly classified under two categories:

(A) crimes identified under the Indian Penal Code (IPC) and

(B) crimes identified under the special laws (SL).

The crimes under the former category include eight types:

(i) rape (section 376 IPC),

(ii) kidnapping and abduction (section 363 and 373),

(iii) dowry homicides (section 302 and 304B),

(iv) torture—physical and mental (section 498A),

(v) molestation (section 354),

(vi) eve-teasing or sexual harassment (section 509),

(vii) importation of girls (section 366B), and

(viii) murder (other than dowry homicides) (section 302).

The crimes under the last category includes four types:

(a) immoral trafficking (1956 Act),

(b) demanding dowry (1961 Act),

(c) commission of *sati* (1987 Act), and

(d) indecent representation of women (1986 Act).

*Statistics of Women's Crimes under Law*

On the total crimes committed in India under the IPC every year, about 6 per cent are crimes against women. In 1995, of the total crimes committed under the IPC (16.95 lakhs), 6.3 per cent were crimes against women (*Crime in India,* 1995: 223). Taking the total crimes against women recorded under the IPC and the SL, 8 per cent were Local and Special Laws cases and 92 per cent were IPC cases.

The statistics collected point out that the total number of crimes against women (under the IPC and the SL) (excluding murders) increased from 68,000 in 1990 to 74,000 in 1991, 79,000 in 1992,

84,000 in 1993, 99,000 in 1994 and 106,000 in 1995 (*Crime in India*, 1995: 223). Thus, in five years (between 1991 and 1995), crimes against women increased by 45 per cent.

*Break-up*

Of the crimes against women committed in 1995 under the IPC and the SL (1,06,471), about 29 per cent are torture cases, 27 per cent are molestation cases, 13 per cent are kidnapping and abduction cases, 13 per cent are rape cases, 4.5 per cent are sexual harassment cases, 8 per cent are immoral traffic cases, 5 per cent are dowry-homicide cases, and 0.5 per cent are other cases (*Ibid:* 222). Broadly speaking, every year, under the IPC, there are about 31,000 torture cases (cruelty by husband and other relatives), 28,000 molestation cases, 14,000 kidnapping and abduction cases, 14,000 rape cases, 5,000 eve-teasing cases, and 5,000 dowry-homicide cases (*Ibid:* 222). Likewise under the SL, there are about 7,500 cases of woman trafficking, 2,800 cases of dowry harassment, 400 cases of indecent representation of women, and 170 cases of importing of girls, and one or two *sati* cases.

*All India Ranking of Crime*

The highest recorded cases of crime are from Maharashtra (15.3%) followed by Madhya Pradesh (14.4%), Uttar Pradesh (11.2%), Rajasthan (8.8%), Andhra Pradesh (8.5%), Tamil Nadu (8.2%) and West Bengal (6%). Of the 1,06,471 recorded cases in 1995 (under IPC and SL) in the country.

*Rajasthan*: In Rajasthan, the incidence of crimes against women has sharply increased since 1994. Many committed by influential and moneyed people who could manipulate things in their favour namely — the Shalini Sharma sex scandal of Alwar; the throwing of acid on Shivani Jadeja in Jaipur; the J.C. Bose (Rajasthan University) Hostel gang rape of a girl by seven persons (including the nephew of a minister, an advocate and a police officer); the alleged rape of a woman in Jalore district by a Jain monk who later committed suicide; and the Chomu firing case over the issue of a woman's rape are some of the more serious examples of increasing crime. A point worth noting is that in all these cases, the women involved were blamed and held responsible through manipulation. Rajasthan thus being designated as Rapisthan.

*Orissa:* In Orissa also, atrocities on women have been similarly on the rise since 1991. Rape cases have registered an alarming increase of about 33 per cent every year. While in 1991, 309 rape cases were registered, their number had gone up to 372 in 1995 and 617 in 1996. Dowry-homicides in the state rose from 98 in 1991 to 169 in 1995 and 354 in 1996, and dowry torture cases from 214 in 1991 to 710 in 1996. The torture of women (not for dowry) was also on the rise with such cases increasing from 183 in 1991 to 361 in 1995 and 405 in 1996. The kidnapping of women increased from 209 in 1991 to 221 in 1995 (*The Hindustan Times,* March 11, 1997).

*Delhi:* The Delhi figures of crimes against women, as revealed in the latest data issued by the Delhi State Commission for Women are simply shocking wherein *Situation of Girls and Women in Delhi,* Delhi's record in rape cases was twice as bad as that of all the three metropolitan cities (Mumbai, Chennai and Kolkata) put together. That the rate of crimes against women in the capital was far higher than that of the national average (34.1 per lakh of population against 9.5) represented one part of the problem. The alarming aspect was that minor girls were particularly targeted as victims. The incidence of rape cases involving girls below 10 years of age in Delhi was four times higher than that of the rest of the country. What was even more shocking, was the fact that crime in 88 per cent of the cases was committed by relatives or acquaintances, and in 89 per cent of the cases, it was committed at home. The problem thus goes out of the control of police or law and order. It underlines a psychopathic condition (*The Hindustan Times,* March 5, 1997).

## Categories of Violence

There are six categories of violence: sexual violence, kidnapping and abduction, dowry deaths, murder, wife-battering, and a few other specific categories of violence like torture, molestation, etc. These have been discussed in the following pages:

### *(i) Sexual Violence*

#### *Rape*

Virginity is valued by man, yet it is man who violates it and commits rape. The important factors in rape are: age, consent (including implied consent and obtaining consent under fraudulent pretext of marriage), duress, state of mind and resistance. Section 376 of the Indian Penal Code describes rape as sex with a woman against her will, or without her consent, or with her consent when the man knows that he is not her husband but she believes him as her husband, or with or without her consent when she is under sixteen years of age. Statistics on rape worldwide show that in the United States, the annual rate of rape offences is about 26, in Canada 8, and in the UK 5.4 per one lakh of total population against 1.38 in India, 3.62 in China and 1.29 in Japan.

There are fewer cases of rape in India as compared to the West. The number of rape cases per one lakh population in 1993 was only 0.5. However, in the last decade, rape cases were more than doubled. Of the 13,754 rape victims reported in 1995, 5.4 per cent were below 10 years, 24.1 per cent between 10 and 16 years, 56.3 per cent between 16 and 30 years, and 14.2 per cent were 30 years and above (*Ibid:* 226). The highest number of rape cases in 1995 was reported from Madhya Pradesh (22.7%), followed by Uttar Pradesh (13.1%), Maharashtra (9.9%), Bihar (9.5%), Rajasthan (7.5%), Andhra Pradesh (6.2%), West Bengal (5.7%), Assam (4.3%) and 21.1 per cent from other states and union territories (*Ibid:* 237).

*Causes of Escalation*

Though it is difficult to indicate the causes of increase in the incidence of this crime, some factors which appear to have an impact on the conservative social morals and on the increasing rate of rape could be identified as :

(i) urbanization and urbanism;

(ii) industrialization and the growth of slums;

(iii) better reporting by the police;

(iv) co-education and co-work;

(v) movies, obscene and pornographic literature;

(vi) changing attitudes towards women;

(vii) decreasing religious restrictions;

(viii) fall in moral values; and

(ix) emergence of the neo-rich people.

It should be clear that these figures do not reveal the true picture. A high percentage of rape cases go unreported either because the victim does not dare to face the shame and humiliation being heaped on her by society, or because of the disgrace it will bring to her family, or because of the police harassment, or threats and consequences by the rapist. Many cases are put behind the action. It is not only the illiterate and the poor but also the educated and the socially advanced victims of rape who are rejected by their own families, and at times forced to take up the oldest profession. Some victims even commit suicide. Social values turn them into outcastes, a disgrace to their family, and unfit to marry. No wonder, therefore, most victims choose to conceal the fact of having been victims of forcible criminal assault.

*Instances*

Shamim (real name concealed), a Muslim girl of seven years, was brutally assaulted in Jandhera village near Meerut in 1994 by a 20-year-old truck-driver, a Dalit from the same village. Shamim's mother, accompanied by two policemen, took the traumatized girl to a hospital in Meerut. The little girl had to be operated upon because of which the doctors said, she would never be able to conceive. The case was brought to the notice of a women's organization—Disha—which got her admitted to a hospital in Saharanpur. The rapist was arrested but soon released on bail. He has since been boasting that "in a state where the Dalits reign supreme (Mayawati at that time was the Chief Minister), no one can touch him". He even went to the extent of taunting Shamim's mother: "Shamim is like the *ber* fruit that can be eaten when it is unripe or when it has ripened." The district magistrate had assured a home to Shamim's homeless family but the assurance remained only on paper. For obvious reasons, the villagers dared not throw the rapist out of the village.

Another instance is, a five-year-old girl who was raped in Pehalwan village in Rajasthan by a shop-owner and his servant. The mother was so traumatized by the incident that she became insane and the father committed suicide. The little girl, who was the butt of cruel jokes and taunts in the village, was moved to an *ashram* in Jaipur.

There is a case of two school teachers, 57 and 52 years old, were suspended and arrested for rape/molestation of three school girls of 12, 13 and 14 years in May 1997 in Uttar Pradesh. They were released on bail by the sessions court which maintained that the medical records did not show rape. It so happened that the teachers had taken the girls to school for coaching in view of the forthcoming school examination. They stayed overnight in the school building. Each child was given five tablets in the night. As fate would have it one child did not take any tablet but the other two took two to three tablets. Two girls were found unconscious in the morning and one was bleeding. They were rushed to a doctor, the husband of an 'anganwadi' worker informed the incident to the parents. The villagers beat up the teachers and rushed the children to a hospital in Saharanpur. After the intervention of the National Commission for Women, the teachers were arrested and suspended. The teachers brought to bear tremendous pressure on the parents to take back the cases. Are these girls to become 'Phoolans' to take revenge?

*The Vulnerable Sections*

The girls belonging to socially deprived classes are not only inclined to be raped, the women employees belonging to socially advanced classes are sexually humiliated and exploited by their employers and thus are equally under the category of possible victims. Similar treatment is meted out to the inmates by the superintendents of hostels, to patients by hospital personnel, to maid-servants by their masters, and to wage-earners by contractors and middlemen. Even the deaf and dumb, lunatics, blind women and beggars are not spared. Women who come from the lower-middle class and who are the main supporters of their families bear sexual abuse silently as a part of life. The reason makes the incidents of rape increase. As culprits are not punished.

At times it is felt that the stories of rape are exaggerated. Women have to deal with these opinions and attitudes as well as with the age-old myths, such as, "a woman cannot be raped unless she wants it". These myths have been coined and propagated by men, for every woman knows that none of these are true, as in India rape is tantamount to death.

The victims are socially ostracized facing disgrace and suffer serious guilt-pangs and personality disorders as a consequence. When pregnancies result from forced rape, all the outraged sentiments of the community are vented on the women. Children are also stigmatized unless their parents marry them, or they are fortunate enough to be adopted into homes sanctified by marriage.

What is the character of rapists? Are they abnormal sexual perverts or ordinary normal men found in all walks of life? Social scientists' contend that by and large they are normal men. A large number of rapes are situational rapes. Criminal assault is instrumental for men either to exploit women or to take revenge. In villages, it is a tool in the hands of the landlords to terrorize their agricultural labourers. One survey on prostitution has revealed that 80 per cent of the prostitutes took up the profession after becoming victims of rape.

*Protection by Law for Women at Work*

Sexual harassment of women at the workplace is also becoming a serious problem day by day. Public interest petitions were filed in the Supreme Court in 1997 by social activists and NGOs to ensure that women be allowed to work freely and with dignity. The Supreme Court directed the centre and the state governments to enforce twelve guidelines to protect women from harassment at the workplace under which it shall be the duty of the employer or other responsible persons in workplaces to prevent the commission of acts of sexual harassment and provide procedures for the resolution, settlement or prosecution of acts of sexual harassment by taking all relevant steps.

Sexual harassment in workplaces, according to the Supreme Court, includes (*Sunday,* September 28-October 4, 1997):

(i) physical intimacy and advances;

(ii) a demand or request for sexual favours;

(iii) sexually tainted remarks;

(iv) showing porn material to women employees; and

(v) any verbal or non-verbal conduct of sexual nature.

*Complaints and Redressals*

There has been a great increase in harassment incidence with more women coming out to work. Between 1992 and 1997, of the total complaints (1817) received by the National Commission for Women, as many as 49 were of sexual harassment at the workplace. A sample survey done by the Delhi-based NGO—Sakshi—among women in the private sector has revealed that 60 per cent of the respondents had at some time or other been victims of sexual harassment and that in almost half the cases, a superior was responsible for the harassment (*The Hindustan Times,* September 21, 1997). Most working women have come to regard sexual harassment as an 'occupational hazard' and society in general believes it is 'normal male behaviour'. In its milder form, sexual harassment is generally abstract and therefore hard to prove. There is no evidence, for instance, of a whispered remark, an obscene sound, or just plain ogling can be provided unless it is persistent and repeated and witnesses are available. The humiliation can be as intimidating, embarassing and annoying as being pinched, shoved or solicited by a stranger. In a survey conducted by Sakshi, 46per cent of the victims chose to do nothing about it because they feared they would not be believed or because of the worry that by complaining they would invite allegations of "taking revenge on male colleagues for relationships besmirched".

Myra Dias who was secretary to the Regional Manager (Western region) of Vayudoot Ltd. was subjected to sexual harassment by the Regional Manager and when she did not yield to his advances, he ensured that she was superseded by her juniors. Myra refused to be cowed down. She appealed to the National Commission for Women who took up the issue and after a six-month battle she was upgraded. Myra's case was an exception. She was brave enough to take up the issue and what is more important is that she won. Less fortunate was Ela Chaudhary, a commercial artist in the Government Directorate of Employment and Training: Ela was molested by her immediate boss. Her complaints to the Director General were of no avail. Counter allegations were made against her like having tampered with the attendance register, etc. Ela took the case to the courts and after an eight-year battle, the remarks in her confidential file were expunged. But it was only after her boss retired that she got justice and her stand was vindicated. Somehow the department delayed the procedure because they wanted him to retire with a clean record (*The Hindustan Times,* September 2, 1997).

*The Unorganized Sector*

Providing protection against sexual harassment may be possible in the organized sector, both in private and government offices, but what about women in unorganized sectors and in rural areas? For example, take the case of domestic female workers or maid-servants or female labourers tilling the land. These women are extremely vulnerable to advances and, having little power to fight such attempts, end up being sexually abused. Caste factor poses another threat. When employees belonging to lower castes are harassed more than those belonging to other castes. In villages, the power structure is controlled by the dominant class. The nexus between the political head of a village and the moneyed gentry is impregnable. Any attempt to quash its stranglehold over the villagers finds with strong resistance.

The court directives to create awareness among women may

be used by NGOs. But what about the harassment which female volunteers with NGOs themselves face carrying out their work? Bhanwari Devi, a Sathin in Rajasthan, displeased many upper caste people for trying to prevent child marriage in her village. She was raped as a punishment. And, of course, her rapists were acquitted by the court.

Eventhough the Supreme Court directives on sexual harassment of women in their workplaces may be well intentioned, they do not appear to be practical. Unless the socio-economic ethos undergoes change, unless women themselves show courage, social legislation is likely to fail to make a difference to the life of those who face the danger of sexual harassment. Trade unions can play a significant role by encouraging women to report cases of sexual harassment and then standing by them. Men should also be sensitized and re-educated. Most of men appreciate and recognize the need for laws and change. Men must be subjected to introspection and to look at the problem in their own context as husbands, employers and colleagues. There is also the tendency to dismiss it as a Western input even though it is very much a part of our own male dominated system.The whole matter should be looked at in the Indian context.

### *(ii) Kidnapping and Abduction*

*Definitions (under IPC)*

Kidnapping (under section 363 of IPC) is taking away or enticing a minor—a female of less than 18 years and a male of less than 16 years of age—without the consent of the lawful guardian.

Abduction (under section 363 of IPC) is forcibly, fraudulently or deceitfully taking away a woman with the intent of seducing her to illicit sex or compelling her to marry a person against her will. Thus 'abduction' differs from 'kidnapping' whereas the latter is committed only in respect of a minor, the former is committed in respect of any person. In kidnapping, the victim's consent is immaterial but in abduction, the victim's free and voluntary consent condones the crime. In kidnapping, the offenders' intent is irrelevant but in abduction, it is an all-important factor. Thus, a girl of 18 and above could only be abducted and not kidnapped; but if she is under 18, she could be kidnapped as well as abducted.

*Statistics*

The incidents of kidnapping and abduction like rape have been increasing in our country by leaps and bounds. The total number of cases recorded in 1990 was 11,699 which increased to 14,063 in 1995 (*Crime in India*, 1995:237). The highest number of kidnapping and abduction cases in 1995 was found in Rajasthan (2,579 out of 14,063 or 18.3%) followed by Uttar Pradesh (16.6%), Assam (7.9%), Madhya Pradesh (7.3%), Gujarat (6.9%), West Bengal (5.8%), Maharashtra (5.6%), Andhra Pradesh (4.8%), and Tamil Nadu (4.7%) (*Ibid:* 237). The rate of this crime per one lakh of population is 2 in our country.

Reports of poor girls being abducted and sold either as wives to rich Arabs or as potential prostitutes to pimps are not unknown. A broker is reported to get from Rs. 5,000 to Rs. 10,000 per girl/woman, and sometimes even more if he caters to every whim and fancy of the prospective customer depending on his economic status. A large number of liaison men and agents are reported operating in big cities. Significantly, the Report of the UN Human Rights Panel has pointed out that the phenomenon—child/girl/woman prostitution—has taken an uglier form in India. The sale of unsuspecting innocent children/girls/women brought from remote tribal areas and villages feeding the big metropolises and other towns and cities has increased.

The number of abducted girls and women rescued is woe-ully small. Some rescued ones are siphoned into the Protection and Correctional Homes. The conditions at Delhi and Agra Nari Niketans which were pursuing flesh trade within their compounds were exposed by the Supreme Court.

***(iii) Dowry Deaths***

The Dowry Prohibition Act, 1961 has banned the practice of dowry, but in reality all that the law has done is to recognize that the problem exists. It is not often that we hear of a husband or his family being sued for insisting on taking a dowry. If anything, the demands for dowry have escalated over the years along with dowry-deaths.

*All India Statistics*

At a modest estimate, the figure for deaths in India that occur due to non-payment or partial payment of dowry could be placed around 5,000 for one year. The total number of deaths was 4,836 in 1990, 5,817 in 1993, 4,935 in 1994, and 5,092 in 1995 (Ibid: 222).

The highest number of cases in 1995 was found in Uttar Pradesh (36.3 per cent), followed by Maharashtra (9.2 per cent), Bihar (7.5 per cent), Rajasthan (7.2 per cent), Andhra Pradesh (7.1 per cent), Haryana (4.3 per cent), Karnataka (4 per cent) and West Bengal (1.7 per cent) (*Ibid:* 237). Under the Dowry Prohibition Act (SL), the number of cases registered in 1990 was 2,155 which increased to 2,679 in 1993 and 2,814 in 1995. Bulk of cases in 1995 were reported from Bihar (982), Uttar Pradesh (653) and Karnataka (337) (*Ibid:* 230).

The Dowry Act, 1961 states that dowry is a bailable and non-cognizable offence and ceases to be recognized if demands are made or met one year after marriage. Most dowry-homicides occur in the privacy of the husband's house and with the collusion of the family members. The inability to convict anyone for lack of proof is therefore a natural concomitant. Sometimes, the police are so callous in conducting investigations that even the courts cast a serious reflection on the efficiency and integrity of the police authorities.

The figures of dowry deaths assuming a large number of unreported deaths are as it is unnerving — leave alone if all figures were included. Having their origins in social, economic and psychological factors, too deep-rooted to be tackled by amending the law their genesis lies in the tension created by persistent demands, accompanied by torture, for dowry. The greed for money, the aggressiveness increased by resistance and the ease with which the weaker sex can be exploited, all combine to encourage family members to take the bride's life.

### *(iv) Murders of Women*

Though all-India figures pertaining to murders and their victims on the basis of sex are unavailable, it is well known that the number of female victims of homicides in comparison to male victims is low. Whereas in the United States, female victims comprise between 20 per cent and 25 per cent of the total victims of homicides (about 25,000 to 30,000 every year), in India of about 38,000 murders committed every year, women constitute about 10 per cent to 15 per cent of the total victims.

#### *Reasons*

Being inspired by many factors, such as illicit relations, petty quarrels, feeling of revenge, the desire to get rid of a person who is to get a share in the property, and so forth, many murders may be disguised as suicides and some are even called 'accidents', as if they are natural deaths in some epidemic.

At times, the victim is believed to be a major contributor to the criminal act. She perpetrates the murder either by her habit of constant nagging, or her illict relations with some other male, or by completely ignoring her husband's or her in-laws' advice, and so forth. The victim may provoke a person into attack, and though the provocation may be slight, if perceived by an egoistic attacker, it may be sufficient to result in homicide. The analysis of the victim-offender relationship in such homicides is, therefore, considered necessary in criminological literature.

*Redressals*

The inability of the kith and kin of the victim to get redressal through courts is a common occurrence. This is due to notoriously long-winded legal procedures and the offender's social and economic status prevents it.

Women's organizations have been galvanized with the rising curve of murders and other crimes against women. The realization has come amongst women that the individual protests are not strong enough to enable them to fight against their collective oppression. They have started forming forums and associations. Moreover the government also keeps on amending the social laws pertaining to marriage and family from time to time. But will the women's voluntary organizations and the government's legislative measures reduce women's oppression. Solving the problem of violence against women is a matter of introspection. What social measures need to be adopted to tackle this problem? These are some of the issues that need our immediate attention.

*Battering of Women*

There can be nothing more shattering for a woman than being battered by a husband who is supposed to love her and look after her and whom she trusted the most. Ranging from slaps, kick to breaking of bones this includes violence torture, attempted murder, and even murder itself. The violence may be related to drunkenesss sometimes but not always. It may also be related to demands for sex, a refusal to obey the husband's commands, extravagance, habit of using vile and disgusting language, and so forth. Battering being occasional or frequent. It may be as frequent as once or twice a week, once or twice a month, or three to four times in a year. In some marital relationships, battering may begin soon after the marriage while, in others it may begin one or two years after marriage. Some wives are held captive by the husbands who insist on controlling their every movement, and knowing every detail of their lives.

*Redressals*

The Indian cultural system rarely gives examples of a wife reporting to the police of having been battered by her husband. Preferring to suffer humiliation in silence, she takes it as her destiny and does not revolt, due to the fear that her own parents would refuse to accept her in their house permanently after the marriage. It is not always the poor and the illiterate who are battered but even the rich and highly educated are similarly undergone to these sort of ordeal by their husbands. Likewise, even those women who earn and are economically independent also face violence.

Male violence crosses class boundaries and has no association with poverty or lack of education. The common public image of the battering husband is of a working-class male. As wife battering is concealed from the public eye, it is difficult to estimate its extent in society. Since divorce cases in the courts are not always related to marital violence, the extent of divorce also does not reveal the nature and extent of wife battering in society. The battered victims and the indignation they face pose a serious problem for society. There is great need to create an awareness for the scientific study of the problem of domestic violence for ascertaining its intensity.

*Miscellaneous Categories of Violence*

*Torture*

Torture of women includes cruelty by husband, in-laws, parents, siblings and relatives. Among crimes reported against women in India, incidence of torture is the highest. Of the total crimes against women (1,06,471) reported in 1995, 29.2 per cent were cases of torture (*Crime in India*, 1995: 222). In a survey, Maharashtra had the highest number of torture cases (28.1 per cent), followed by West Bengal (10.7 per cent), Rajasthan (10.3 per cent), Uttar Pradesh (10.2 per cent), Andhra Pradesh (9.1 per cent), Madhya Pradesh (8.5 per cent) and Gujarat (6.2 per cent) (*Ibid:* 237). Generally, husbands and in-laws are more accused of torture cases, but an exceptional case from Rajasthan in October 1997 shows that brothers and fathers also torture their sisters and daughters. Here, a girl of 22 years was locked in a dark room by her brother for more than two years for her refusal to live with her husband after the marriage. When ultimately the case was reported by a neighbour to the police, she was rescued and admitted to a hospital in Jaipur. The brother and the father of the victim were not arrested till two months after detecting the case.

### *Molestation*

Molestation after torture, is another major crime against women. This constitutes 25 per cent of the total crimes committed against women in our country. While the total number of molestation cases in 1990, 1991, 1992 and 1993 ranged between 20,000 and 21,000, the number increased to 24,117 in 1994 and 28,475 in 1995. The rate of this crime in 1995 was the highest in Madhya Pradesh (25.8 per cent), followed by Maharashtra (12.2 per cent), Andhra Pradesh (9.4 per cent), Uttar Pradesh (9.2 per cent), Rajasthan (7.4 per cent), and West Bengal (4.6 per cent) (*Ibid:* 238) thus accounting for about 70 per cent of the reported cases.

### *Eve teasing*

Eve teasing or sexual harassment is widely prevalent in India. While the total number of these cases was 8,620 in 1990, their number increased to 12,009 in 1993 but decreased to 10,496 in 1994 and 4,756 in 1995. The highest crime rate in 1995 was reported from Tamil Nadu (22.7 per cent), followed by Maharashtra (17 per cent), Andhra Pradesh (16.2 per cent) and Madhya Pradesh (16.1 per cent) (*Ibid:* 238).

### *Importation of girls*

Importation of girls is an insignificant crime in our country. Only 167 cases were reported in 1994 and 191 in 1995. Still the police has to be concerned about this crime. About 80 per cent of the total cases of this crime occurred in the following six states—Andhra Pradesh (33.5 per cent), Punjab (14.1 per cent), Gujarat (11 per cent), Madhya Pradesh (8.9 per cent), Maharashtra (6.8 per cent), and West Bengal (6.3 per cent).

### *Violence: Concept and Definition*

An aspect of power dynamics of social situations 'violence' is not simply aggression or injury committed by one individual (man) against another (woman); it is more precisely the abuse of power; it is a behaviour in which a more powerful person takes advantage of and abuses a less powerful one. This relationship of power differential is clear in sexual violence against women (rape), in their kidnapping and abduction, in physical battering of wives, as well as in dowry deaths and murder of women. In rape, either a man in authority position victimizes a girl in a subordinate position or a male takes advantage of his physical power and assaults a female. In wife battering, a similar principle of the stronger victimizing the weaker operates. High risk category include women who have less power by virtue of not being an earning member, by virtue of being excluded from participation in decision-making because of being considered socially immature, and by virtue of having no education or less education than her husband. This underlies the need for research in the dynamics of power and how it operates in and outside family.

*Violence: Consequences*

Violence has been defined as "injurious and destructive behaviour which damages the victim physically, mentally and/or financially". The three consequences of 'violent behaviour' are: (a) pain to victim, (b) social disapproval and public concern, and (c) realising the need for enacting legislation. That violence against women generally occurs in the privacy of the home or in the privacy of the working places or in the institutions away from the public eye sharply reduces the likelihood of a complaint.

*Crime Against Women*

'Crime against women' refers to crimes in which a woman becomes victim. The phrase contains two terms, viz., 'crime' and 'against women'. While the latter term refers only to those crimes in which the victim is female, the former term is meant by the acts which are legally forbidden, intentionally committed and punishable by courts. If we use the definition of crime as "conduct which incurs the formal punitive pronouncements of the courts", or that crime is "the violation of conduct norms of the normative groups", the scope (of crime) becomes broader and more meaningful vis-a-vis violence against women.

*Aggression*

'Aggression' refers to injurious behaviour. BUSS (*The Psychology of Aggression*, 1961) defines it as "a response that delivers noxious stimuli to another person". Berkowitz used the term to denote "behaviour aimed at the injury of some object". Many issues cloud the definition of aggression.

*Intention*

Is injury to the victim the goal of the perpetrator, or is such injury a by-product of some other goal-seeking behaviour? This issue of intention centres on two things:

(a) whether the perpetrator had a reasonable expectation that his behaviour would injure the victim, and

(b) whether such injury was in fact desired by the offender.

Kaufmann (*Aggression and Altruism*, 1970) opine that unless the person performing, he/she had some expectation that the behaviour would deliver noxious stimulation to the recipient the act would not be considered aggressive. Berkowitz maintained that for an act to be considered aggressive, the injury to the victim had to be reinforcing.

*Injury*

*Another issue is, whether the injury need be only physical or whether there can be psychological injury too. Those definitions which limit aggression to acts that physically injure the victims have the advantage of being precise and operational. Psychological injury refers to disparagement, scolding, coercion, harassment, and a variety of other non-physical agonistic behaviour.*

Buss distinguished 'angry aggression' behaviour that is reinforced by pain or injury to the victim, from 'instrumental aggression' in which aggression is a means to an end. Delivery of electric shock or verbal criticism are two milder forms of instrumental aggression.

*Aggression Vs. Violence*

The term 'violence' may be used for more extreme forms of aggressive behaviour that are likely to cause significant injuries to the victim. Although violence refers to physical aggression, it is also applied to psychological stress that causes suffering or trauma. Broadly, the term 'violence' has been applied to the narrow issue of physically striking an individual (Kempe, 1982) and causing injury (Gil, 1970), to the act of striking a person with the intent of causing harm or injury but not actually causing it (Gelles and Strauss, 1979), to the act where there is the high potential of causing injury, and to the act where there is no actual hitting at all, such as verbal abuse or psychological and emotional violence.

Megargee (1982) has defined violence as the "overtly threatened or overtly accomplished application of force which results in the injury or destruction of persons or property or reputation".

Where does one draw the line between aggression and violence? The rapist, for example, uses coercion to obtain sexual advantage over a non-consenting victim. When that coercion involves the overt or threatened use of physical force, it clearly constitutes violence. But what of psychological coercion? A husband may pressurize his wife to submit to sexual relations. This constitutes sexual harassment. Some writers, however, feel that sexual harassment by husband is not an act of violence whereas some others attempt to resolve the issue by making a distinction between 'force' and 'violence'. Hofstadter (1970) defined acts of force as "those which inhibit the normal free action of movement of other persons, or which inhibit them through the threat of violence". Luckenbill and Sanders (1977) have maintained that some actions, for instance rape, are considered violent yet may involve only force. This would exclude acts like kidnapping from the roster of violent crimes, unless the victim is injured.

Thus, if we wish to use the term 'violence' to denote an observable reality, it (violence) must be recognized as a specifically human phenomenon in as much as it consists of the freedom of one person to encroach upon the freedom of another.

# Eight

# Physical Torture

Women who are married at a younger age are at higher risk of physical violence. The women who got married at younger age were more victims of physical violence by their husbands in contrast to those who got married at later age. Further, it was noted that there was a progressive decrease in the percentages of victims of physical violence from lower age at marriage category to higher age group. Out of 60 respondents who got married below the age of 18 years, 45 per cent were the victims. In contrast to this, who were married after the age of 21 years, only 24.71 per cent were the victims of physical violence.

It is also interesting to note that median age at marriage of victims of physical violence was lower than those of non-victims. It can, thus, be concluded that those women who married at lower age were at high risk of physical violence in comparison with those who got married at later age in the Indian society, although the age at marriage is increasing yet in the rural areas it still remains quite low that is, 17.81 years. Therefore, class and situational factors may play an important role in determining the age at marriage, which in turn may be associated with violence because young couples are under lot of stress to adjust to new role responsibilities.

A few studies indicate that wives of younger age group are at higher risk of abuse as compared with those of older age group because older women are not prone to file assault charges either because of traditional attitudes or because of the possibility of divorce. The results of National Family Violence Survey conducted in America indicate that all forms of marital violence occur most frequently among those under 30 years of age. The rate of marital violence among those under 30 years of age was found to be more than double the rate for the age for 31 to 50 years.

The data for the present study were tabulated to find out association between the age of the wife and her being victim of physical violence. The respondents were distributed into four age categories. There was a progressive decrease in the percentages of victims of physical violence from lower age category to higher age category. Among the victims of physical violence 45.45 per cent were below the age of 30 years. In contrast to this those who were in the age group of 50 years above, only 18.18 per cent were the victims.

Similarly, if the median age of the victims of physical violence is compared with non-victims, it was noticed that median age of victims was 35 years in contrast to 39.24 years median age of the non-victims. In short, an inverse relationship was found between the age of wives and their physical abuse. In other words, physical violence against wives of younger age group was more frequent as against those of higher age groups. The data of the present study support the findings of studies cited above.

Wife abuse can occur at any age but the data on age indicate that wives of younger age are at higher risk of being abused. It may be due to the fact that younger couples are still learning to make adjustment with each other and addition of children in the family puts enormous demands and stresses on the younger people.

Presence or absence of children in the family is likely to affect the quality of relationship between husband and wife. Further, presence of more children in the family would create problem of management and proper training of the younger ones. Researches on the impact of children on marriages consistently show that the level of marital satisfaction and marital adjustment goes down after the birth of the first child.

An additional child would imply a decrease in time for parents to pursue their own interests. Further, each additional child increases the work load and conflicts. In the traditional societies like India, child care still remains under the domain of mothers and for any deviance on the part of child, it is the mother who is blamed. Further, more children put a lot of stress on the limited resources of the family.

Among the victims of physical violence it was found that the rate of violence against mothers who had five or more children or no child was more than double the rate for those who had one or two children. Keeping in view the number of children it was noted that there was a progressive increase in the percentages of victims of physical violence from one to two children category to women having five or more children or with no child. In short, it can be concluded that a large number of children in the family become a source of conflict resulting into violence against wife or mother.

The highest percentages of physical violence was found in those house-holds which had no child. It may be attributed to their younger age as well as wives' inability to have children because children are valued in the Indian society and those women who are unable to bear a child are ridiculed.

In the patriarchal society like India, greater importance is given to the male child. The female child is not only considered a liability because of associated dowry problems, but mothers who give birth to female children only do not get much respect in the family as compared with those who give birth to male children. Lately with the help of amniocentesis the couples would like to know the sex of the child. In case the foetus is of the female sex, they go for abortion. A study of 8000 cases of abortion showed that 7999 of them involved a female foetus. The high female foeticide reinforces the sex preferences prevalent in our society. The victims of physical violence were almost equally divided in the categories of those who had only male or female children of both the sexes. In the present study sex of the children in the family was not found to be associated with wife abuse.

Wives living in extended and joint households are required to make adjustments with a large number of kin in contrast to those who are living in nuclear households. Further, patrilocal residence and patriarchal structure of the family places women into subservient position. The men are more likely to act as sons rather than husbands. The parents-in-law and other kinsmen continue to have greater affiliation with the sons as compared with daughters-in-law.

A number of cases have been reported where because of backbiting, the husbands have maltreated their wives. Hence presence of a large number of members in the family not only creates the problem of adjustment but they also act as instigators for wife abuse. Although there was no marked difference in the percentage of victims living in nuclear and extended households, yet among the victims a relatively higher percentage (36.67) were found to be living in joint and extended households in contrast to those living in nuclear households (32.94). Similarly, among the non-victims no marked difference was found with regard to their pattern of living arrangement. Hence, the composition of household was not found to be associated with wife abuse.

From the foregoing discussion on the demographic correlates of wife abuse, it was found that the younger age at marriage, young wives and those having no child or a large number of children were at higher risk of being victims of physical violence. However, no association was found between the sex of the children as well as living arrangement and wife abuse. Based on the results of this exploratory research, the following hypotheses can be formulated for verification in future researches.

1. The younger the age at marriage of the women, the greater is the possibility of their being battered.
2. The younger the age of wife, the greater are the chances of her being victim of physical violence.
3. The greater the number of children, a woman has the greater is the possibility of her being victim of physical violence of her husband.
4. The absence of child is likely to result in wife battering.

An individual's social milieu not only influences his social position, network of relationships and contents of learning but also his social behaviour pattern. Social behaviour is a function of the life situations which may be physical, economic, social or cultural or an interplay of these elements. It is assumed that persons having differential life situations would react differently to the same stimuli. It is, therefore, essential to explicate the role of these social variables for understanding the quality of conjugal relationship. The social variables considered for the present study are educational and occupational status of the respondents, their social class background, their caste and religious background, their attitudes regarding traditional gender roles in the family and their value orientation in favour of use of violence for the resolution of conflict. Formal education helps an individual to know what is happening outside one's immediate surroundings. It also facilitates him to develop rational outlook towards life. Education widens the horizon and makes the individual more knowledgeable. Education also helps an individual to get jobs of high prestige and with high economic returns. Further, higher education enhances one's social prestige. Efforts have been made to find out association between the level of education one has and the quality of interpersonal relations.

A few studies indicate that the less education a person has, the more likely he or she is to approve of and support violence. Some other studies, however, contradict their findings and on the other hand, they are of opinion that couples with the lowest educational levels are less prone to violence than those who had attained higher education. It is argued that low education level does not cause violence but it aggravates the frustration.

The reason for more violence among those who have higher education, may be that women with high education may not endorse the traditional role relationship and this may be considered as threat to the dominant position by their husbands. However, education can provide people with alternatives for resolving family disagreements. It is, therefore, expected that with the help of education, individual learns different mechanisms to resolve the conflict in the conjugal relationships.

The educational background of the victim wives indicates that those who have low educational attainment or higher educational attainment had over representation as compared with those who had moderate level of education. There is a progressive decrease in the percentage of the victims from illiterate educational category up to graduation with the exception of those who had higher education. This curvilinear distribution of victims of violence indicates that women who have no education or have higher educational attainment are more prone to physical violence by their husbands.

The women with low education designate their complete dependency because with low educational background they will not be able to have economic independence or would be engaged in occupations with low economic returns and low prestige. In the case of those who have higher education they may be in better position to gain economic independence and with the higher education they may start questioning the dominant position of their husbands. Such a threat is not tolerated by the husbands and they use physical violence as their ultimate resource to maintain their dominant position in the family.

Occupation is an important indicator of a person's position in society. It is believed that the higher the education one has, the higher the occupation one holds and the higher the prestige he gets in society. Conversely, the lower the occupation, the lower will be the economic returns and as a consequence thereof, there are likely to be higher frustrations and greater marital conflicts.

Many studies indicate that persons engaged in occupations of lower prestige are more likely to resort to physical violence against their wives to give vent to their economic stresses. It is also argued that women who stay at home and are not engaged in paid work outside their homes are at somewhat greater risk of being physically abused than those engaged in paid work. This is probably because housewives are perceived to contribute less to family subsistence and are consequently valued less than women who are engaged in paid work outside the home. Wife beating is far less common in societies in which women have independent economic and social resources, perhaps because these resources are valuable enough to make a husband think twice before acting in ways that might force his wife to terminate the marriage.

In the sample there are only 65 women respondents who were found to be engaged in paid work. Out of these, 47.69 per cent were victims of physical violence of their husbands. On the other hand, out of those not engaged in paid work outside their homes, only 26.67 per cent were physically abused by their husbands. The results of the present study support the findings of Homung et al. who, in one representative sample, found housewives had a lower risk of violence than working wives.

The reason housewives are abused less than working wives is because keeping in view their economic dependency they may have "Learned helplessness" with the result they have developed tolerance of such violence and do not share with outsiders that they are being abused or they would endorse the traditional gender roles and would not question the authority of their husbands. Hence, they do not provoke their husbands to use physical violence to maintain their dominant position in the conjugal relationship.

On the other hand, the working wives may not accept the dominant position of the husband in family decision-making and raise questions about asymmetrical conjugal relations. Such a situation may prompt the husband to use physical force to retain his dominant position. The general contention that working gives economic independence to women, hence, they would be relatively free dependence to be correct in the present from abuse is also not found to study. On the other hand, it is the working women who are than the non-working women. The association abused more, status and her physical abuse will between wives' working which these become more clear if the type of occupation in which women are engaged in is taken into consideration.

As the number of respondents under the working category were limited to 65 cases only, their occupations were grouped under three categories, i.e., occupations with low prestige, medium prestige and high prestige. The data reveal that the percentage of the victims goes on decreasing from low occupational prestige category to higher prestige category. In short, there was inverse relationship between occupational prestige and physical violence, i.e., the lower the prestige of paid work, the greater was the violence against wives. The results indicate that it is not the working status per se which provides women freedom from physical violence of their husbands but it is the nature of the occupation and associated prestige and economic returns which facilitate women to be free from physical abuse.

## The Concept of Social Class

The concept of social class has been defined by several sociologists. They have, however, given emphasis to different attributes. One salient feature of different definitions is that members of a class group have common style of living and value orientation. Wolfgang and Ferracuti in their study of subculture of violence have even divided a class into subclasses depending upon value orientation of the members. Similarly, a number of scholars have tried to find out association between class background and family violence. One set of studies maintains a positive association between lower class and wife battering. Whereas some researchers do not endorse their findings and they have contended that wife battering transgresses the boundaries of class.

An attempt has been made to find out association between class background and wife beating. The class background of the respondents has been worked out based on education, occupation and income of the husbands of the respondents because a majority of the women respondents were not found to be working and hence, had no independent income of their own. While selecting the sample their living arrangement was taken into consideration and 50 cases from each house type were included in the sample, which were redistributed into different social classes. The class background of the respondent was also divided into lower, working, middle and high for the purpose of finding out differential behaviour pattern, i.e., wife abuse in different classes.

The data indicate that in contrast to 19.23 per cent victims of physical violence in the upper class, there were 51 .85 per cent victims in the lower class. There is a progressive decrease in the percentages of victims of physical violence from the lower through the middle to the upper class. Similarly, among the non-victims the higher per cent (80.77) belong to the upper class. In short, women belonging to the lower class were at a higher risk of being physically abused by their husbands. The results of the study indicate inverse relationship between class background and wife battering.

These findings support the contention of those researchers who found that women belonging to the lower class were at a higher risk of physical violence which was attributed to their way of life. The use and approval of physical violence in the lower class has been attributed to what Lewis calls, the culture of poverty. The concept implies that the poor people have a distinct subculture. Due to common experiences they have developed certain attitudes and behaviour pattern which have been transmitted from parents to children. These include the casual resort to physical violence, an inability to plan for the future, seeking of immediate gratification, weak impulse control and fatalistic attitude towards the future. Davis while describing the class linked, violence contends that physical violence in the lower class families is normal, socially approved and socially, inculcated type of behaviour. Similarly, Whitehurst while making a distinction between the middle and the lower class families with regard to control over violence, maintained that violence-responses were much more built into lower class subculture as a means to achieve some goals to assert independence and masculinity.

The members of the lower class are subject to a lot of economic pressures and strains and they cannot show their resentment and frustration, against those who are highly placed and hence they give vent to their frustrations at the slightest provocation by beating their wives on whom they can exert their power. On the other hand, members of the middle and upper classes have more resources and can keep their violence private and additionally, because of the sensitivity of the issue and embarrassment, the victims are not likely to admit its existence in their conjugal' relationship.

Individual's social status is determined by his ascriptive and acquired attributes. In the Indian society ascriptive attributes, like caste, determine not only his social milieu, as castes are hierarchically placed but also his opportunities to acquire new attributes. Although an individual is now theoretically permitted to achieve any position and support any ideology. Yet caste plays an important role in influencing his behaviour pattern. Keeping in view the importance of caste in the Indian society, it will be worthwhile to find out an association between caste and wife battering.

The distribution of the victims of physical violence according to their caste background indicates that respondents belonging to the lower castes group and those who have not specified their caste were more victims in contrast to the respondents belonging to the higher castes. Among the twice-born, the respondents belonging to trading castes were at a higher risk in contrast to Khatris and Aroras. Similarly, among the non-victims the higher percentages of respondents were found among the twice-born.

The higher frequency of physical violence present among the members of the lower castes may be attributed to their lower class background. Similarly, among those cases who have not specified their caste, most of them belonged to Muslim and Christian religion and these respondents were having lower socio-economic status. The association between caste background and physical violence would remain incomplete unless their economic status is also considered. Preceding analysis has indicated that members belonging to the lower class were more likely to resort to physical violence for the resolution of conjugal conflicts.

Religion is an important institution which instills a particular philosophy of life in an individual. His outlook towards himself and others as well as his behaviour pattern are likely to be influenced by his religious belief system. Is wife abuse a characteristic of a particular religious group? To find out an answer to the question, religious background of the respondents was considered. No clear-cut association was found between religious background and physical violence against wives. Among the two main religious groups present in Chandigarh, there was no marked difference in the percentage of victims.

In case of Muslims and Christians 50 per cent of the respondents belonging to these religious groups were the victims of husband's violence. This again may be attributed to the low economic status of the respondents. The results of the present study do not establish any association between religion and wife battering.

The family as a social institution lays down norms and values to regulate the behaviour of the members of the social group. Family as a social group is structured in such a manner that one member, usually the husband, assumes the dominant position and the other members take up subordinate positions.

The family provides a social setting where husband and wife play complementary roles. One of the conditions which maximises the cooperative elements in the family is the similarity of social values and ideologies which promotes not only cohesiveness and harmony but also helps in the proper functioning of the group. In the patriarchal traditional societies, like India, sex role expectations favour male dominance in the family. Traditional ideology promotes and serves to justify male dominance as well as helps in cultivating a belief system among the husbands and wives as to how they should behave in the marital relationship.

Motivated by traditional ideology, division of labour in the family was worked out into a male provider and a female to focus more narrowly on the domestic realm. Such a task specialization and differential evaluation helped men not only to have greater control over economic resources, but also a greater access to power in the family. The power structure in the family is maintained through the actions of the members involved in the relationships. Those at the top of the power structure behave in dominant ways and they do not hesitate to use coercive methods to retain their dominant position.

Attempts have been made to find out association between traditionality and wife abuse. A number of studies have concluded that men who were more traditional in their attitudes towards women were more likely to become wife abusers. Some importance is also given to sex role orientation of the victims. Walker is of opinion that non-traditional wives if paired with traditional husbands are at higher risk of being abused. An attempt has been made in the present study to find out correlation between wives' traditional orientation and their being victims of abuse.

Traditional sex role orientation of the respondents was worked out based on the responses to eight statements. The level of traditionality was further divided into three: High, Medium and Low, to find out association between level of traditionality and wife battering. It is assumed that respondents who have low level of traditional role orientation are at higher risk of physical violence than those at high level of traditionality because wives with low level of traditional orientation are more likely to question asymmetrical power relations in the family.

In contrast to 22.86 per cent of the wives showing high level of traditional sex role orientation, 40.32 per cent wives indicating low level of traditionality were the victims of physical violence by their husbands. Similarly, among the non-victims, their percentages go on increasing from low level of traditionality to high level of traditionality. In short, it can be concluded that wives with non-traditional sex role orientation are at higher risk of being physically abused- The reason for wives showing less traditional sex role orientation being victims of physical violence may be attributed to their attempt in questioning the traditional power structure in the family. The husbands in such situation are likely to use physical force as the last resort to maintain their dominant position.

The norms and values relating to intra-family violence indicate cultural contradiction. On the one hand, there is a myth of family non-violence which reflects cultural norms for the family as a group characterised by love and harmony. On the other hand, there seems to be social norms which imply right of the family members to strike each other. The legitimation of violence in the family is explicit and mandatory as in the case of rights and obligations of the parent to use a necessary and appropriate level of physical force to adequately train and control a child.

Violent wives as well as violent husbands express more approval of violence than do non-violent husbands and wives. Levinson in his cross cultural study on family violence came to the conclusion that wife beating was more common and frequent in societies in which adults solved conflicts by resorting to physical, violence, indicating attitude in favour of violence.

The cultural norms and values permitting and sometimes encouraging husband to beat wife actually reflect hierarchical and male dominant type of society like India. The right to use force exists, to provide the ultimate support for the existing power structure of the family in which the wife assumes a subordinate position.

Respondents' values in favour or against use of violence in the family were obtained from their reactions to 12 statements. Their scores were divided into three categories depicting low, medium and high scores. This exercise was done with an assumption that the respondents with high score on values in favour of violence in the family would be at a higher risk of being victims than those with low score. The data did not depict any clear-cut association.

On the other hand, it was noted that those respondents who had medium score on values favouring use of violence to resolve family conflict were more victims in contrast to those who had high or low score. The reason for lack of association may be attributed to the fact that there is a lot of gap between values and actual behaviour pattern. Secondly, the values were taken of the wives rather than the husbands who were the perpetrators of physical violence against their wives.

The respondents might be holding values against the use of violence but had no control over the values and behaviour pattern of their husbands.

The above discussion on social variables highlights certain salient features which contribute to husbands' physical violence against wives. Lower caste background, low and high educational attainment, lower working status, lower social class background and low level of traditionality were found to be contributing factors for husbands' physical violence against wives. However, no association was found between religious background and value system of the respondents and their being victims and non-victims of physical violence.

Dependency is a state, both physical and mental, depicting assistance from a person or persons for continuing living in the community. The human child has to depend upon his parents for his growth, development and social recognition. The Indian society has placed women in a state of dependency as a daughter on her father, as a sister on her brother, as a wife on her husband and lastly as a mother on her son. Further, sexual division of labour and gender roles accentuate these differences.

Additionally, patriarchal social norms not only grant control of family resources and property to men but also provide dominant position to them. To maintain their dominant position, the husbands are likely to use coercive methods including physical violence against their wives. Sometimes physical violence is used as a means to an end and at other times as an end in itself. Dependency is also treated as a cause of physical violence in the conjugal relationships. Researches have utilized this explanation in two ways. In case, a wife is completely dependent, both physically and socially, her husband exploits her dependency and uses violence at whim to reinforce his dominant position in the conjugal relationship. A few scholars are also of opinion that when a husband is dependent upon his wife he resorts to physical violence as a last resort against his wife as he is afraid of losing his spouse or a person on whom he can exert his dominant position. Hence, dependency of husband over his wife is also treated as a cause of wife abuse.

As the present study is limited to wife abuse, the analysis is limited to wife's perception regarding the conditions which make her dependent upon her husband and how this state of dependency results into her being abused. To find out association between wife's dependency and her abuse, dependency has been divided into objective and subjective. It does not, however, mean that we can draw watertight compartments between the two. In certain cases objective dependency may lead to subjective dependency, whereas in other cases even though there is no objective dependency yet the individual remains subjectively dependent upon her spouse. It can, however, be assumed that a wife who experiences both objective and subjective dependency is at higher risk of being abused in contrast to those who have only objective or only subjective dependency.

For the purpose of analysis, wife's objective dependency stands for conditions like not working, i.e., being economically dependent upon husband; not having any property in her name; not receiving any financial assistance from her family of orientation; inability to live alone; inability to do shopping alone, and inability to go outside the city alone.

Further, level of objective dependency may vary from case to case. Hence, objective dependency is further divided into three levels: low, medium and high. The wives who are objectively dependent upon their husbands are at higher risk of being abused. Because it would be difficult for these women to come out of the abusive relationship as they do not have the resources to live alone. Their objective dependency is also known to their spouses who may fully exploit the situation knowing fully well that their wives would not be able to leave them. It is further envisaged that wives who have high level of objective dependency are at greater risk of being abused.

Wives with high level of objective dependency are physically abused more in contrast to those who have low level of objective dependency. This is evident in the percentages of the victims at different levels of dependency. Similarly, the percentage of non-victims goes on decreasing to high level. There were 33 respondents who had high level of objective dependency, out of which 60.61 per cent were not the victims of physical violence.

The results of the study support the contention of a few scholars who are of opinion that high level of women's marital dependency is not associated with wife abuse, because husbands of dependent wives can maintain their dominant positions without resorting to violence as their wives are in no position to question their dominance. Although no cause and effect relationship can be established between dependency and wife abuse yet the data show an indicative trend that wives who have high level of objective dependency are abused more as compared to those who have low level of objective dependency.

A few scholars contend that objective dependency, of the wife per se does not result into her abuse but is mediated by her tolerance. One may, however, raise the question why she develops this tolerance to abuse? One reason may be that she remains subjectively dependent upon her husband because her social reality has not been constructed outside the marital relationship. In Indian society marriage is a must for every woman, unless she adopts a life of celibacy. Remaining unmarried or living a life of a divorcee is looked down upon. Hence, whether a wife is objectively dependent upon her husband or not she remains subjectively dependent. It is not, however, true in the case of husbands.

Remarriage after divorce or separation is easily available to a man than a woman. Such a discriminatory practice perpetuate subjective dependency in the wives.

Subjective dependency in the present study stands for, not leaving the husband even under adverse circumstances; divorce not considered good; perception that married women even if abused enjoy higher status than divorced; lack of support from kin; greater commitment and more devotion to marital relationship. It is also expected that wives are likely to have different levels of subjective dependency. Depending upon their scores they are divided into three categories: low, medium and high. It is expected that wives having higher level of subjective dependency will be at higher risk of being physically abused in contrast to those having lower level of subjective dependency.

In contrast to 23-94 per cent wives having low subjective dependency, more than 42 percent of the wives with high level of dependency are the victims of physical violence of their husbands.

There was a steady increase in the percentage of abused wives from low level of subjective dependency through medium level to high level of subjective dependency. Taking into account 38 cases having high level of subjective dependency it was noted that more than 42 per cent were the victims of husbands' physical violence and approximately 58 per cent were free from being physically abused.

Although, no positive correlation could be established between subjective dependency of wife and her being victim of physical abuse yet the high percentage of victims having high level of subjective dependency designate a partial association between subjective dependency and her being battered. The reason for high percentage of such victims can be attributed to wife's commitment to marriage and her inability to use alternative mechanisms to get out of the abusive relationships. Such a situation forces her to cultivate tolerance and continue living in the abusive relationship.

Similarly, the husband uses coercive methods to assert his dominant position in the familial network of relationship because he is confident that his violent behaviour would not be challenged and he can attain the desired goal, that is, subduing his wife. The results of the present study on subjective dependency and wife abuse partially support the findings of other researchers.

Subjective dependency in certain cases may be treated as a consequence of objective dependency. In other cases subjective dependency may not be the outcome of objective dependency. It was for this reason that these two facets of dependency were treated separately, however, to find out the impact of dependency on wife abuse, both objective and subjective dependencies have to be combined. In other words, to find out the validity of dependency framework to explicate wife abuse, both the facets of dependency are combined to find out their combined effect on physical violence.

The total dependency scores of the respondents have been arranged into three categories—low, medium and high. The data indicate that wives with higher level of dependency are at higher risk of being abused in contrast to those with lower level of dependency. In contrast to 27.42 per cent of wives with low level of dependency more were the victims of husbands' physical violence. The percentage of non-victims goes on decreasing from lower level of dependency to higher level.

# Nine

# In House Exploitation

Living in a society which is largely patriarchal though centered around the wife, the family has its share of marital violence in which the woman bears the brunt in spite of being the pillar of the home.

To maintain their dominant position in the home, men inflict some or the other kind of violence on women and harass her throughout her life. A common name given to wife battering is silent crime. Others are considered as domestic violence like spouse abuse and similar ones. If we examine the variety of names it is known by, besides wife battering, two points emerge at once: that the violence is located at home and the attacker is the husband. The side of violence being the home and the attacker being the 'husband' has distorted, confused and is responsible for the gross trivailisation of the crime.

Wife battering is a crime that is 'victim precipitated'. This has been largely proven by three aspects—social, legal and psychological—with large help from recent cases, at home or abroad and through the numerous myths or sayings. It is a widely prevalent crime that is under cover for being 'too private' to be spoken of. Being an old problem; it is assumed by some to have begun with the first monogamous pairing. What is new, however, is that the fact that the public admission of violence against women occurs in a civilised society and the insistance by the government and responsible citizens that such violence is no longer acceptable, that we are therefore compelled to discuss the problem of such a form of violence and search for solutions to alleviate it.

In the context of marriage, violence towards women becomes more significant when a husband who is supposed to love and protect his wife, batters her. It becomes a big setback for a woman, being battered by a man whom she trusted most.

### Culture as Reinforcer of Brutal Attitude

Wife battering has been largely supported by various cultures down the ages. It was part of the Napoleanic code until a decade back. The very code says: "Women like walnut trees must be beaten every day". In North Africa, the expression "women and camels need to be beaten" is still common. In Europe, they used to say that a man had the right to beat his wife with a stick not thicker than his thumb. In Indian culture we have the quotation of Tulsidas such as "Drums, donkeys and women need to be beaten". So religion has played more or less a crucial role in reinforcing brutal attitudes to women which include "mortification of the flesh" deemed religious and more appropriate to the female. In fact over the ages, religions have constantly admonished woman to stay with her husband, no matter how cruelly he treated her".

**Common Reasons of Violence**

Wife battering is the most prevalent form of violence against women which is commonly caused due to maladjustments between husband and wife. Also prevalent among working women as most mothers-in-law, who are non-working and under complete dominance of their husbands feel jealous of and frustrated at the sudden independence and freedom of their daughter-in-law. She counters by poisoning the ears of her son antagonising him against his wife.

The batterer rationalises his battering saying that it happened as he was not satisfied by the conduct of his wife. So she is made to feel guilty of her performance at home — be it cooking or general upkeep of the home. A housewife of Rajouli was beaten to death by her husband as she was not cooking good food and the house being untidy, for which she alone, often at times, is not responsible. Implicit in this viewpoint is that the husband has a right to beat his wife if she does not behave according to what he desires. A young woman of village Taaddih under Amarpur police station of Banka was battered to death by her husband and in-laws as she refused to go out in rain to bring *ganja* for her husband. While attempting to amend her husband a pregnant woman of Samastipur was mercilessly beaten and sent to her parents' house by her husband. The battering resulted in abortion. Her husband along with his two brothers used to commit dacoity. When the wife protested against this, the dacoit started battering her mercilessly. Consequently, an abortion took place and she objected to the illicit relation of her husband. A young housewife of Dalsingsarai was mercilessly beaten to death by her husband when she objected to his having illicit relations with his elder brother's wife.

## Acceptance and Tolerance by Women

To tame a woman who does not accept the traditional role of submissiveness and subordination, any means including violence is justified. Ironically counsellers and social workers also contribute towards this ideology when they question a woman who gets beaten: 'what did you do to provoke him? Due to this she often begins to have serious doubts about herself, to the extent that she starts questioning her identity as one who is responsible, intelligent or knowledgeable. The women continue to live in a state of fear and uncertainty as it is unpredictable when, where and under what circumstances the violence may suddently erupt. The consequence of this is that she develops an inferiority complex, so much that she begins to look down upon herself and underestimates her value and potentialities loosing confidence in all her moves.

It is undeniable that some women are so arrogant, haughty, uncompromising and intolerant and make the husband's life so miserable through calculated and well planned acts of social misconduct that even the most reasonable man would lose control of himself beyond a certain limitation and beat up the erring woman. Cases of women suspected of adultery come under this category. A man of village Janui under Nargar Police Station of Garhwa hacked to death his 28-year-old wife as she had illict relations with a man of the same village, in spite of being told to mend her ways, she paid no heed. In a fit of rage he hacked her to death.

Until the mid-1970s and the re-emergent women's movement wife battering was almost completely ignored. In USA many researchers in this field agree with Justice Stewart Oneglias' estimate that 50 per cent of all marriages involve some degree of physical abuse of women. Such statistics are not available in India, but there is no doubt that they would far exceed the American statistics. Being the most frequently referred to "crime in India" reports do not provide information on wife battering. So widely and pervasively is wife battering accepted and tolerated that very rarely it is publicly talked about and still much less written about in the media.

## Prevalence of Male Biased Attitudes in Society

Wife battering is seriously under-reported crime and the data hard to obtain because of its location, the home... "Gelles Straus and Steinmetz reported that physical assault occurs in one-third of all homes. "In Mumbai, HELP, a voluntary group received over 300 calls in less than a year in which more than 80 per cent were calls for marital violence.

No one dares to interfere or question the man even if he is seen battering his wife because it is considered purely something their family affair. The society also implicitly supports this attitude by leaving the husband and wife to themselves to settle their affairs. On the other hand, if two neighbours get into a fight, the people around immediately intervene to see justice prevails. But in the case of a husband battering his wife, the neighbours tend to be mute spectators. Wife battering is commonly accepted by society and not many people take much notice to it. If the wife happens to retaliate, she is considered a woman of low morals. It is ingrained in the mind of people that no decent woman would beat her husband. Whereas battering one's husband is considered shameful for the husband as well as for the wife, there is no shame attached to wife battering, society being what it is.

## Legislations on Wife Battering

Wife battering falls under the general category of assault, under sections 319-326 of Indian Penal Code. Sections 319 and 321 are non-cognizable offences, i.e., the cases in which the police can take no action against the assaulter. Thus, there is no legislation against wife battering.

### *Grievous Offences*

Under Section 320 of the I.P.C. the following kind of offences have been described as grievous:

(a) Emasculation;

(b) Permanent deprivation of the sight of either eye;

(c) Permanent deprivation of hearing of either ear;

(d) Deprivation of any organ or joint;

(e) Destruction or permanent impairing of the power of any organ or any joint;

(f) Permanent disfiguring of the head or face;

(g) Fracture or dislocation of a bone or both;

(h) Any hurt which endangers life or which causes the suffer to remain for twenty days in severe bodily pain or unable to follow his ordinary pursuits. Section 324/326 of I.P.C. cover those cases where the assaulter uses dangerous weapons or means.

Thus, unless the wife is grievously beaten up resulting in one or more of the above injuries, the offence is non-cognizable, i.e., not punishable by law.

**Course of Action Taken by Women: Options**

Wife battering is the most under-reported crime in India. No woman wants to bring her agony and personal life to courtroom and throw herself open to having her *bonafides* questioned and her character maligned. She would rather prefer to cling on to a broken marriage that break up her family reputation.

The first point to be noted is that these laws are ineffective for protection of a woman under the general law of assault. Very often, because a woman's lack of interest in a separation with her husband, people say that she enjoys the batterings. But there are currently very few alternatives to help women to live an independent life. The alternative for her is to go to her parents, only if they are in a position to maintain her with children which is often a rarity. Another option for her is to go to a women's rescue home run by the government which in the Indian context are very few and ill-maintained. Moreover, if she has children over the age of eight, then the children would be sent to a children's remand home. Both these centres are largely, centres of exploitation. A woman can leave her husband for cruelty but it is a ground only for a judicial separation and not for a divorce. It is essential that laws be changed to make wife battering a ground for immediate divorce. Custody of children of such women who are compelled to take divorce is another problem. A woman can get custody of children only after undergoing a lot of legal problems involving time, knowledge, money and of course judicial patronage. These hardships come in the way of making a decision of divorce for the woman and often she is forced to look back and face her destiny and torture.

Women belonging to the poorer groups are more easily swayed by emotions, can leave their husbands and start living alone. Being used to the hardships of life, they can rough it out even living alone. Their society gives them shelter and helps them start a new. Women belonging to the middle class, however, are more guided by social taboos and bindings. Right from the time of maturity, they are taught to be loyal to their husbands, to mould themselves to the whims and caprices of their husbands, bearing stoically the brunt of all hardships and all the abuses their husbands put them to. Under such conditions; they prefer not to leave their husbands in spite of extreme hardships and torture.

Causes of wife battering are high level family conflict, stress and violence in society, family socialisation in an environment marked by violence, cultural norms and sexual inequalities. (Straus, 1983). Wife abuse is seen as a reaffirmation of male self image as an aggressor which has been internalised and encouraged during childhood (Cotlin, 1974). According to (George, 1977) child abuse in own families or parental violence, alcoholism and the husband experience of childhood battering are some of the factors leading to wife battering. Moore (1979) looks into the social, legal, psychological and personal factors to explain the causes of wife battering. Newman hypothesised that the intake of alcohol, hostile dependency, extensive brooding on the part of the husband, husband's frustration in his work and other activities, and the husband having been battered by his parents in childhood, contribute to wife battering.

## Frustrations Leading to Wife Battering

There are two levels of frustration in a man's life, individual and societal.

### *Individual*

Man's expectations of himself and his inability to face problem and failures which lead to a sense of insecurity lead to individual frustration. If frustrations in a man's life lead to violence, why is it that the wife is always an inevitable target of his violence? Frustrations build up in a woman's life as well, but why is it that this does not lead to spouse abuse? Some cases have been put forward to answer these questions:

1. The unquestioned authority of man in his home/marriage.
2. The consequent subservient role of the wife.
3. The wife's total dependency on her husband.
4. The social status which the husband provides to his wife.
5. Male confidence that he can make a woman forget and forgive the worst with a show of love and gifts.

6. The fact that a wife is least likely to show resistance to her husband's batterings.

7. If a man has witnessed wife battering during childhood or has been physically abused as a child, he is likely to adopt it as an acceptable way of resolving problems in his marital life.

*Societal*

The most fundamental factor which leads to wife battering is linked with the sex structure of the society as well as the family. The fundamental rights grant a man and woman equality but as long as the authority of man remains rooted in our culture and in the eyes of the law, wife battering will be perpetuated in society.

It has been seen that while economically dependent and independent women are equally likely to be battered, an economically dependent woman is more likely to stay on in a violent home. Lack of education and poor job opportunities force the middle class women to remain married to men who constantly batter them. This, along with the burden of child care and parental responsibility forces women to remain in violent homes. Knowing this, men continue abusing their wives with relative impunity. They can be relatively confident that she will not leave him because:

(i) She is not economically independent;

(ii) She has no place to go and;

(iii) She has the burden of bringing up the children because society feels that child care is exclusively a mother's job and women who leave children behind became social outcastes.

*Immediate Causes*

However immediate causes of wife battering may be noted as:

1. Monetary causes
2. Jealousy and suspicion
3. Instigation by in-laws
4. House work
5. Impact of alcohol

6. Economic independence of wife or wife's high self-esteem (she thinks too much of herself)
7. Dispute over children
8. Extra-marital affairs of husband.

**Myths Regarding the Battered**

There are some myths common to all cultures about the "kind of women" who get beaten.

1. The first myth is that middle class women do not undergo wife battering. In reality women come from all sections of the society, belonging to different religions, educational levels and from all socio-economic classes. If we hear more about wife battering in slums or in chawls, it is because these women have less privacy. The middle and upper class women are battered behind closed doors. They live in total isolation and keep up the pretence of a successful marriage. Working class women talk, quite openly about the violence that they experience in their homes, and generally it seems to affect them less psychologically as they do not see it as being something unrelated to them as individuals whereas middle class women begin to question and doubt themselves.
2. The second myth is that the victim of violence is a small, fragile, helpless woman belonging to the working class. In reality, women holding responsible jobs as doctors, lecturers, journalists and models get beaten by their husbands. Many of them are quite capable of managing their lives. So there is no stereotype of a battered woman.
3. The third myth is that of provocation. This myth conveys the message that women who get beaten are masochistic and they want to get beaten. It further victimizes the women. The burden of guilt falls on her, increasing her shame and degradation.
4. The fourth myth is that the women who don't leave their husbands do not mind the batterings or that they

actually like it. It is often asked: why women continue to live in a situation where they are eventually murdered or are driven to suicide. Why don't they seek a way out? The theory of learned helplessness gives an insight into the mental stage of passive resignation experienced by women. According to this approach, some events occur in the battered women's life during childhood and onwards with sufficient regularity due to which they acquire feelings of helplessness and poor self-image and resigning themselves to fate or accepting blame. Some important events in women's early lives which suggest a susceptibility factor include a high level of violence by members of their families in childhood (e.g. being battered by the mother, battered by the father, the father battering the mother, the father-mother battering other children) perception of critical or uncontrollable events in childhood, and experiencing such conditions which place them at high risk for depression in future. The fear of losing the husband's affection and the fear of disruption of their home life status quo also prompts them to tolerate the husband's battering. The battered wives are thus afraid to stay and at the same time terrified to leave for fear of inescapable reprisals. They prefer to choose the devil than foray into the deep sea.

**Myths Regarding the Batterer**

As there are myths about the type of women who get beaten, there are myths about the type of husbands, who beat their wives.

1. We generally tend to take it for granted that if a man beats his wife, he must be from the lower strata of society, being frustrated in his job, an alcoholic, or a paranoid person, aggressive in his relationship with the world at large and his wife being one of the victims. The act of wife battering is found elsewhere too, where the males are either professionals like lawyers, teachers, doctors, etc. or the well off economically like businessmen, politicians, etc. In some cases, the males

are not alcoholic but they too are not free from this very act towards their wives.

2. The myth that loving husband does not indulge in wife battering is also false. Sometimes some males are quite sober, gentle and lovable to their wives but they too involve in wife battering in case of some frustration.

Hence, more or less from what is found, the wife battering is a general phenomena among all sections of male community of the society throughout the world.

**Suggestions for Effective Action**

1. A preventive rather than a curative approach to the problem should be taken by the institution which tries to deal with the problem of wife battering. Unless the structure of the family changes, the help given to battered wife will prove to be only superficial. This does not mean that we should ignore the desperate and immediate situation in which millions of women find themselves, and live their lives in constant fear of violence and death. Despite occasional successes to expect lone women to fight individually against institutionalised family violence is both cruel and unrealistic. There is not only a desperate need for more homes for battered women, where such women can take refuge when their lives are threatened, we also need homes which will look at the problem of wife battering from a pro-women point of view, and which will help the women rebuild their shattered lives and induce faith and confidence in themselves. These can serve as important educational institutions and consciousness raising places. The time spent here can be utilized in teaching the women useful skills which can eventually make them self-sufficient. In case a woman chooses to go back to the husband, the home should lay down rules that the husband allows her to continue her job training and should not send the women back on their husband's terms. In most cases

the husband is more anxious to get the wife back once she leaves, and this is the only time, terms and conditions can be laid for the man. This can be very useful in maintaining contact with the woman, so that when the batterings recur, prompt action can be taken against the husband.

2. There is a need to create an awareness in society so that the attitude of society — doctors, counsellors, institutions, social workers and the police is more sympathetic towards victims of marital violence.
3. Community action like having a *morcha* or a *dharna* outside a wife-battered house goes a long way in acting as a deterrent to marital violence. Men and society at large should recognize once and for all that women are no longer going to take batterings lying down.
4. Support structures for women who decide to break away like legal aid, a place to stay and a job go a long way in bringing a feeling of security to the tortured and oppressed woman. The homes for battered women should be linked up with organisations which help women take up self-employment ventures. We need more committed lawyers who are sympathetic and understanding and would help to provide legal protection and relief to the women who are battered.
5. In cases where the marriages are resolved and reconciled, full precautions should be exercised so that any future attack on her is frustrated. This can be done by getting help from her neighbours, locking herself in a room, running away from the house, throwing objects or chilli powder at the husband can at times, deter a husband from being violent. There may be several hurdles to a religious mind which is conditioned to accept the husband as lord and master, but unless women can stand upto the batterings and fight back, the power relationship within the family will not change.

6. The situation of assaults by a husband on a wife being quite specific where the wife is economically dependent on the husband, and that the assault occurs in the house of common residence, it is essential that the police operate under different laws than those which cover general assault. A law such as Domestic Violence Act should be passed.

The point that women are often their worst enemies should not be forgotten. Mother-in-laws and sisters-in-law often instigate men to violence. Do they not poison the ears of their sons and brothers respectively and antagonise them against their wives? Voluntary social workers uphold women's dignity through glittering sessions and often have double standards as they subject their own maidservants to cruel humiliations.

Unless women are able to organise themselves, they cannot fight male domination. There is a need, therefore, to set up women's organizations in every area to fight this aspect of women's oppression. Forming into groups will help them raise their voices louder against the men and get them the desired results one day.

Ten

# Marital Violence

The very foundation of a happy family lies in cordial husband-wife relationships. It affects all — the children, the home and the family. A cordial relationship makes the children feel more secure in their home and relate to everything more effectively, whereas an uncordial relationship makes them dull and inefficient. The suffering of the wife is not to be forgotten. Thus, marital conflict only leads to familial disorganisation and has negative consequences on the children's upbringing. Thus, the quality of interaction between a husband and wife has repercussions on the whole family. Keeping in view the importance of the husband-wife relationship in the family as well as the distinctive nature of quality of the interaction between them, it would be most appropriate to investigate the causes of violence in conjugal relations.

Different studies around the world have shown that wife-beating is the most popular form of violence. Husbands use violence against wives to reinforce their dominant position, because use of coercive methods by husbands against wives have societal approval. Women being women, they tolerate the torture silently keeping it all within themselves sometimes to keep the family fabric intact.

Because of the gender relationships down the ages, women are used as instruments of reproduction with no independent status outside family thus maintaining systemic inequality over time. Further male authority exposes them to swift retributions and confirm their vulnerability. Ganley (1981) suggests that men who batter their wives have learned certain cultural and social values about masculinity and their roles in families that support their aggression and violence. Males are socialized into roles that encourage aggression towards females. Socialization and sex role conditioning appear to be instrumental in defining the attitudes that males have toward violence and are major factors in determining the power relationship between men and women that allows violent behaviour to take place. Unless women raise their voices this process will continue in times to come.

## Patriarchal System and Male Dominance

With male values superseding female values and emphasis on submission and timidity for women and strength for men as cherished values, it becomes clear that man is born to rule. The first and indeed the life-long recipient of male violence is the female (Krishnan, 1988). Thus within the family the husband enjoys higher status than the wife, who is considered inferior and subordinate. Social pressures force women to maintain the status quo. A woman who does not accept the traditional role of submissiveness and subordination needs to be tamed into accepting this position and any means specially, violence is justified in achieving this goal (Agnes, 1988).

## History of Wife Beating Worldwide

Being a historical phenomena, wife beating has been studied by many historians who have documented the informal and formal sanctions by society that have encouraged wife battering (Davidson 1978; Martin, 1976; Pleck, 1987). Scottish and English laws permitted a husband to discipline his wife physically without prosecution for assault and battery. As a few Scottish sociologists observed about both the United States and Great Britain: "Prior to the late 19th century it was considered a necessary aspect of a husband's marital obligation to control and chastise his wife through the use of physical force." (Shupe *et al.*, 1987). This view can be traced back to the Roman Empire and medieval times in "Laws of Chastisement" found in many countries as well as in selected passages of the Old and New Testaments in the Bible endorsing male authority over women.

For many centuries, during the Dark and Middle ages as well as the Renaissance, women were routinely subjected to physical punishment that accompanied their accepted inferior status and justified by the so-called "laws of chatisement" which went unquestioned. Such violence was simply taken for granted as part of the divinely ordained order of things.

Wife beating was condoned in American culture via the English law. The infamous rule of the thumb which permitted a husband legally to beat his wife with a rod not thicker than his thumb was a formal sanction of British Common Law. Ironically, it was originally intended as an example of compassionate reform to limit how harshly men abused their mates. Thus, man's right to use violence in managing their homes was very much an accepted pattern.

It was only in the 20th century, that the law finally condemned wife abuse and considered it to be a criminal offence. It was not until the women's liberation movement in the 1970s that identified and responded to wife abuse recognising it as a "social problem" (Tierney, 1982). Prior to this time its existence was overlooked and even denied, although it continued to exist. Various historical circumstances led several social scientists to explain that men abused women basically because they are permitted and encouraged to do so (Gelles, 1983).

The patriarchal system of society relegated women to a subordinate position always obeying orders of men. For them, the husbands were *Pati Parmeshwar* (God). They meekly suffered discrimination in shape of female infanticide, Sati Pratha, dowry, denial of widow remarriage, denial of education, denial of share in family property, etc. because of their dependency and lack of alternative support system.

During the nineteenth century, educated Indian elites namely, Raja Ram Mohun Roy, Ishwar Chandra Vidyasagar, Mahatma Phule, Karsandas Mulji and many other social reformists attacked the social practices of child marriage, *Sati* and harsh treatment of widows. They advocated women's education, widow remarriage and such other social reforms. They engaged in advancing the status of women by requiring that the law to take cognizance of their rights by providing them some basic rights such as the right to live.

*Pre Independence Legislations Protecting Women's Rights*

Lord William Bentick outlawed the practice of *Sati* in 1820. Sati had always been an exaggeration of the Hindu ideal, never practised by the majority, and was therefore successfully eradicated. In 1856, Widow Remarriage Act was passed. It was, however, less successful. The Britishers also passed Infanticide Act in 1870 to abolish this practice to female infanticide. In 1860, following much agitation, the age of consent was raised to ten years and in 1891 it was raised to twelve years. The Sarda Act of 1929 raised the age still further to fifteen. In spite of such legislations there was no visible change in women's status. The British were unwilling to interfere with Indian customs as per the populous measures to keep their government stable. The dogged persistence of their Western-educated Indians compelled them to move, if at all.

*Post-Independence Legislations Protecting Women's Rights*

There were serious attempts made to elevate the status of women only after Independence. Only in 1955, by passing the Hindu Marriage Act the law forbade polygamy for Hindus, allowed divorce by either husband or wife on the same grounds and specified the marriage age for girls as 15 and for boys as 18. Secular and mixed marriages were legalised by the Special Marriage Act of 1954. These acts were followed by the Hindu Succession Act of 1956, poviding that a son, daughter and widow/mother could inherit equally. The Hindu Adoption and Maintenance Bill of 1956 provided separate maintenance for women under certain conditions, where legal separation or divorce was not sought. The Dowry Prohibition Act was passed in 1961 as an effort to end the practice of demanding dowry. The Act was modified by the Dowry Prohibition (Amendment) Act of 1984, which has again been modified by the Dowry Prohibition (Amendment) Bill, 1986. Other major legislative measures to improve the position of women have been the passage of the State Maternity Benefit Acts and the Termination of Pregnancy Act in 1972.

*Literacy among Women*

Another force for improvement in the status of women apart from legal reform of social customs is education. After more than four decades, the literacy figure for women is 39.42 per cent as opposed to that of men, which is 63.86 per cent (1991 census). Though education for women, was restricted to a very small upper-class elite, yet it played an important role in opening up avenues for women in gainful employment outside their homes.

Whereas urban upper and middle income group women have changed the rural women and urban poor women still suffer like before. Thus, neglect and exploitation of women continue in its characteristic fashion. According to Desai (1982) the conditions of women in general do not show much improvement and the social economic measures of women's upliftment have not significantly affected their economic status practices, such as the denial of remarriage of upper caste Hindu widows, polygamy and dowry continue in our society despite being illegal. Thus, there is no let up in the suffering of women in spite of legal measures. The widespread incidence of bride burning and dowry deaths still continues. What was known as female infanticide has come in newer form of amniocentesis after sex determination tests in urban areas.

**Women Organizations: Shields for the Oppressed**

A small percentage of women who have gained economic

independence are facing the challenge of an exploitative social order. They no longer accept male dictates and are now claimed an egalitarian way of living, which implies change in the traditional relationships between husband and wife. Men being what they are not likely to accept the new position of the wives and may use violence to retain their traditional position. To highlight the plight of women victims, some women organisations, which are however, mostly urban-based, have emerged. These women organisations are engaged not only in militant activism to assert women's right but also have made serious attempts to articulate their thoughts on the root causes of oppression of women. Their main purpose being to create public awareness against the existing exploitative system in society. In the beginning these women organisations took up the issue of dowry, wife beating and subsequently they took up different types of exploitation of women which were not confined to intra-familial relations, for example, sexual harassment at the work place. Women organisations are thus playing an important role to highlight the problem of wife abuse not only in the West but also in India and seek public cooperation for this.

**Incidence and Prevalence of Wife Abuse Around the World**

Having been given little attention, wife abuse is perhaps the most prevalent form of family violence. It was during the mid-seventees that social scientists in the West started conducting studies to find out the nature and the extent of violence against wives while trying to identify the precipitating factors which led to violent relationship between the marital partners. The research of almost two decades led them to work out not only the coping mechanisms adopted by the victims but also different treatment programmes for the batterer and the battered. Comparatively India, has very few studies which have been conducted in this area. A few isolated attempts have been made after the late 1980's to find out the nature of the problem as well as the precipitating factors which lead to violence against women.

In David Levinson (1989) study of 90 pre-literate and peasant societies of the world it was concluded that beating is the most common and frequent form of family violence.

According to a 1976 national survey in America, violent against wives had reached "epidemic" proportions with nearly 2 million women battered every year. At least one act of violence occurs per year in 16 per cent of all married couples. Nearly one-third of all married couples experience physical abuse at some point (Straus et al., 1980). It was estimated that actually over one-half of all wives will be assaulted sometime during their marriage (Walker, 1979). Other studies in the United States have suggested that incidence is as high as fifty per cent (Straus, 1978). Data from the Second National Family Violence Survey conducted in the United States (Straus and Gelles, 1986) reveals that incidence of battering has decreased as much as 20 per cent since the mid-1970s. Some scholars are of the opinion that wife battering is quite widespread in all the cultures though the problem is hidden away in some cultures as a "private matter" (Seager and Olson, 1986).

There has been no nationally representative sample survey conducted to find out the extent of the problem. Besides a few isolated studies conducted to find out the frequency of wife abuse in India.

A study of dowry victims shows that one in every four were murdered or driven to commit suicide and more than a half (61.3 per cent) were thrown out of their husband's house after putting up with harassment and torture for long. (Ranjana Kumari, 1989). According to the Anti-Dowry Cell set up by the Police Commissioner, New Delhi, in 1983, 690 young women died in Delhi alone of whom 23 were burnt alive (Jain, 1992).

Mahajan, M. (1992) in a study of 200 cases at Chandigarh found that with the exception of 13 families, all the other cases reported presence of one or another form of violence in the relationship thus observed that violence in conjugal relation is common. In 33.5 per cent cases, there was a presence of physical violence against the wives.

Bhatti (1989), while taking into account various forms of violence concluded that 88 per cent of women in lower class were the victims of physical and verbal violence in contrast to 43 per cent from the middle class and 35 per cent from the high income class. With regard to emotional and intellectual violence, he found that representation of the upper and middle classes was more as compared to the lower class.

Devasahayam *et al.* (1991) in a sample of 153 cases of K.V. Kuppan Block (a village in Gujarat) found that approximately 21 per cent admitted the existence of marital violence. Alcoholism was the major cause of violence in their families. Singh (1985) in a study conducted in a village of Punjab found that violence in different forms existed in 50 per cent of the cases and physical violence was present in 9 per cent of the cases out of the sample of 114 cases belonging to different caste groups.

Different studies thus establish that wife abuse is a widespread phenomena around the world.

**The Offender and the Victim**

The precipitating factors leading to wife abuse have been studied by various scholars and some have attributed abuse to the personality factors of either the battered or the batterer or both. It is assumed that either one or both the spouses possess certain characteristics that make them prone to wife battering. A few sociologists have tried to identify the social variables which are responsible for differential behaviour pattern attributing it to socialization, normative pattern, value system, etc. They attempt to explain the legitimization of intra-familial violence and the victimization of women through social approval.

It is often assumed that batterers suffer from various personality disorders. Men who assault their wives have low self-esteem and use violence to compensate the feelings of inadequacy (Boyd, 1978: Coleman, 1980; Gayford, 1975; Gelles and Cornell, 1990; Rosenbaum & O'Leary, 1981a; Walker, 1979). Violent and abusive men have also been described as feeling helpless, powerless and inadequate (Aggarwal and Thatte, 1988; Ball, 1977; Bhatti, 1989; Weitzman and Dreen, 1982). Wife beaters have been described as sadistic, passive-aggressive, addiction-prone, pathologically jealous, dependent and pathologically passive (Faulk, 1974; Margolin *et. al.*, 1988; Shainess, 1977; Snell *et al.*, 1964) or suffering from neurological or biochemical disorders (Elliott, 1977; Schauss, 1982). These researchers are of the opinion that these personality disorders directly involve abusive behaviour. But comparison studies fail to substantiate that these features are distinctive. Although the negative traits identified by descriptive studies are linked to battered males, they share these traits with non-violent males in distress (Browning, 1983; Dvoskin, 1981; Rosenbaum and O'Leary, 1981; Stark and Flitcraft, 1988; Telch and Lindquist, 1984).

According to Douglas and DerOvanesian, 1983; Hughes and Rau, 1984; Rosewater 1984; Telch and Lindquist, 1984; Walker, 1984) women who have been battered tend to suffer from depression, anxiety and have elevated MMPI profiles. They have often been described as dependent, having low self-esteem and feeling of inadequacy and helplessness (Ball, 1977; Hilberman and Munson, 1977; Mahajan, 1989; Shainess, 1977; Walker, 1979). According to Adams and McCormick, 1982; Bhatti, 1985, 1989; Dobash and Dobash, 1979; Lata, 1989; Mahajan, 1989; Shah, 1989; Straus *et al.*, 1989; Weitzman and Dreen, 1981). Battered women are picturised as shy and reserved and have a tendency to blame themselves for the violence.

As per (Ball, 1977; Graff, 1980; Scott, 1974; Snell *et al.*, 1964) battered women are aggressive, masculine, frigid and masochistic being a totally opposite personality profile. Star (1978) reported that battered women exhibit more independence and ego strength. In a study of issues provoking violence Finn (1985) emphasized the importance of power balances in the relationship and suggested that the abused victim has a better sense of reality than her assailants, particularly with respect to sexual relations.

It is however argued by Gelles and Cornell (1990), that it is not possible to present personality profile of the battered women, as one never really knows whether the personality factors found in battered wives were present before they were battered or are the result of the victimization. As with other studies of family violence, personality studies of battered women frequently use small samples or clinical samples and often fail to have comparison groups. Thus, generalizing from these studies is difficult and demonstrating that battered women are actually different from non-victimized women is nearly impossible using these data.

## Factors Responsible for Wife Abuse

Other than personality factors, researchers have shown that various other factors are also responsible for wife abuse. Due to lack of longitudinal research and failure to differentiate samples according to dimensions, it is difficult to predict factors responsible for violent outcomes, alone or in combination.

### *Violent Homes of Origin*

Violence in the family of origin accentuates both a woman's vulnerability and a man's propensity to abuse his wife and/or children. It is said that men who have experienced violent childhoods are more likely to grow up and assault their wives than are individuals who have not experienced childhood violence. Researchers have found that both offenders and victims had violence-ridden childhoods (Fagan *et al.*, 1983; Roy, 1977; Schulman, 1979; Straus *et al.*, 1980). Studies also find that observing parental violence is related to spousal aggression (Pagelow, 1981; Rosenbaum and O'Leary, 1981). However, two-designed studies using multiple comparison groups and collecting data from men and women found no significant effect of childhood violence on later victimization (Rosenbaum and O'Leary, 1981; Telch and Lindquist, 1984). Although, the chances of being an offender and victim are increased if one grows up in a violent home, there are many violent people who had limited exposure to violence as children and some people who experienced extremely violent childhoods and grew up to be non-violent. (Gelles and Cornell, 1990; Stark and Flitcraft, 1988).

*Income and Domestic Violence*

There has been an inverse relationship between income and domestic violence reported in various studies. Researchers have highlighted that wife beating is more common in lower classes (Ahuja, 1987; Bhatti, 1985; Gaguin, 1978; Gelles and Cornell, 1983, 1990; Grewal, 1982; Jain, 1992; Mahajan, 1992; Prescott and Letko, 1977; Saunders, 1982; Stark, 1984; Steinmetz, 1974; Straus *et al.*, 1980; Young, 1963). On the other hand, (Berk *et al.*, 1983; Dobash and Dobash, 1979; Giles-Sims, 1983; Hilberman, 1980; Mahajan, 1989; Martin, 1979; Walker, 1979, 1984) show that wife battering cuts across the class boundaries.

*Employment Status*

Wife battering is found to be more in families where the husband is unemployed (Fitch and Papantonio, 1983; Gaguin, 1978; Gayford, 1975; Lewis, 1987; Prescott and Letko, 1977; Pathy, 1987; Rounsaville, 1987; Straus *et al.*, 1980). Men who are employed part-time have even higher ratcs of violence, probably because they cannot avail of unemployment benefits (Straus *et al.*, 1980).

Wife abuse is inversely related to wives contribution to the household income. Women who stayed at home and were fully dependant on their husbands income had a greater risk of being abused (Iwarimie Jaja, 1989; Levinson, 1989; Mitchell and Hodson, 1983; Schwartz, 1992). Hornung *et al.*, (1981) held a totally opposite view that housewives had a lower risk of violence than employed women.

There are proofs showing that women's risk of victimization increases if their occupational and educational status are inconsistent with that of their husbands. When some inconsistency develops in the status of either husband or wife, wife abuse results (Bhatti, 1989; Dobash and Dobash, 1979; Jain, 1992; Martin, 1979; Mohan, 1989; Parihar, 1989; Yllo, 1983).

For the victims of abuse, pregnancy is a high risk period when they experience violence at unusually high rates (Dobash and Dobash, 1979; Gelles, 1972, 1988; Helton, 1985; Kaplan, 1972; Pagelow, 1981a; Strak *et al.*, 1981; Teske and Parker, 1983; Walker, 1979). Factors react unfavourably at the prospect of a new entrant in the family regarding the child as an intruder — thus they indulge in violent behaviour.

*Alcohol Use and Abuse*

Studies of marital violence typically find a relationship between alcohol use and abuse (Ahuja, 1987; Bhatti, 1989; Bordin, 1981; Brekke and Saunders, 1982; Coleman *et al.*, 1980; Grewal, 1982; Mahajan, 1989; Mohan, 1989; Parihar, 1989; Shah, 1989; Snell *et al.*, 1964). Coleman and Straus (1983) reported that men who drink often are likely to abuse their wives 15 times more than non- drinkers.

Some cross-cultural studies of alcohol use and studies of marital violence points that men drink to have a socially acceptable excuse for violent behaviour (Gelles, 1974). Alcohol is not an immediate antecedent of violence in the majority of families in which violence occurs (Kantor and Straus, 1987). Still, Byles (1979) and Orne and Rimmer (1980) in a comprehensive literature review concluded that a casual role for alcohol cannot be supported. Alcohol is a factor in fewer than eight per cent of the domestic abuse cases, where police were called (McClintock, 1978). In sum, although alcohol probably increases the risk of abusive violence, yet in absence of conclusive evidence it should be considered a contextual factor to be treated separately.

*Power-imbalanced Relationships*

Power-imbalanced relationships are associated with spousal abuse, especially when the males power is threatened (Harris and associates, 1979). Wife beating occurs more often when all the decisions are made either by the wife or the husband (Adler, 1981; Bower, 1983; Coleman and Straus, 1986). It is believed that wife beating tends to decrease in frequency when decision-making becomes more egalitarian (Bowker, 1983; Coleman and Straus, 1986; Straus *et al.*, 1980). Hauser (1982) however argues equal power is seen as a lower position for the husband and as a higher position for the wife, as a consequence, husbands refuse to accept egalitarian way of living and violence continues. The above noted studies on the precipitating factors leading to wife battering highlight one or the other factor. Studies which highlight the characteristics of the battered couples; however, fail to explain adequately why some spouses resort to violence whereas others remain non-violent in spite of being unhappy.

**Programmes and Coping Mechanisms for the Batterers and Battered**

Coping mechanisms and different treatment programmes for the batterer and the battered have been worked out by scholar in the West on the basis of experience of more than two decades of experience (Andersen *et al.*, 1991; Brockner and Rubin, 1985; Gondolf and Fisher, 1988, 1991; Rieker and Carmen, 1986; Sonkin *et al.*, 1985 and Turner and Shapiro, 1986).

The battered women specifically resist the notion that they should leave their battering husbands (Walker, 1979) and seek outside help only as a last resort when violence becomes intolerable due to long-drawn-out rehabilitation procedures (Kaushik, 1988; Pandhye, 1988; Sriram and Bakshi, 1988) as well as lack of alternative support system, self-image, social stigma, dependency, presence of small children and fear of living alone and embarrassment to admit that she has stayed in such a bad situation for so long etc. which force a woman to hide violence against her in the family and to remain in the violent relationship (Bhatti, 1989; Bergman *et al.*, 1988; Chapman and Gates, 1978; Edgell, 1980; Finch, 1983; Kalmuss and Straus, 1982; Kertzman, 1980; Mahajan, 1992; Martin, 1979; Parihar, 1989; Roy 1977; Russell and Von, 1976; Shah, 1989; Strube and Barbour, 1983; Walker, 1979).

Some researchers say that many abused women opt for leaving such a relationship. This category includes women who are employed, who get support from their family of orientation, friends or those who do not have children. (Gelles, 1976; Moore, 1979; Okun, 1988; Strube, 1988).

Different treatment programmes for the batterers, such as individual therapy, marital and family therapy, psycho-educational or psycho-therapeutic group approach, community intervention and anger control techniques have been suggested by researchers. (Adams, 1988; Adams and McCormick, 1982; Gondolf, 1985; Roberts, 1984; Rosenbaum, 1986; Sonkin *et al.,* 1985). A variety of counselling approaches have been proposed for battered women (Gondolf and Fisher, 1988, 1991; Rieker and Carmen, 1986; Turner and Shapiro, 1986). It is believed that such programmes are not very successful in checking the abusive behaviour of the batterers (Gondolf and Fisher, 1991; Gondolf and Russell, 1986). Most of the researchers feel that the root cause of wife abuse can be traced to societal values. Unless social definitions are changed and women are allowed to have egalitarian way of life, wife abuse in one form or the other would persist.

Literature available on violence against woman helps in research. A theoretical and holistic approach is absent in literature available and the empirical studies conducted so far.

**Theories Explaining Wife Abuse**

A theoretical framework is needed to explain the phenomena of wife beating in greater detail. Various scholars have propounded different theories in order to explain wife abuse such as: resource theory, symbolic interaction, social control/exchange theory, sub-culture of violence theory, conflict perspective, patriarchal perspective and general systems theory. Dependency framework has been used for this study to explain the nature of wife abuse in the Indian context. As it can be used both at micro and macro levels to understand the victimization of women at socio-cultural level.

*Dependencys Framework*

Dependency factor in a woman is a need for which the victim has no control. These conditions may be her economic dependency or social definitions which force women to trace out her identity through her husband which makes her more committed to marriage. Dependency framework has been used in three ways to explain wife abuse. Firstly, dependency is treated as a cause of wife abuse. Secondly, it is treated as a condition forcing a woman to assume the role of the victim and thirdly, partial non-dependency also results into wife abuse.

In the first approach, there is a positive association between marital dependency and wife abuse (Dobash and Dobash, 1979;

Marsden, 1978; Straus, 1976; Truninger, 1971; Walker, 1978). Women, enter into marital relationship as subordinates to their husbands. Moreover, they are brought up to be submissive and trace identity through their husbands. Such a situation provides a dominant position to the husband and he uses violence against his wife to maintain his dominant position in the marital relationship. Those who suggest a positive relationship between wife abuse and dependency do not argue that women's marital dependency directly causes wife abuse. They, however, suggest that violence is instigated through women's tolerance of physical violence inflicted by their husbands.

In the second approach, dependency has been considered as a condition of wife abuse. Women who are unemployed, have a low educational level, have children and rely on their husbands for financial support, find themselves it is impossible to leave the abusive partners as they do not possess sufficient alternative resources to negotiate changes in their husband's behaviour (Gelles, 1976; Martin, 1979; Roy, 1977, 1982; Strube and Barbour, 1983; Strube, 1988). According to Roy (1977) and Mahajan (1986) women's explanations for putting up with abusive marriages included economic dependency, young children, fear of living alone, perceived stigma of divorce and lack of alternative support systems.

The third approach is that with partial non-dependency, wife starts questioning asymmetrical power relations which results into her abuse. Economic independence gives a better position to wives challenge their husbands' right to dominate. Since men benefit from the current system of sex stratification, it is unlikely that they will voluntarily give up their prerogative. Husbands, on the other hand, may resort to violence if the struggle for sexual equality increases. Further, violence may be used as the ultimate resort by husbands to keep wives in their place (Allen and Straus, 1980; Brown, 1980; Goode, 1971; Mahajan, 1989). A new type of role relationship will develop between husband and wife based on the ideology of egalitarianism (Kalmuss and Straus, 1982).

### *Objective Dependency*

Dependency has been divided at two levels: objective and subjective. Objective dependency is characterized by conditions that tie a woman to marriage. Objective dependency has been operationalized as :

(a) lack of independent financial resources.

(b) low level of education.

(c) physical insecurity.

(d) presence of young children.

(e) fear of living alone.

(f) fear of physical assault, harassment, etc.

It does not, however, mean that women who are free from objective dependency are not abused by their husbands. They may be economically independent or have no children but are still the victims of violence by their husbands as they remain subjectively dependent.

*Subjective Dependency*

Women's subjective dependency on marriage refers to how a woman perceives herself to be tied to the marital relationship. This dimension of dependency is a psychological state that may or may not reflect objective conditions. Their social reality has not been constructed outside their marriage. The alternative social identity as a "worker" is not available to them. Their social identity is traced through men. Further, it is the wife and mother's role which gives her a respected position in the society. Subjective dependency has been operationalized as :

(a) differential sex role socialization,

(b) emotional investment in marriage and children,

(c) stigma attached to divorce,

(d) fear of rejection by parents, and

(e) lack of social support system etc.

While for some women, subjective dependency may be a direct function of objective dependency, for others it may not be so in spite of situational and objective factors do not make them particularly dependent. Some women may feel strongly dependent on their marriages. Others who are structurally bound to the relationship because of economic ties may not perceive subjective dependency. Further, the degree of dependency may differ from one segment to another.

**Empirical Study: Dadu Majra (Chandigarh)**

In order to verify the dependency framework, an empirical study has been carried to find out:

(i) The nature, extent and frequency of wife abuse.

(ii) The frequency with which physical, psychological and verbal violence is used.

(iii) Whether dependency objective or subjective or both is the cause or condition or instigating factor for wife abuse.

(iv) The reasons why abused women continue to stay in the abusive relationship.

As it becomes really difficult for the researcher to probe the personal lives of the respondents because it is treated as a "private affair", only a few studies have been conducted.

The study has been conducted in a village (Dadu Majra) on the outskirts of Union Territory of Chandigarh. 115 households belonging to lower class were selected for the sample. It was decided to limit the study to those households where conjugal unit lived together.

Out of 115 cases 87 wives, i.e., 75.65 per cent confided that their husbands have acted violently against them. Out of 87, 58 per cent admitted that it was a regular and patterned behaviour. Others, however, confessed that it was not a routine with their husbands. Out of 87 cases of violence 65.80 per cent admitted that violence against them is verbal only, 60.38 per cent labelled it as psychological violence whereas 39.16 per cent, that is 45 cases admitted to the existence of physical violence along with other forms of violence.

Statistics clearly indicate that wives with high level of objective and subjective dependency are abused more in contrast to those who have low level of objective and subjective dependency. Similarly, the percentages of non-victim goes on decreasing at high level. The results of the study, thus do not support the contention of those scholars who are of the opinion that high level of women's marital dependency is not associated with wife abuse because husbands of dependent wives can maintain their dominant positions without resorting to violence as their wives are in no position to question their dominance (Allen & Straus, 1980, Brown, 1980; Goode, 1971; Whitehurst, 1974).

Marriage holds an important position in Indian society where remaining unmarried or living a life of a divorcee is looked down upon. Whether a wife is objectively dependent upon her husband or not, she remains subjectively dependent. It is for this reason that subjective dependency is positively associated with the wife being a victim of her husband's violence. The reason for high percentage of such victims can be attributed to the wife's commitment to marriage and her inability to use alternative mechanisms to get out of the abusive relationship. Similarly, the husband uses coercive methods to assert his dominant position in the familial network of relationship, because he is confident that his violent behaviour would not be challenged and he can attain the desired goal, that is, subduing his wife. The results of the present study on subjective dependency and wife abuse partially support the findings of Kalmuss and Straus (1982).

Most of the women victims reported the fact that their husbands abused them in order to subdue them. They admitted that they behaved according to the wishes of their husbands after abused. When the wives were asked, 'why don't you have the abusive relationship?' they confessed that they had no place to go, after of being humiliated. The study reveals that violence in the family occurs when neither the family nor other support systems meet the needs and demands of the individual. When a violent mode of expression is readily available and when it is endorsed and rewarded. The results of the study show that violence in one or the other form persists in the conjugal relations, because it is associated with positive consequences for the abusers. Finally, it shows that wives continue to suffer and stay in abusive marital relationship because of their dependency.

## Incidents of Wife Abuse

### *Case One*

Ms. Harjit is a 48-year-old matriculate belonging to a Jat Sikh family. Her father was a small shopkeeper. She has two brothers and a sister. She is the youngest of them all. At a very young age, she lost both her parents. When she was 16 years old, she was married to a small shopkeeper of the neighbouring village who was an alcoholic. Her husband is under matriculate, but the only son of his parents. She tried her best to dissuade her husband from indulging in heavy drinking but he did not like her interference and started ill-treating her. Initially such incidents were very few but subsequently it became routine. She tried to seek help of her in-laws but they did not pay any heed to her requests.

During her married span she gave birth to three daughters. Her first daughter, however, died within three months of her birth due to insufficient medical attention and negligence on the part of her husband. Her husband and mother-in-law always blamed Harjit for giving birth to female children only.

Often the husband did not come home for two to three days at a stretch. Whenever Harjit tried to enquire from him of his absence, she was admonished. Very often, on the slightest pretext he would beat her very badly. His attitude towards his daughters was also very rude. She put up with all the sufferings. Her brothers consoled her and advised her to remain submissive and to look forward to a happy future. Left with no alternative she reconciled to her fate and accepted her husband's drunken behaviour and waywardness.

Her sufferings increased. Her husband became all the more rude and harsh towards her when her parents-in-law shifted to Delhi. She was not given money even for household expenses. Her husband started bringing his friends home for drinks and forced her to sit with them. Whenever she refused to oblige him, she would be severely beaten up by him in front of his friends. She realized that her husband could go to any extent only when he asked her to have illicit relations with his friends. She refused to oblige him and locked herself in a room. Finally she fled away from the home along with her daughters and went to stay with her parents-in-laws. She informed them about her husband's behaviour. However, her husband did not come to meet her. This continued for ten years till her daughters passed their matric exams and they wanted to study further, but Harjit's in-laws denied them permission for higher studies. On the other hand, they started looking for matches for them. Harjit realized that if she did not act promptly, her daughters lives would be ruined. She resented her father-in-law's decision. They became very annoyed at Harjit's interference and she was asked to leave their place. Left with no alternative she came back to her husband only to find that he had ruined his life due to his drinking habit. He had sold his shop and household articles. She pleaded with her husband to change his ways and to realize the fact that he is a father of two grown-up daughters. Her pleadings, however, had no impact on him. On the other hand, he would become angry at her. He would call her names and beat up. Her daughters, however, tried to protect her but they too were abused. In spite of constant arguments and ill treatment, she stayed with him for the sake of her daughters. But when Harjit's husband attempted to sell his daughters to clear off his previous loans, she could not control herself and abused her husband. All limits were crossed when her husband pushed her and broke his empty liquor bottle on her head and fled away. She was badly hurt and her clothes were stained with blood. Her daughters called the neighbours for help.

Harjit was forced to make up her mind to leave her husband for ever. Thus, constant threat of physical insecurity of her daughters and herself forced Harjit to take this step. She went to her elder sister in Chandigarh who was full sympathies for her but could not provide her shelter because of her poor economic condition. She, however, made Harjit's living arrangement in a Short Stay Home for Destitute Women. Women Organizations in Chandigarh tried to resolve her marital conflict. Her husband was invited to Chandigarh but he did not come.

Presently Harjit is staying in a Short Stay Home for Destitute Women in Chandigarh. Her elder daughter is working as a storekeeper in a private company, whereas her younger daughter is undergoing vocational training in typing and shorthand. Harjit wants to make her daughters economically independent, so that they can face hard realities of life in a better way. Although Harjit has left her husband for the sake of her daughters, she would like to go back to her husband, once her daughters are settled because she does not want to be stigmatized for the rest of her life.

*Case Two*

Ms. Kiran Khullar is a 30-year-old graduate, who works as a clerk in a private company. She belongs to a Hindu Khatri family. Her father is a Superintendent in a Government Office at Chandigarh and her mother is a housewife. She has two younger sisters and an younger brother. She got married at the age of 23 to a science graduate of her own caste. Her husband is four years elder to her. He is working as an Assistant in a private firm at Chandigarh. He has two elder brothers and two sisters. All of them are married and well settled. Her father-in-law had died before her marriage. Before settling the marriage, Kiran's parents had expressed their inability to provide any dowry. Her husband and his brothers had also expressed negative views regarding dowry. Kiran's parents thus readily agreed to their proposal and accordingly performed a simple marriage. They did not give her anything in dowry.

Kiran started facing the hostility on her husband's side and his relatives for not bringing any dowry immediately after marriage. Her parents expressed their shock at the changed attitude of her husband regarding dowry. Moreover, they bluntly refused to oblige him. Her husband felt insulted and he humiliated her parents, who did not say anything and tolerated everything silently. He became rude to her. He adopted hostile attitude towards her and would abuse her on flimsy grounds.

Her parents consoled her and advised her to patch up and tolerate. As she was working, her salary was taken away every month after giving a paltry sum as pocket money.

Her husband never took her out with him and would her to go out of his sight as he disliked her. He warned her that she could stay with him, provided she maintained no contact with her family of orientation. Further, when her younger sisters visited Kiran, her husband also insulted them. As a consequence they too stopped visiting her. Thus, she was made socially isolated. Her husband not only denied physical and economic freedom but also made Kiran victim of his jealous and suspicious nature. In case she came late from the office, he would accuse her of immoral character.

Instead of arguing with him, she would prefer to keep mum in order to stop the quarrel because she was in the family way. Throughout her pregnancy, her husband harassed and humiliated her. Her mother-in-law, who had come to stay with them was also instigated by her son against her. She had to work throughout her pregnancy and her husband did not show any concern for her. She suffered malnutrition and mental agony. Her husband even threatened to kill her if she gave birth to a female child. It was only after the birth of her first son that she felt relieved. She thought that things might improve for her. But her hopes were shattered when her husband did not accept sweets from her parents and abused them. When they left, she was humiliated and she accepted taunts helplessly.

After a gap of two years, she gave birth to another son, but no change was found in the behaviour of her husband. Her husband always looked for an opportunity to humiliate her. He would even try to find fault with her dress, make-up and other personality configurations. She felt very annoyed and sometimes lost her temper. Whenever she resented his remarks, her husband would become furious and beat her. Kiran's husband would not even spare his children. On simple mistakes he would beat them up very badly. She was beaten up also whenever she tried to protect them.

The final and ultimate blow was when Kiran went to see her ailing father in the hospital without taking permission from her husband, she realized that she was a slave in her own home. As she had to stay in the hospital a little longer. On her return her husband refused to open the door and she had to seek the intervention of the neighbours. When the neighbours left, he locked her in the bedroom and started beating her. He refused to listen to her and made insulting remarks about her father. The beating continued till he himself got exhausted. As a consequence of severe beating, she had a black eye and a broken tooth and was also denied any medical aid. She cried and cursed her fate and developed a feeling of insecurity to her life. She even thought of committing suicide, but her love for her children stopped her from taking such an extreme step. She however, decided to seek help from some outside agency. With the assistance of her friends, she contacted a woman organization and sought its intervention. On her request, the members of that organization went to her husband's office and tried to plead her case. In their presence, Kiran's husband did not utter single word but on returning home, she was again beaten by him. She was kicked, slapped and strangled. He even beat both his sons. He threatened to kill them if she even tried to lodge complaints against him.

After this incidence, Kiran become so depressed that she lost the will to fight. She became so pessimistic that she felt that only some miracle can change her husband. Kiran has lost all the hope for her future and continues to suffer. She feels herself that she would either die herself or her husband would kill her one day.

*Analysis of the Cases*

The above case studies help us analyse the problem of wife abuse. Ms. Harjit belongs to working class became the victim of excessive drinking nature of her husband. It was when her husband tried to force her and her daughters into prostitution that she was compelled to leave her home. Ms. Kiran who represents the middle class is a dowry victim, being educated and working she tried to raise objections to asymmetrical marital relations. Her efforts to have egalitarian conjugal relationship seems to have resulted in her abuse. In both the cases, it was found that these women were objectively dependent because it was difficult for them to live alone. Further, they did not have any support from their family of orientation. Their objective dependency encouraged their husbands to fully exploit the situation knowing fully well that their wives would not be able to leave them and stand alone on their own.

In spite of her economic dependency, presence of female children and no support from informal group. Ms. Harjit separated from her husband when violence became unbearable and her husband tried to force her daughters into prostitution. She still nurtures hopes of living with her husband because of her subjective dependency and hopes that things will improve one day, she does not want to be stigmatized as a separated woman. Kiran, on the other hand, continues to stay in the abusive marital relationship in spite of the fact that she is educated and working. She is unable to feel accepted in society without her husband. Further, social pressures from her family of orientation forces her to continue staying in the abusive marital relationship. Formal agency has also failed to put any end to the wife battering. Additionally, their intervention further deteriorated marital relationship. Thus, we can say that both objective and subjective dependency is related with wife abuse. The women continue to suffer in the marital relationship because of their upbringing and socialization. Dependency thus is a prime condition forcing women to continue living in the abusive marital relationship as they lack alternative support system.

In sum, in India, marriage institution is considered as a religious obligation. More relevant in case of Indian women, whose destiny in life has been marriage and motherhood. The Indian women, values from their childhood are to be submissive, expected to develop patience and courage to face different odds in life but not to seek separation from their spouses. Although legally, she is allowed to seek divorce because of the atrocities of her husband, yet social definitions, values and norms have not undergone appropriate changes to create congenial situation for her to go for divorce, even if circumstances demand so. Divorce for women being stigmatized, it is not easy for her to terminate the marital relationship even though it is abusive. Additionally, she may be economically, psychologically and socially dependent upon her husband or have so much emotional investment in her marital relationship and children that she prefers to suffer rather than to go for separation or divorce and keep the social fabric intact.

# Eleven

# The Dowry Menace

Dowry is generally believed to be given by the girls parents to the groom to ensure her a happy married life by fulfilling the basic necessities to give a comfortable living. But the greed of the groom's family is growing day by day. Starting from basic needs, the custom has become rigid enough to become an evil associated with social status and family prestige. Monetary considerations receive priority over the merits of the bride. Never before have the demands for dowry been so exorbitant and so widespread as today. It has taken the form of bridegroom price and has developed into a great social evil. There is hardly a day when the cries of dowry victims are not echoed by the media. One day we read that the bride was burnt to death, as she could not bring the expected dowry. The next day, we come across a case where the bride was taken out on the pretext of sightseeing, and pushed from the hill top or into the swelling river. And these are just those cases which are reported in the media. There still remain countless other cases which do not come to the notice of the media or the police or the women's organisation.

*Meaning*

Dowry normally means gifts given during the marriage to the son-in-law or his parents in cash or kind. From the point of view of women's status, however, dowry has to be looked at as constituting:

(a) what is given to the bride, and often settled before and announced openly or directly; the gift though given to the bride may not be regarded as exclusively her property;

(b) what is given to the bridegroom before and at marriage; and

(c) what is presented to the in-laws of the girl.

The settlement often includes the enormous expenses incurred on travel and entertainment of the bridegroom's party. The gift-giving ritual continues throughout early married life, during festivals and celebrations.

*The Justification*

Indirectly it is assumed that it is a way of providing a girl with a share of the family property. The Hindu laws on property and ownership do not, in their present form, grant women their due share of family income and property. The Hindu Succession Act gives women the right to a share of the family property. But tradition dies hard, and in most cases the property of the family is given to sons. Daughters usually do not contend this, and hence inadvertently strengthen the argument that the dowry system alone ensures them fair share of her father's property, which will help them tide over any crisis. The latter also explains the importance attached to gold and jewellery and other constituents of dowry. For, unlike land and other immoveable property, they are both easily transportable and readily converted to cash. Demand for dowry is justified on many grounds. Firstly, since they have to pay dowry for their daughters, why not take it for their sons? Secondly, fathers of educated boys want to get back the money spent for their sons' education.

*Non-fulfilment of Demand: Consequences*

Dowry today is being demanded and paid without any relation to the bride's father's income and wealth: One Ganaur Mahto of Keshopur village under Sakra police station of Muzaffarpur self-immolated as he failed to meet the dowry demand of his son-in-law even after five years of his marriage. With the increased desire for quick money and the luxuries of life, these demands are not confined to the middle class alone. Dowry is being demanded by all levels of people, be they high, middle or low, items of dowry may differ ranging from flats, cars, electricals, furniture, clothes, cash and jewellery. Failure to meet these demands results in ill-treatment to young wives, often driving them to commit suicide. A 22-year-old bride of Banka committed suicide by throwing herself into a well after constant nagging by her in-laws over inadequate dowry. In many instances they have been murdered. These deaths are generally represented as accidents to save the future of the children and the parents from social stigma.

*Growing keenness among Girls*

Surprisingly now-a-days girls themselves are keen to collect their own dowry without any consideration of the plight of parents and the future of younger brothers and sisters. It is surely their socialization and the influence of the social milieu which have shaped their attitudes and expectations. If they have no rights of membership in the natal family, they also have no obligation to contribute towards its maintenance. Their main concern is to establish themselves in the new family and acquire status there. They look upon dowry as a necessary contribution towards this process and a compensation for their share in the family property.

*The Concept*

Social scientists differ widely in their interpretations of the concept of dowry reflecting the particularistic features of the societies which they have studied. It is very difficult to arrive at a universal definition from these varied explanations. The sociologists who have analysed the dowry system in South Indian societies define dowry as "female inheritance" because dowry is often termed as 'streedhanam' in South India. On the other hand, those who have studied dowry system in north India emphasise the *daan* or the gift aspect of dowry as it is variously called *daan dahej* (in Bihar) and *Dayaj* (in the Awadh region). They also view it as a compensation related to the institution of hypergamy.

The problem of protecting young married women against harassment on account of dowry has been engaging the attention of social workers and women's organisations for quite sometimes. Unnatural deaths of newly married young women beat headlines in the newspapers. Hardly a day passes without a news item on a tragic event like this. Some social organisations have been urging the government to make suitable provisions both, legal and administrative, to give protection to young married women against cruelty at the hands of their husbands and in-laws.

*Women as Perpetrators*

Women being the enemy of a woman in cases of bride burning is an interesting feature of this crime. It has been usually found that attitude of a woman as a mother is different from that as a mother-in-law. As a mother she gives all what she has to the daughter but as the in-law she attempts to extract the maximum possible dowry and can go to the extent of causing death of the bride, if the demands are not met to her satisfaction. In other words, in bride burning cases, crime is normally abetted and even committed by the women themselves. It is ironical that in many cases where one woman is killed for dowry another woman with a more handsome dowry is prepared to "console" the bereaved husband.

The government of Bihar set up "anti-dowry cell" in 1976 headed by a Superintendent of Police to give protection to women and Harijans against atrocities against them and the name of this cell was subsequently changed to "Offences against Women Cell". What is interesting is the fact that during the wedding season in 1983, IAS and IPS officers, engineers and doctors fetched more dowry; as IAS officer was paid Rs. 10 lakh as dowry and his marriage ceremony was attended by high officials (*The Statesman,* 18 August, 1983). Thus, if government servants are the perpetrators what more can be said and done is a matter to ponder.

**Dowry Prohibition Act**

The first attempt by the Government of India to recognise dowry as a social evil and to curb its practice is the Dowry Prohibition Act of 1961. The Act was modified with the Dowry Prohibition (Amendment) Act of 1984 and 1986. Women's organisations have played a key role in this process of change.

The 1961 Act defines dowry and makes the practice of both giving and taking dowry, a punishable offence. Any agreement on dowry is void. If it is given at all, it will be the women's property. With increased awareness of dowry deaths and consequent public condemnation, women's organization made a thorough analysis of the implication of 1961 Dowry Act and criticised it for being theoretical and lacking in clarity.

*Amendment 1984*

The Dowry Prohibition (Amendment) Act, 1984 makes the offence cognizable by enlarging the meaning of the term "Dowry".

The main features of the Amendment Act are as follows:

> Any property given or agreed to be given in connection with a marriage to the bride or bridegroom or any other person is considered as dowry. It is not necessary to show that the same has been given as consideration for the marriage. It also provides for the preparation of list of presents which are given at the time of marriage to the bride or bridegroom in accordance with the rules made under this Act.
>
> Any person giving or taking dowry or abetting the giving or taking of dowry is also punishable with imprisonment which is not less than six months, but which may extend to

two years and with a fine which can extend to Rs. 10,000 or the amount of the value of the dowry whichever is higher.

Neither the bride nor the persons giving presents to her at the time of marriage is liable for punishment if the presents have been given to her without any demand on that behalf and the presents are entered in the list maintained in accordance with the rules.

Demands of dowry continue in spite of this significant new amendment of the Dowry Prohibition Act 1961, failing which the bridegroom or his parents take to violence against the bride and sometimes such violence results in her death. Further there is a need for legal registration of gifts to be made compulsory, so that women may not be cheated of her dowry. The 1984 Amendment however makes it a cognizable offence and empowers recognised welfare institutions or organisations to take cognizance of the offence.

*Amendment 1986*

The Dowry Prohibition (Amendment) Bill 1986 was introduced in the Rajya Sabha. It attempts to tighten the provisions of the Act and includes dowry deaths in the list of offence in the Indian Penal Code. The Bill provides that if a woman dies within seven years of her marriage due to causes other than natural, her property would be transferred to her children and if she has no children to her parents. The burden of proving that no dowry demand was made will be on those who took or abetted in the taking of the dowry, the aggrieved person will be subjected to prosecution. This amendment bill has made the offence non-bailable and raised the minimum punishment to five years and fine upto Rs. 15,000. Provisions for appointment of dowry prohibition officers and their advisory board with two women members had been made. According to this new amendment in the Indian Penal Code whoever, being husband or related to the husband of a woman, subjects such woman to cruelty shall be punishable with imprisonment which may extend to three years and shall also be liable to fine. The cruelty for the purpose of this provision means any wilful conduct which is of such a nature as is likely to drive the woman to commit suicide or cause grave injury and danger to life, or health (whether mental or physical) of the woman. The cruelty also includes harassment of the woman where such harassment is with a view to coercing her or any person related to her to meet unlawful demands for any property or valuable security or on account of failure by her or any person related to her to meet such demand. Under this amendment the police have been empowered to investigate and report cases of unnatural or suspicious deaths of women.

*Factors Initiating Investigation*

Further, they have been empowered to investigate in the following cases: when

(i) The case involves suicide by a woman within seven years of her marriage, or

(ii) The case relates to the death of women within seven years of her marriage in any circumstances raising a reasonable suspicion that some other person committed an offence in relation to such woman; or

(iii) There is any doubt regarding the cause of death.

**New Legislations**

A new Section 198A has been inserted in the Cr. P.C. 1973, providing that "No court shall take cognizance of an offence punishable under Section 498-A of the I.P.C. except upon a police report of facts which constitute such offence or upon a complaint made by the person aggrieved by the offence or by her father, mother, brother, sister or by her father's or mother's brother or sister or with the leave of the court, by any other person related to her blood, marriage or adoption".

The Section takes into account the various circumstances under which a court can take cognizance of an offence registered under Section 498-A of the IPC.

A new Section 113-A has been added in the Indian Evidence Act, 1972, to the following effect, in relation to the burden of proof:

> "When the question is whether the Commission of suicide by a woman had been abetted by her husband or any relative of her husband and it is shown that she had committed suicide within a period of seven years from the date of her marriage and that her husband or such relatives of her husband had subjected her to cruelty, the court may presume, having regard to all the other circumstances of the case, that such suicide has been abetted by her husband or by such relatives of her husband".

This Section empowers the court to assume that the suicide has been abetted by the husband or a relative of the husband, unless otherwise established. Under this provision, the burden of proof is shifted from the prosecution to the accused. Thus, there is a total departure from the fundamental rules of evidence. The guilt of the accused is assumed if the death of the woman is caused within seven years of marriage and if cruelty against such woman at the hands of the accused is established. However, the accused is at liberty to prove his innocence. He will not be entitled to any benefit of doubt, provided under the law of Evidence.

In spite of this amendment, dowry deaths in the country have not undergone any decline.

**Latest Trends Related to Dowry**

The names vary. The circumstances differ. The amounts in question are vastly dissimilar. But the victims of dowry death all share one thing in common—an untimely, unnatural, grisly end. Shorn of superficial differences, each story reads the same: the demand for goods and/or money by the boys' side, the inability or the unwillingness, of the girls' parents to pay up: the lack of support structures available to the girl and, therefore, her incapability to walk out of the marriage; the mental, and often physical torture that follows. The barbaric bestial act turned on by the flick of a match stick on kerosene drenched victims marks the end to a helpless being. The demand for dowry and the victimization is carefully planned and plotted by the culprits so as to leave minimum evidence of the crime which they term as accident. The culprits allow some time to pass to give the impression that the couple had good relations. Demands for dowry are conveyed to the bride's father and others in a variety of direct and indirect ways. When demands were made after marriage, it is perceived either as an exercise of the rightful prerogative of the groom and his family, or to express discontent at what was given at the time of marriage or in social comparison with neighbours, at a later date, the dowry was perceived as inadequate.

The list of dowry demands are numerous and diverse and stretch beyond imagination ranging from cash for starting business to TV, tape recorder, motor cycle, refrigerator, car, even wrist watch, cycle or few *tolas* of gold. There are even demands for buffalo or a fan or a job for the groom or transfer of name of husband in fixed deposit. Demands of a grand wedding, share in property of bride's father are also few other demands which may precipitate into serious consequences.

No correlation exists between the level of the education of the bride and her murder on dowry issue is a matter of great surprise. Parent's belief that proper education of their daughter will diminish the margin of dowry is proving wrong . The more a girl an educated, the greater is the demand of dowry. A sixth year Chemistry student of Bihar University was burnt to death by her in-laws and husband for a car. Her parents are said to have given Rs. 4 lakh a few days before she was married. Her father said that a week back his son-in-law had sent a letter threatening him with dire consequences if he was not given a car. In the meanwhile due to constant pressure her father sent two ceiling fans, one cooking range, one table fan and four electric irons. Even working women are not spared for dowry.

Victimization starts immediately after the marriage in most of the cases. But sometimes victimization starts even after several years of marriage. In Gaya town even after eight years of marriage, a mother of two children narrated a woeful tale before the police after regaining consciousness that her husband and mother-in-law with the help of other members of the family inflicted hot iron injuries from her waist to chest till she became unconscious as father of the victim had expressed his inability to comply with the demand of her husband and this led to inhuman treatment with her.

**Trends in Bihar**

A total of 1635 cases of bride burning have been reported during the period 1981-88. This was analysed to examine the rural-urban differences and then regional variation across four regions, namely, Magahi, Maithili, Bhojpuri and Adivasi.

The per cent of distribution of dowry deaths shows increasing trend in Magahi region. When the figure is compared with other regions it is found that all other regions showed a decreasing trend. This result showed that dowry system is more rampant in Magahi areas than in Maithili and Bhojpuri areas, while Adivasi people did not have concept of dowry.

Statistics reveal that incidence of dowry death was always double in urban areas compared to the rural areas during the same years in the four regions. The gap between rural-urban cases was the biggest in Magahi region (39.71) followed by Maithili (35.42), Bhojpuri (29.60) and Adivasi regions (26.21) in that order.

Harassing brides in the name of dowry is not caste or community specific. The dowry deaths are not confined to the Hindu community alone, they are now noticeable among the Muslims. A Muslim girl of Siwan was murdered by her husband. First of all, the boy refused to take his wife to his house. Soon he took her to a place and after a month he sent a message of burning in an accident of her parents. A young Sikh housewife was allegedly murdered by her husband and in-laws for dowry in Punjabi Colony, Chitkohra in Patna.

**Prevalence of Dowry Among Muslims**

Though dowry has been widely prevalent among Muslims in Bihar "dowry deaths were relatively unknown. It is only in recent times that such incidents have been coming to light. A glance at media reports over the years make it amply evident that no longer are Hindu women alone victim of dowry-related violence, it is taking place among Muslims as well although data available on the topic is inadequate. It is beyond doubt that the incidents of dowry deaths among Muslim is much lower in absolute number, yet their occurrence can no longer be described as a "stray incident" or "an isolated case". Wife battering and torture have always been indulged in by men in a male dominated society. Even Muslims come from the same kind of society and so the problem exists among them too and they are no exceptions to the nature of men all over. But burning of women has been rare occurrence in comparison to Hindus reason being that Muslims have recourse to divorce, a provision in Islam much misused by Indian Muslim men. There are also cases of Muslim brides who are constantly harassed physically or mentally for failure to bring sufficient dowry. Approximately thousand applications of women are pending before the Imarat Sharia, Phulwari Sharif, seeking to get their marriage dissolved as Muslim women have as such right as men to get out of an unhappy marriage through *Khula*. Many of these applicants have complained to the religious heads of the constant torture by their husbands for dowry and gifts. Maulana Mujahidul Islam, Head Qazi, of the Imarat Sharia told that increasing number of applications seeking divorce in the last two years, have forced the religious leaders and Muslim intellectuals of Bihar to sound a warning to Muslims to distant themselves from such practices in future and not to fall prey to the evils that have gripped the Hindu community of late. If this is not done, the dowry death and burning of brides among Muslims would become common. (Muslims asked not to take dowry, *Times of India*, Patna, April 2, 1992).

## Categories of Victims of Dowry

Domestic violence related to dowry takes a particular form of reporting. A dowry victim would be one who is harassed, beaten up, mentally tortured by her in-laws or her husband for failure to bring in the demanded dowry or more dowry; or would be one who has been harassed or deserted; or one who has been burnt to death; or who has committed suicide due to excessive harassment.

Though the dowry death is generally perceived to be the murder of a woman on the dowry issue but before the act of killing, several forms of harassment and humiliation take place against the victim. An innocent bride of Hazaribagh was kept confined in a room without food for days together before being murdered.

## Methods used in Dowry Killings

It has been gathered from the newspapers that five different methods were alleged to have been adopted in killing the victims.

Sometimes the victims are first strangulated and then hanged from the roof to make it look like suicide. We shall not attempt to define what exactly is meant by harassment and cruelty, since they are largely subjective terms. At best, some of their physical manifestations on death or injury to body are cognisable. What is more important is that it must be recognised.

## Putting up with Harassment and Torture

The most common form of harassment of a woman in her in-laws family unfolds in the forms of taunts, abuses, threats, which generally escalate to battering, even abettement to suicide or murder in some cases. However, what remains hidden from us are experiences of woman battered by their husband — for various reasons including inadequacy of dowry. This is viewed by the police as a simple case of domestic assault and by the society as "normal interaction among intimate couples". Women will be women, always striving to keep the family fabric intact. Blinded by the patriarchal notions about the privacy of family matters and because of their assumed weakness, woman seldom choose to get out of these relationships or even complain about it. Putting up with violence becomes the order of the day for an indefinite period until it becomes unbearable when thev have to take hard decisions and escape torture by suicide or walking out. Keeping relationships together, despite violence, is also important for practical reasons such as financial support and shelter. Setting out is almost as bad as staying in the relationship. The threat of male violence outside the home is an acutely intimidating reality of women who endure violence within their won homes. Living among constant threats of killing and desertion become a daily ordeal for them, they have to take it or leave it, in most cases they keep taking it.

The mother-in-law, sister-in-law nexus along with an unsympathetic husband make life a living hell for them. Indian conjugal relationships are typically much less closer than those between mother and son: frequently the mother-in-law instigates the harassment against the young bride using her son as her agent. The actual or supposed inadequacy of dowry becomes an excuse for the mother-in-law.

On the slightest pretext the bride is sent back to her parental home—usually to refurbish her "inadequate dowry". To make matters worse and continued harassment, the quality and quantity or whatever she gets from her parents are made the excuse.

On the other extreme the girl is discouraged from frequently visiting her parents. Her isolation from her earlier natal source of support being complete, her natal family is kept in the dark under the impression that all is going well not having an inkling of idea what their daughter is going through. That torture and harassment could reach such limits can be seen in cases where clothes for daily wear were given to the woman by mother-in-law each day; where for a pair of slippers and handkerchiefs she was not given money but was asked to get these from her parents; where every time, she went to her parents, she was not given the rickshaw fare, but was asked to make her parents pay it where the battering has permanently disfigured her finger, where a newly married bride tried to commit suicide because of the hopeless situation she was in and had a miscarriage; where she was not allowed to sleep with her husband or communicate with him for one whole year after marriage; where a woman was tied with a rope, beaten, after which she was burnt, where a woman was burnt within a week after her marriage, and where a girl had been accused of being insane and cast out. These are few of the many instances of harassment the women may have to undergo each day of their lives.

## Opting the Hard Way Out : the Indian Woman

### *Reasons*

The question that confronts us now is why do so many girls

come back even after they have undergone such torture beyond endurance? The first reason being the wish of the girl herself who really sees no respectable position outside her husband's house. Women often feel inadequate to cope with self-sufficiency and consequently the lack of self-confidence often acts as a trap to keep a woman within a violent home. Putting up with physical abuse is the very reason that there is no decline in domestic violence against women.

A daughter's change of status and her transfer from one family to another have a strong cultural sanction. It is said that at marriage the girl dies and is reborn as a new person. The formal advice given to her is that as long as she is alive she is not to leave the house she is entering. The parents themselves ignore the case of the daughter who is being harassed and wishes to come back. They advise her, pressurise her or even force her to stick to the "real" home and try to adjust. They are afraid of the stigma of a married daughter leaving her home and returning to her parents. Their constant advice to her is to "adjust" to maltreatment, the common saying being. "It is nothing unusual or so unbearable—so many women are coping with it". In most cases of wife murder, suicide, maltreatment, the women feels so burdened by the expenditure undertaken by her parents, that she feels duty bound to present a brave picture of "silent courage".

Parents justify their succumbing to these demands, saying that it was done for the daughter's well-being ... the well-being of continued torture, within the four walls rather than independent survival for their daughter. Most women would also undoubtedly opt for the former precisely because they have been conditioned to think along similar lines. Both society and religion sanctify the patient and suffering women.

Women see their recognition in society through matrimony and for this she has to sometimes pay a heavy price. A home for a woman is synonymous with the home her husband would provide her. This is the general understanding of the man, of the parents, of the women, and indeed of Indian society in general. In our culture divorce or widowhood for a woman is worse than death. However, this is in many cases not true for the women of lower castes, as there is greater autonomy to women among them.

**Adjustment Problems Related Deaths**

It is not always dowry which can lead to woman's burning there are other problems related to adjustment which confront her after her marriage and precipitate into serious consequences. After marriage an young bride joins a new family and she is expected to "adjust" her needs, her behaviour, her personality and her entire self - according to her husbands and his family needs as soon as possible. This adjustment problem creates conflicts between husband and wife and daughter-in-law, and father/mother-in-law and brother/sister-in-law. In this situation of conflict the husband does not always know when and where to side with his wife. Over small conflicts, therefore the girls go to their parents home to get their (parents) sympathy The parents generally advise them to go back and adjust. The girls, therefore remain frustrated; unable to cope with the harsh realities of married life and getting no emotional support from their husband or their own parents, they seek the easy way "ending it all" by committing suicide. Some of the cases thus reported as dowry-deaths are in fact cases of impulsive suicides. Earlier, it was held that women in the autumn of their life had suicidal tendencies. But nowadays psychologists are of this view that teenagers form the highest risk group, because in this age, rapid hormonal changes in her body which make them more excitable, depressive and vulnerable. When they experience tensions after marriage instead of love and affection from the husband and the family, they take their own lives, often on filmsy pretexts. The young girls with dreams in their eyes fall victim to tension on experiencing small disappointments making them big issues. This amkes them excitable and prone to suicide.

A lady Commissioner of Police in charge of the Anti Dowry Cell of Delhi corroborates the view that 90 per cent of the cases that have been registered with Anti Dowry Cell have no link with dowry and many of them are directly related with the problem of non-adjustment between husband and wife due to variety of factors like physical or mental incompatibility, the wife resenting her mother-in-laws domination and wanting to live separately etc.

Earlier also there were suicides and murders due to conflicts, but now they are reported in the newspapers, due to the awakening of womens rights and the pro-bridal wave. Many women's organisations take up the issue of the so-called "silent sufferers". Thus, it is not that all of a sudden in-laws and husbands have been savages, but that the mass media gives these cases prominence, at the same time not declaring mother-in-law as completely innocent in case of dowry death.

*Circumstances Leading to Killings of Wife*

It is gathered from newspapers that there are many circumstances in which, ill treatment of young wives, often driving them to commit suicide and many times they have been murdered, take place which are not linked with the dowry death in any way.

It is, however, desirable to be remembered that all broken and problematic marriages do not have dowry as the roots. There are cases where a girl who had been married by the parents against her will, may be because she did not like the proposal or intended to marry some one else with whom she was in love before, cannot adjust with her husband or in-laws and concocts a story of cruelty against her, returns to parents and sends a legal notice levelling dowry and torture charges and uses blackmail to demand a handsome life time maintenance. If this is not met, she might involve the husband and his parents in a criminal case under the Dowry Prohibition Act. Such cases are coming to light in which ultra-modern working women are involved. They do not re-marry but live in adultery with men of their choice.

The laws and bouts of propaganda have created panic, trauma and suspicion all round, without helping to do with the dowry menace. To a great extent, the matrimonial relations in general and the rapport between the parents and in-laws, in particular have deteriorated under the stress of suspicion. It would, however, not be forgotten that the dowry deaths and ill treatment of married women are not as common as they are made out to be, by the recent publicity. In comparison with number of happily married couples and contented families, they are a microscopic minority. So, the generalisation of plights of some particular brides and rampant in-laws baiting will cause immense harm to the social fabric. Every case has to be dealt with individually as all aberration and not as a part of the general state of affairs. After all, marriage is still the cementing factor of the social edifice and nothing should be done to weaken it.

**Calling Parents and Potential Victims of Dowry**

In some rare cases parents are also equally responsible for the plight of their daughters. Why do they select such boys for their girls for whom they even have to borrow money or spend all their life savings? Why do they marry their daughters in dowry—greedy families? Why do they not bring back their daughters from their in-law's home when they come to know of their harassment? Why are they so concerned about the social stigma and send back their daughters to their in-laws when they are tortured by their husbands and parents-in-laws? Why do they acquisce in the demands of their daughter's in-law? Why do they sacrifice their daughters for the sake of the legality of a tag marriage? Why do they spend thousands of rupees on dowry as demanded rather than spending a little less amount on their daughters to make them economically independent? We may therefore come to a conclusion that the parents of the girls and the girls themselves cannot be absolved of the responsibility. In several instances, the girl has been known to have written to her parents or visited them, just before she died and told them about the cruelty.

The girls as victims to oppression are equally questionable as to — why do they submit to oppression? Why do they not realize that a divorce is better than a marriage where money is the all and end-all of all relations? Why do they not walk out of their marriages and try to stand on their own legs? Why do they not realize that by committing suicide, they are creating problems for their children and an emotional trauma for their younger sisters and parents. Marriage is not the ultimate end in life but happiness certainly is.

Ideally the parents of the girls should take a firm decision to report the matter to the police and to the court, as well. At the same time the girl must also take a decision as to her future course of action. She must decide whether she would continue to live in a state of growing tension, or whether she would prefer to secure release from that tension once and for all.

There have been suggestions for special or separate courts may be established to deal with cases of dowry and bride burning. These courts would contribute to the speedy and efficient disposal of dowry death cases.

Moreover, court proceedings should be made time bound laws amended to make it more effective, particularly by giving recognition not only to written but oral dying declarations made in the presence of a doctor, or a police officer or a magistrate or any respectable citizen. Neighbours who can really be vital witnesses should come forward more often and be involved in a dying declaration.

There is no let up in the rate of crime despite the law. What can be done to prevent dowry violence and crimes related to dowry? People should stop exhibiting dowry items. They must socially boycott dowry seekers. The young girls must fight dowry and take a pledge not to marry those who demand dowry.

Along with amendments and changes in the present law and providing more teeth to police force, the girls, their parents, their husbands and the people at large who matter, can only prevent the bride burning. There is also need for structural changes like assuming easy and less costly education, taking effective measure to reduce unemployment among educated youth devising a system to eliminate bribery in the process of getting employment, providing housing facilities to the employed and simplifying the procedure for lodging complaint to the police, may definitely go a long way in minimizing the rate of bride burning.

Moreover, mutual respect for each other and a degree of tolerance of opposing viewpoints will, in a great measure, contribute to harmonious solution. Men have to be taught to respect women and not treat her as an object of exploitation. Further on, only if women respect themselves can  command respect from others.

Twelve

# The Rape

The Oxford Dictionary defines the word rape as "forcible or fradulent sexual intercourse imposed on women". In the words of Susan Brown Miller, "Rape is the only crime for which the victim cannot have a revenge." It represents as "act of violence and humiliation in which the victim experiences not only overwhelming fear for her very existence, but an equally overwhelming sense of powerlessness and helplessness that hardly a few others events in ones life can parallel" (Hilberman, 1976).

## Meaning

The word rape in many Indian languages, is *balaatkar* derived from the root *bal* meaning strength, basically in a physical sense. But it is also a beastly crime because the time and place where the rape is committed, finds the victim defenceless, weak, alone, or vulnerable. In other words, at that particular moment she is in no position to defend herself against physical assault. Rape for a woman should simply mean a criminal invasion into personal integrity. Seen from the angle of the patriarchal society, it has primarily meant an assault on the legally recognised male rights of possession where he has the right of possession of an unblemished woman. The Hindi phrase for rape is *Izzat lootna* which literally translates as "the robbing of honour".

## Definition under Section 375 IPC

According to Section 375 of the Indian Penal Code, rape is committed when a man has sexual intercourse with a woman:

(i) against her will, or

(ii) without her consent, or

(iii) with her consent, when her consent has been obtained by putting her or any person in whom she is interested, in fear of death, or of hurt, or

(iv) with her consent, when he by deception, makes her believe that he is her lawful husband, or

(v) with her consent, given an account of her unsoundness of mind, or intoxication, when she is incapable of understanding the consequences of her consent, or

(vi) with or without consent, when she is under 16 years of age.

'Against her will' means an act is done against a woman's will when she is fully conscious and capable of consenting and a decision-making power and is aware of what is being done and resists or objects to it. 'Without her consent' means that she is insensible and incapable of rational consent, due to fear, shock or intoxication or any other cause.

Rape is the most calculated, cold blooded, deliberate and heinous of crimes committed by one human being on another by virtue of the simple and biological fact that the one who commits rape is physically stronger than this victim. Being by no means accidental or committed in the heat of the moment on a passionate impulse, there is no anger or vengeance involved either.

In a rape, the aggressor is a man, the rapist and the aggrieved party is also a man, the father or the husband and the woman being the damaged property. The woman is the victim and it is she who has to carry the stigma for the rest of her life. The social and religious values make her an outcaste, an untouchable and a disgrace to her family. It is an exceptional crime where harassment, guilt, shame and social disapproval are attached to the victim, not to the offender. Society at large looks down on a victim with suspicion. The woman is made to feel guilty as myths about rape such as "no woman can be raped unless she wants", dressed like that she was asking for it, or "women like being raped", etc. are current in society. This makes it even more difficult for the victim to reveal her tragedy. Often men consider women tempting in any dress good or bad. When she is alone, she can be taken as inviting man and she can be considered flirting when she is socialising.

All women perpetually suffer from the fear of being raped irrespective of her age, health, appearance, mental state, shelter and relations. No woman is immune from being the victim of rape.

The scourage of rape continues to wreak havoc on the nation's thousand of innocent women. Various examples have been gathered, the rape case reported in newspapers that high class men or men in power rape Harijan women.

- Two Harijan girls were allegedly raped, their huts were demolished and a well was polluted by landlords in separate incidents in the interior of Nawada district.
- Teachers rape their students, three minor girls were raped by their teacher in mohalla Machharhatta of Barh Bazar.
- Sometimes the colleagues residents of Myar village under Noorsarai P.S. witnessed the rape of a female teacher at the Myar Middle School by her male colleagues in the school building.
- Students rape their fellows. A young girl, victim of an attempt of rape in the hostel of a local college of Patna, was handed over to her parents by the Pirbahore police after medical examination.
- Doctors rape their patients in hospital and nursing home. Two doctors of Nalanda Medical College Hospital were arrested by Sultanganj police on the charge of criminally assaulting a female patient; Employees rape their co-workers. A nurse of Sadar Hospital, Giridih was criminally assaulted by two employees of the hospital.
- Prison staff rape their undertrials. A Harijan woman undertrial prisoner was allegedly raped to death by the jail staff in Giridih.
- Landlords rape their tenants. A twelve-year-old girl in Barmasia locality of Giridih district was assaulted and raped by her landlord as the parents of the victim were out of the town.
- Tenants rape their landlords. A middle-aged woman of Tekari road, Sultanganj area of Patna was raped by one of her tenant.
- Masters rape their maid servants. A 15-year-old girl working as a maid servant in the lodge in Dhaneshwar

Ghat Mohalla under Bihar Sharif Police Station was raped by some students.

- Domestic servants rape the housewives. A domestic servant was arrested by the Bankmore Police of Dhanbad on the charge of criminally assaulting a housewife when the other family members of the house were out.
- Old men and young men alike enjoy the pleasure of sex out of wedlock and even women suffering from T.B. and other ailments undergoing treatment become victims. A poor, sick woman was gangraped by some identified people in village Berhna under Police Station of Patna while she was relaxing under the shade of a tree. A girl of 17 years, living with her sick mother in the hospital of Chaibasa was raped by unknown persons, after disconnecting electric line. A pregnant woman of Sinhpur village under Kasmar Police Station of Bokaro was brutally beaten by three miscreants when the victim resisted their attempt to rape her. An adivasi minor blind girl of Lakha village under Mofussil Police Station was gangraped by three identified persons. An Adivasi woman under treatment for leprosy at Nav Kusth Ashram of Bhagalpur was gang raped by four criminals. Their physical appearance need not be always attractive.
- Sometimes the rape victims are reported to be baby girls. A man was arrested at Jamshedpur on the charge of raping a three-year-old girl.
- Old women have also been raped.
- An old woman of Agrer village under Sasaram block of Rohtas district was raped in her house by some goondas in a drunken state when his husband was out of station. Later on she was strangulated to death.
- Women may not be safe even in their families. A 20-year-old woman was raped and murdered by her father-in-law at Sheonar village of Mokameh.

Rape of women cuts across barriers of caste, class, education, looks, age and status. The rapist may be any person—a holyman, a doctor, a teacher, a servant, a landlord or a farmer, a student, a neighbour or a co-villager, a relative or a criminal. Therefore, the rapist is one among ourselves. He has no distinct identity. There are an umpteen numbers of instances and a plenty of evidence to show that rapist may be no stranger to the victim and the offence could just as easily occur in family setting—offices, educational institutions, hospitals and even homes. The aggressor could even be a boy friend or acquaintance. He could be an employer, or landlord who wields power, a neighbour or a member of the family.

Sexual harassment is unknown in the dingy corridor and cubicles of office and factories in metropolitan and industrial towns. Working women are harassed by their bosses and colleagues. Those who come from cultured families and also have some financial means give up their job as a protest. But women who come from the lower middle-class and are sole supporters of a family or their income is an indispensable supplement to their husband, beat their bosses sexual overtones silently. It is a mistake to assume that all rapists are perverts, normal men do rape. There are the cases male members of the victim's family have even lost their lives in a bid to save the female members from being raped.

It would be more precise to state rape is mostly used to express or to assert class power or as an instrument of class oppression. Rape an assertion of male power as a terrorising instrument of punishment, is indulged in by the elite, by the guardians of the law and order on woman from the rural areas, woman from the scheduled castes and tribes. Why is it that educated women are raped less frequently than illiterate and ignorant women? Why is it that high caste women are raped very rarely. A 19-year-old girl was gang raped by a number of Harijans in village Neura of Barh subdivision in broad day light and the rapists prevented the victim's family from going to the police station and in their bid to do so they opened several rounds of fire. While low caste tribal woman and women from minority communities who are also poor raped quite often? And finally, women from the upper, middle and affluent classes are hardly raped while women from the economically poor classes are subjected to rape every other day. Rape among the middle and upper classes is another taboo subject. Even among middle class women, the general attitude towards rape is that it is something which happens to lower class women, something the rest of society is protected from by virtue of caste or class. In parts of the country even today, landlords demand 'first night' privileges. It is the common allegation in rape case where the authority is the offender and helpless, poor women are the victims that these women are of loose moral character.

The question is: how can the investigating authorities make any positive conclusions about the moral character of any woman, whether she is raped or not, without having any knowledge about her lifestyle except the fact that she is poor, illiterate and belongs to a backward and oppressed community? Even if the women who have been victimised are women of loose morals, what has character got to do with a man's right to rape her? These questions remain unanswered in this male dominated society. It may be known that — a woman is a woman just as man is a man. One human being's moral or immoral or a moral stand does not in any way justify another person's humiliation of her or him, sex notwithstanding. If one were to reverse the theory, then what would women do with men who have loose morals? But women cannot do anything specially if they are poor, illiterate and belong to the backward classes as long as it is the men who man the law and judicial machinery of the country.

Rape is one language often used by two groups of warring men to get even with each other, not considering that the people who are used for this, are flesh-and-blood thinking and living beings because they are women. Rape is not always necessarily for the perverted sense of sexual pleasure of man as was commonly believed for ages together. Brownmiller states that populations have been terrorised by rape : (i) in the two World Wars, (ii) in the wars of Bangladesh and Vietnam, (iii) during partition riots in India in 1947, when there was mass rape of both Hindu and Muslim women. Rape, therefore, has been systematically and calculatedly used as an instrument of intimidation in India, not only for women, but also to humiliate and demoralise the men. After the assassination of Indira Gandhi, about 2000 women were raped in Delhi in the riots following her death.

Rural-urban difference in the incidence of rape in Bihar revealed the following trends.

**Trends of Rape Incidence: Rural/Urban**

(i) Percentages of rape in rural areas were slightly higher compared to urban areas in all the years except 1981 and 1988.

(ii) In urban areas higher rate of incidence was in 1981 and 1988 when the percentage of incidence was 50.61 and 51.05 respectively.

(iii) Both rural and urban areas demonstrated decreasing as well as increasing tendencies in the rate of rape cases.

The data were further analysed to examine the difference between rural and urban areas within each region.

Studies in Bihar indicate that the incidence of rape was always higher in urban compared to rural areas except in Adivasi region where the incidence was double in number in rural areas compared to the urban areas during the same years in the four regions. When the rape cases were analysed region-wise, the rural-urban differences became more vivid as well as region-specific. In Magahi, Maithili, and Bhojpuri region urban areas contributed more towards the incidence than the rural one. On the other hand, in the Adivasi region it was rural side which reported higher rate of rape cases.

## Types of Rape

### *Rape of Dalit and Tribal Women*

It is an all-pervasive fact that Dalit and tribal women are oppressed by society at large; rape is simply being used an instrument to oppress women. Dalit and tribal women are raped for a variety of reasons not least of which is the fact that they are vulnerable women and raping them is not likely to result in any punishment. They are also raped as a way of demoralising them in their struggle for an improved existence. For the last two decades Bihar has seen many gruesome violence taking place in different parts of the state. The incidents at Belchi, Pipra, Parashbigha, Arwal, Kansara, and Gua are some of the most prominent ones, where women had been targets of rape and molestation. A big demonstration by about 5000 tribal including women was held in front of the office of the Deputy Commissioner demanding immediate action against the policemen who had allegedly misbehaved with tribal women while they were on their traditional 'Janishikar'.

### *Rape on the Job*

The rape of working women is a national scandal which is at least as widespread as custodial rape, yet it does not receive as much attention. They are harassed by their bosses and male workers.

Domestic servants are molested by employer or the relatives or friends of employers. The headmaster of an English medium school at Bhurkunda, 30 km from Ramgarh Cantt was taken into police custody for raping a lady teacher of his school. A nurse of Sadar Hospital, Giridih was criminally assaulted by two young employees of the hospital.

***Rape by Strangers***

Women are not safe anywhere, may it be the street or the fields or even her own home.

A married woman of Chandi mohalla of Barh was brutally assaulted by six youths at her residence as the other members of the family were out. A Harijan girl of village Musapur under Sarairanjan police station of Dalsingsarai was raped and murdered by identified persons in her house while she was sleeping with her mother.

***Rape of Minor***

Rape of minor is particularly horrifying and now it has become a common crime. Newspapers regularly print accounts of the rape of minor girls. One person of Jamshedpur was taken into custody on the charge of raping a three-year-old girl. A five-year-old girl was lured away from a Ganesh Puja pandal and raped by an unidentified man and she was taken to the intensive care unit of the Tata Main Hospital in an unconscious state.

***Rape in Journey***

Women are not safe even while travelling. A minor girl waiting for a particular bus at the Harding Park bus stand of Patna was taken to a lonely place by a worker of a transport agency on the pretext of guiding her to the said bus and was raped. Two women train passengers were kidnapped from North Eastern Railway Dighwara station and allegedly gangraped.

A young woman passenger was criminally assaulted in a compartment of the Munger-Jamalpur local train after locking the gates and her husband who tried to resist them was thrown out of the running train.

***Rape of Sick***

Even women suffering from T.B. or other ailments undergoing treatment, pregnant, blind women and women suffering from leprosy are the victims of rape.

A sick women of Patna who went to a hospital for her treatment was allegedly raped by three persons.

A pregnant women was brutally beaten by three miscreants when she resisted their attempt to rape her.

A Adivasi minor blind girl was gangraped by three youngsters.

An Adivasi woman under treatment for leprosy was gangraped by four criminals.

***Rape within family***

Women are not safe even in their own family. A 20-year-old woman was raped and murdered by her father-in-law of Sheonar village in Mokameh. A young married woman deposed before the Judicial Magistrate that her father-in-law entered her room and committed rape on her and it was why she stabbed him.

Thus, it is observed that women are raped at work, on the street, in the fields, at bus or railway platform, in train, in school, in their homes by men who are their employers or employees, their acquaintance, their neighbours, their relatives, and their in-laws. It is not only Dalit women who are victims and not only landlords who are rapists.

**Categories of Rapists**

There may be at least three categories of rapists. There is one whose assault is the explosive expression of a pent-up sexual impulse; he is motivated by sex desire only. In such cases the rapists has no respect of age or looks. The second group is motivated by an impulse to punish and hurt the victim, rather than sex desire. Gang rapes by dacoits after committing a dacoity, rapes on Harijan women, rapes on women during communal riots, rapes due to family dispute and gang rape by policemen all come under this group. And there is a third group of rapist, the aggressive criminals, who is out of pillage and rob, like the soldiery of a conquering army.

Gebhard in a psychological study of rapists found the following five categories of rapists:

(i) *Sadists:* who have a past history of violence, a strong hostility to females, and who obtain sexual satisfaction only when it is accompanied by physical violence.

(ii) *Moral delinquents:* who are not hostile to females, use force to get what they want and commit rape to satisfy sexual desire without taking interest in victim.

(iii) *Explosives:* who are normally "upright" citizens. A disturbed family background usually underlies the behaviour of these offenders.

(iv) *Drunken variety:* who after drinking delude themselves into thinking that a female is trying to seduce them.

(v) *Double standard:* who divide females into "good" and "bad" and rationalize the use of force, if necessary, on "bad" girls.

**Characteristics of a Rapist**

The sex, instinct, indeed had been a very powerful motivation since the time immemorial. In a way, every man in this world is a sexual criminal at the unconscious level. But what matters is the action. People who translate their latent feelings into action give way to the doctrine that pleasure is the chief god. Through psychoanalytic studies, it has been revealed that the rapists are persons with poor judgement and inadequate impulse control. They lack the power of reasoning which leads them to sexual perversion. A man with a well developed personality and a strong moral standard would never indulge in such activities.

Rape is also attributed to unhappy family life which may be due to various incapabilities such as potency, temperament, habit and economic conditions, as a result of which marital life turns annoying and frustrating. Broken homes and constant friction in family turns children into sex delinquents.

Pornographic literature and the modern movies depicting crude rape and bathing scenes are also contributing to the desire to rape among adolescents and youth. Disregard of moral values and lack of religious sanctions also give rise to urge of rape.

Sex crimes also occur due to psychological factors like desire to rape, exhibition of potency, experience of pleasure in the pain of others (Sadism), taking revenge on a woman and like. A major study of forcible rape (Amir, 1971) has shown that in 85 per cent of all reported rapes there was some form of overt violence such as beating or choking. It may be stated that rape is an act of aggression and violence and it is committed by persons who are not motivated by sexuality; rather they are motivated primarily by power, hostility and the urge to brutalise, humiliate and debase their victims.

According to Mackellar (1975), "The man who rapes does so because he lacks a better means for making the point, 'I am a man,' while Bart (1975) has stressed the anger in rape: "Psychiatrists say a gun is a substitute phallus. Rape is a power trip, not a passion trip. The rapist is more likely to rape in cold blood, with contempt and righteousness, than with passion".

Thus, rape is a universal phenomenon. Its etiology is complex and the manifestations are extremely varied according to time, place and person. It also varies with historical periods, modes of life, economic conditions and social attitudes.

**Victimization: Ways and Consequences**

The victims of rape are victimized in sundry ways and rape is pregnant with momentous consequences for its victim. We may distinguish three ways of victimization of, and three types of consequences for, the victim of the rape: psychological, physical and social.

*Psychological Victimization*

Psychological victimization of the victim and its consequences can be understood in three phases of rape: before, during and after rape.

The fear of rape troubles all women, it is a source of mental anxiety to the victim. Research on the fear of crime and on public opinion, about crime shows that the very possibility of being victimised troubles many people. Freedom from criminal victimisation is a social good, much like any other social good of a just society.

Rape affects all women whether or not they are actually victimized. According to Griffin (1970) who verbalizes as follows, the experience of many women: 'I have never been free of the fear of rape. From a very early age I, like most women, have thought of rape as part of my natural environment something to be feared and prayed against like fire or lightning". Women are under perpetual fear of being raped which induces a continuing state of psychological stress in women due to which they resort to several safety precautions which, in turn, seriously restrict their freedom, such as not moving alone, or avoiding to go to certain places, or going out with certain men. Several studies attest to these consequences of the fear of rape on all women, all the time, everywhere, who may not have been victimized but who, nonetheless, are subjected to the threat of rape and to the concomitant forces of social control.

The actual commission of rape is a "crisis situation" full of stress and strain for a victim thus far leading a normal life. And it is a strange sudden crisis—a crisis with which the victim must deal herself. If she surrenders sexually, then her life is spoilt personally and socially, and if she resists, then she runs the risk of being destroyed physically at the hands of the rapist.

The post-rape period poses a more lingering as the ordeal for the rape victim. The terror of the criminal justice system, social stigma, and the physical injury, combine together to cause psychological malaise beyond description. In her post-rape life, she begins to nurture distrust in men and society, confronts difficulties in her sexual adjustment, and suffers from a host of psychological disturbances, including fear, insomnia, anxiety, dreams, hallucinations and others. Many a time, the victim reconciles with the mental trauma caused by her by taking refuge in suicide.

*Physical Victimization*

In the process of preventing the rapist from raping the victim incurs a wide variety of physical injuries, depending upon the location and the extent of resistance put up. The injuries from the physical attacks of the rapist are on various parts of the body, throat, neck, cheeks, thighs, legs, arms and genitalia. And injuries themselves are varied 'scratches, bruises, at times being knifed or shot at.

Varieties of physical complaints and complications begin to appear in post-rape period: physical pain in different parts of the body, skeletal muscle tension, gastro-intestinal irritability and genito-urinary disturbances, to cite a few.

The victim's large number of complicated physiological problems warrant immediate medicare. For instance, there is a possibility of contracting venereal diseases and conceiving, besides other physical injuries in course of her struggle to resist the occurrence of rape. It is the victim alone who has to bear the cost of the medicine, besides bearing the physical pain and mental agony. Needless to say, the hospitals lack physicians with special training in handling physical and emotional complications which rape victims are exposed to. Furthermore, the hospitals are not adequately equipped to treat even the physiological damages, what to speak of psychological treatment, facilities which are practically non-existent throughout the length and breadth of the country.

*Social Victimization*

*The Victim's Plane*

Rape has several far-reaching social implications both for the victim and for the society. Although it involves a limited number of men and women on the face of it, rape is basically a social problem (Rose, 1977) of great magnitude. On the victim's plane, the implications of rape depend upon whether she is married or unmarried, child or adult, having first sexual experience or not. In case the victim is unmarried, it creates problems in the settlement of her marriage if it becomes public. And, if she is married, there is a possibility of a breakdown of the marriage. Even if the marital life continues, or marriage of the unmarried happens to be solemnized, the sword of the fear of rape being divulged, and consequently being disturbed when it becomes known it always hang will over the head of the rape victim. And, if per chance the rape remains concealed throughout, the psychological stress caused by sexual assault remains for ever.

The volume of physiological pain due to sexual assault differs to different age groups of the victims but psychological complications also vary. The severity of the impact of rape felt by the victims varies depending upon whether the victim is a child or a younger or older or an adult.

In all these, and many other ways rape has a chain of negative consequences in the life of the victim as a wife, a daughter, betrothed, a beloved, a child, parent, working women, and so on. In this manner, rape threatens the very existence of the victim in society.

*The Social Plane*

Rape is one instance where the atrocities of men against women become naked. Rape is in fact, not the rape of women but the rape of morality and the noble ideals of the society as a whole. The rapist remains a man and, at times, he is honoured in society, whereas, the victim of the same rapist is treated as a 'bad' women. In a male-dominated society, females are subjected to all sorts of subjection—physical, social and psychological. On the social plane, the threat of rape serves as a weapon in the hands of men and the society. They dominate to maintain social control of women by keeping them in a state of perpetual anxiety and by encouraging the self imposition of behaviour restriction in quest for safety (Riger and Gordon, 1981: 71-92). Rape is a crisis for the victim's family members and friends who also need emotional support (Krishna, 1988). If the rape is her first sexual experience, she may find herself quite confused about the relationship between sexuality, violence and humiliation. On attempting to leave her house and have an independent identity, her sense of adequacy is challenged by her feeling that she really cannot take care of herself. The women who have an ongoing sexual relationship may prefer not to disclose it to their man/men for fear of disrupting the relationship.

Rape of women is simultaneously a crisis for the victim's family. The very feeling that a woman of the family has been raped is a kind of shock, difficult for a family to bear. In such a crisis situation, the family members become emotionally disturbed. The prestige of the family in society is lowered, if such cases become public through the court or otherwise. In many cases, raped wives and daughters are not accepted by their husband or parents as the case may be. Many a time they are thrown in the lap of prostitution. Even if the victim survives the shock and remains in the family, social stigma labels her as a 'bad' woman throughout her lifetime.

Rape cannot be consummated until after force and prolonged resistance have been overcome. So if there is no outward evidence of resistance such as a black eye, bruise or scratch, there evidently was no resistance. Right from the beginning the victim is subjected to embarrassing queries which hinge on whether she had resisted sufficiently, and generally the accused gets the benefit of doubt. Rape is a personal crisis in the sense that the victim must deal with the impact and meaning of the event for herself. The stereotype that a woman should always attempt to prevent the rape through struggle leaves women in a double mind. If they do not struggle, they have a very hard time in court. If they do struggle, they run the risk of incurring even more injuries at the hands of the rapist.

Rape involves at least two major crisis for the women. The first is the rape itself. The second is her experience of going through the medical examination and the criminal justice system, with her appearance in court being the most painful part. While it is difficult to provide all the long-term psychological problems of the victim, some of the issues which seems to re-emerge at a later date are mistrust and avoidance of men, sexual disturbances, phobic hallucination, delusions, insomnia, terrifying dreams, anxiety and depression often precipitated by seemingly trivial events which symbolise the original trauma. Due to sexual repulsion and fear there is a decline of interest as well as withdrawal from one's partner. Post-rape adjustment is one of the most important psychological problems, which must be tackled properly in time by counselling. Psychologically problems are more severe when the rapist is a near relative. There is no law that can obliterate the trauma with which she must live.

**Need for Change in Attitudes**

The evidence of resistance required in case of rape victim is not required for dacoity, etc. The rape victim is subjected to embarassing questions. The social stigma attached to such cases is deterrent enough to reporting such cases. Under Rule 228(A) of the Act, the identity of the victim and all details of the rape itself will be kept in the strict confidence of the trying court. The entire legal proceedings will be held in camera.

Values and attitudes regarding rape should be changed. When a woman is raped, why should she be held guilty. The man has committed the rape on her person should be held responsible for the shameful act. Why should her identity remain secret? Why should she feel ashamed or guilt or both? Because she is the subordinate and less important sex? Because if she is unmarried, her chances of a good marriage may be lost for ever? Because she has lost her virginity if she is unmarried, and her chastity if she is married and these two things are held at the premium in a society where social values are decided by the males?

Thus, social attitudes towards the victims need to be changed. Thousand of girls and women are victims by society for no fault of their own. Taking unfair advantages of the social stigma, the rapist lead the victim to prostitution. Forms and values of the society should not be misinterpreted for the cause of women. If a sexually active man is perceived as a sexually active man; a sexually active woman should also be perceived as a sexually active woman, not as a bad woman. The objective 'promiscuous' should not be applied only to her. The problems cannot be solved adequately unless we change the Victorian attitude of male dominated society.

## Suggestions

Some of the suggestions which need proper attention are as follows:

1. The accused should not be permitted to question the victim regarding her character or previous sexual relations with any other person.
2. Rape victims should not be maltreated at the hands of the police whose assistance has been sought during the crisis. They should not be submitted to the countless questions about her own sexual mores and behaviour by the police investigator.
3. The victims should be thoroughly examined by an expert doctor and immediate cure of physical injuries, prevention of veneral disease, and prevention of pregnancy should be taken.
4. It is advisable that the burden of proof be shifted from the victim to the offender. Let him prove that he did not rape her. Let it not be the woman's burden to prove that she was criminally assaulted.
5. In recent years, cases of false accusation have come to notice for the purpose of blackmailing the accused to extort money or women offenders, during arrests and search, to level false charges of rape against policemen. Therefore, when women are involved in a crime she must be arrested and searched by a woman police officer. Report of rape victims should be recorded by women police officers and women investigators are to be appointed to investigate such cases.
6. The burden of stigma should not be attached within the victim and his family rather it should be shifted from the victim to the offender.
7. Victims of the rape deserve emotional support and sympathy by family members for post-rape adjustment rather than being disowned by them.
8. No woman should be arrested between sunset and sun rise.

9. Sex education should be imparted to adolescents and youths in order to prevent the crime against women. Parents should not feel ashamed in discussing sex with their children.

Our study of rape shows that the status of women continues to be low, and crime continues to be directed against them. Changes must be brought in the mind, heart and behaviour of men and women in the various compartments of our culture and in our social institutions so that the age-old sex anarchy of rape of women is removed.

# Thirteen

# Abduction and Kidnapping

Kidnapping and abduction is a heinous crime. It affects adversely the career of a large number of girls and women every year. Normally it has been noticed that the abductors and abducted victims are acquainted, rather not strangers to each other. The initial contact between the abductor and his victim frequently occurs in their own homes and neighbourhood rather than in public places. On the other hand, father is too busy with his own world. The mother too has developed a circle outside the home. Thus, the parents do not know or even ask their sons and daughters where they spend the evenings. There is lack of parental control. The bond of love, affection and respect seems to be vanishing from Indian families.

As discussed earlier on the taking or enticing away of a girl less than 18 years of age or of a male less than 16 years of age without the consent of the lawful guardian constitutes kidnapping. Abduction is the forcible, fraudulent or deceitful taking away of a woman with an intension of seducing her to illicit sex or compelling her to marry a person against her will. Thus, "abduction" differs from "kidnapping". The latter is committed only in respect of a minor, while the former in respect to any person. In kidnapping, the victim's consent is immaterial but in abduction, the victim's free and voluntary consent condones the crimes. In kidnapping, the offender's intention is irrelevant but in abduction, it is the all important factor. Thus, a girl of 18 or over, could only be abducted and not kidnapped; but if she is under 18 she could be kidnapped as well as abducted if the taking is by force or the taking or enticing was by deceitful means.

### Circumstances Leading to Kidnapping/abduction

There are different circumstances and motivations leading to kidnapping or abduction. Sometimes it is politically motivated, sometimes economically and sometimes it occurs due to some personal reasons. The political kidnapping of famous filmstar Rajkumar, Veerapan attracted much attention. Economically motivated kidnapping is mainly for ransom and sale for prostitution. In this study we are chiefly concerned with the kidnapping of woman for marriage, sex satisfaction or for sale for prostitution.

Kidnapping/abduction may occur with or without the consent of the girls. Sometimes the victims "run away" from their homes willingly to marry persons of their choice and when caught their parents describe the act as an "abduction". Sometimes the victims "run away" from their homes willingly to marry boys of their own choice as they fail to get the consent of their parents and their parents knowingly report to the police, the act as an "abduction". Sometimes even married men "run away" with married girls as even after marriage their affair did not end finally. Sometimes the abduction is done by a man not getting a marriage proposal which drives him to this madness. Sometimes abduction is done by an ascetic. Sometimes abduction of Harijan girls is done by their landlords to demoralise their men in their struggle for an improved existence. Sometimes mishap victims are kidnapped by criminals. A married woman of Mara village under Khagaria Police Station, a victim of the Mansi train disaster of June 6 was kidnapped by a notorious criminal and compelled to live a life of shame. Sometimes abduction is done due to old enemity. A 34-year-old woman of Chandpura village under Begusarai was raped and murdered after being abducted from her house. Old enemity with a fellow villager was said to be the cause of this crime. Sometimes women play major role in abduction for sale and immoral purpose and the women involved in this trade are themselves abducted women.

## Cases of Kidnapping and Abduction

### *Consequences of Kidnapping and Abduction*

In the majority of cases abductor and the victim are known to each other. Sometimes they kidnap the girls as an adult, sometimes as a minor. Sometimes the consequences of kidnapping is rape and murder. A young unmarried girl of Manpur in Gaya was enticed away by her lover and after the rape murdered her for fear of being detected, and later her body was found in the dry bed of the river Falgu. Sometimes it ends in marriage. A young girl of Shastrinagar Police Station of Patna filed a petition in the Court of Chief Judicial Magistrate, Patna, stating that she was a major (19 years) and nobody has kidnapped her. She also stated that she had married with her own consent and free will at Muzaffarpur and since then she was living with him as his wife. Sometimes kidnapping leads to communal tension. A former student of the T.P. College, Madhepura who had kidnapped a daughter of a noted businessman of Madhepura surrendered in the court. Both told the court that they were married to each other and demanded protection in view of the communal tension mounting in the area due to their marriage. Sometimes parents accept the marriage and choice of their wards. The Chief Judicial Magistrate of Patna ordered the release of the couple after the girl's father had filed an affidavit before the court stating that the case of kidnapping of her daughter filed by him was done under misinformation. He said his daughter was a major and had married on her own. Another affidavit was filed by the boy's father that he had no objection to the marriage. Sometimes, the parents of the victims even after marriage do not accept the choice of the girls and lodge a kidnapping case against their husbands. A school-going girl of Shastrinagar area at Patna returned after marrying a young man in a temple at Muzaffarpur. However, the parents of the girl did not accept the choice of the girl and lodge a kidnapping case against her husband.

**The Kidnapper**

A kidnapper may be any person irrespective of his age, education, religion, caste, creed, and culture. He may be a priest. More than 30 young girls were liberated from the Ashram of a Yogi at Gopalganj. According to the police the fake Yogi trapped innocent young girls, women and gents at the gun point. The wife of the temple's pujari near Sataquat Ashram was kidnapped by a frequent visitor of the temple and she was recovered from Vaishali, the kidnapper was holding a respectable position of society. A doctor of Patna Medical College Hospital was arrested by the Kadamkuan police on the charge of kidnapping, wrongful confinement and attempt of criminal assault on a minor girl. Some armed men raided a house in Mehadia village under Arwal police station of Jehanabad, lifted a young girl after taking some household articles at the gun point and escaped. A school clerk of Madhupur was taken into custody by the local police with the co-operation of the Darbhanga police for kidnapping the minor daughter of his landlord. A young girl of Rajendra Nagar near the Station of Patna stated before the Magistrate that she had been kidnapped and criminally assaulted by a person living in the ground floor of the house. An umarried girl of Chausa police station of Madhepura was kidnapped by a co-villager who was arrested by the Delhi police. A student of R.N. College, Hajipur kidnapped a 15-year-old girl student in collusion with some anti-social elements. A girl of 16 years of Mandi village of Begusarai ran away with her servant and was arrested at Lakhminia railway station. A school girl of Giridh was allegedly kidnapped by her tutor about seven years ago, was recovered from a farm at Ludhi in Punjab. A teenage school- going girl of village Jeetpur of Madhepur was kidnapped by her servant. While preparations were being made to sell the girl, the police could find her and arrested two persons in this connection. A young daughter of Munger has accused her father of trafficking in women.

Abduction is definitely related to the absence of parents' control over the victim and non-harmonious relation in the family.

But in the eyes of law kidnapping is proved on three grounds. First involves the age of the victim, second the absence of the consent of the victim and the third is the use of force and physical resistance.

Kidnapping and abduction are very common offences unleashed against minor girls or women. Minor girls are enticed away by unscrupulous persons while young women irrespective of age, fall prey to any sort of deceit or force. What is important is that one should clearly understand the offence that is made out, which would depend upon the nature of allurement or force and the age of person.

**Sections 366-373 IPC**

A person who kidnaps or abducts a woman with the intention that she may be compelled to marry another person against her will, commits an offence under Section 366 of the IPC. Even the knowledge that she may be compelled to marry or have illicit intercourse against her will, even if there is no intention, would add to the gravity of the offence and would be punishable under this section. Abuse of authority, or criminal intimidation as defined in the code, or any form of compulsion used for inducing a woman to go from one place to another with the knowledge or intention that she may be forced or seduced for illicit intercourse is also similarly punishable. This section provides a deferrent punishment to persons who resort to the use of force or fraud, for the purpose of marriage or illicit intercourse. However, in all such cases, the intention or the knowledge has to be proved apart from the main ingredients of the offence of kidnapping or abduction as the case may be.

Minor girls have been the victims of various types of nefarious activities by anti-social elements. Sections 366A, 372 and 373 of the

IPC take care of such cases where minor girls are subjected to illicit intercourse, sale or purchase. Thus, inducement of a minor girl under the age of eighteen years to go from any place or to do any act with the knowledge or intention that she will be seduced or forced to an illicit intercourse has been made punishable with 10 years imprisonment. The means used for inducement are irrelevant. The basic ingredients of the offence are that she:

(i) should be a minor girl below the age of 18 years;

(ii) she should be induced by whatever means;

(iii) inducement should be to go to any place or do any act;

(iv) there should be knowledge or intention on the part of the person that she will be seduced or forced to an illicit intercourse by another person.

This section would, therefore, help those cases where innocent girls are allured with promises of a good life and are then exploited by anti-social elements for sexual offences, prostitution, etc.

Selling or buying minor girls for the purposes of prostitution is an offence under section 372 and 373 of the IPC. The selling, buying, hiring and disposing of or obtaining possession of a minor person with the intention or the knowledge that the person will be used for prostitution, illicit intercourse, or any unlawful or immoral purpose are the essential ingredients of the offence. It is not necessary that the person should be immediately put to such an abuse. The knowledge that such a person would be used in future for such a person would also constitute the offence. If a minor girl is sold, bought, lent or hired or disposed of to a prostitution or the brothel keeper or is so obtained, there is presumption that she will be used for prostitution. In other words, it is not necessary to prove the intention, as the circumstances amply point out that the girls would be used for illicit intercourse. Illicit intercourse has been given a very wide definition and would include any sexual intercourse between persons not "united by marriage" or any union which is not recognised as marriage by the personal law of the persons.

The provision made in the Indian Penal Code on kidnapping and abduction, particularly where the intention is to seduce a minor girl or force her to an illicit intercourse, provides ample safeguard against the exploitation of innocent girls and women of tender age by anti-social elements.

In spite of the various sections of IPC. that take care of such notorious activities as kidnapping and abduction, the trend of this crime is rising. According to official police records, around two out of every one lakh women are the victims of abduction and kidnapping annually in our country. But the true rate of victimization is far greater than this. Estimates have placed the figures at 2 to 10 times the official rate. This difference can mainly be explained by the reluctance of the victims' parents to report the incidents to police.

**Gangs of Kidnappers**

Trafficking of women and girls has become a highly organised and inter-state business. A gang engaged in kidnapping girls from Bihar and Assam and selling in many districts of UP has brought to light. A gang of kidnappers engaged supplying the girls to middle east has been noticed. A gang of kidnappers usually consists of both males and females, who operate everywhere, in rural as well as in urban area. Female kidnappers have been found to work as domestic servants who facilitate kidnapping of girls. They have been found to be very active in places of public entertainment, educational institutions, hostels, hospitals and in folk festivals, busy railway stations, bus stands etc. and entice away girls.

The gangs of kidnappers and abductors have their own secret methods of transporting girls and shuttle them to and fro, from city to city, to minimise the risk of their being rescued. The kidnapped or abducted girls are escorted by respectable looking men and women so that they cannot be checked or interrogated by the police. They have their agents at the bars, in courts, and in newspaper offices, they have friends in every political organisation and plenty of funds is given to those who can protect from the law. The police have in many cases extorted money from these unspeakable scoundrels. It cannot be denied that corrupt policemen with the help of dishonest politicians in power have made systematic collections from this source. Sometimes male members of the victim's family are killed or injured in a bid to save them from abduction.

**Types of Abduction**

We can classify the victims into four groups by taking all cases "willing" and "unwilling" victim:

1. *Forced abduction:* This group of victims who clearly do not consent to accompany their kidnappers are forcibly abducted by the offenders.

2. *Willing abduction:* This group of victims willingly agree to live with offenders because they (victims) intend to marry them against the wishes of their parents.

3. *Accessary abduction:* This group of victims neither give their consent nor oppose it, thus, aiding or contributing a secondary manner to the abduction activity. The abduction stands in a relationship "power" over the victim because of being older, being an authority figure or some other reason. The abductor then gains access to the victim and pressurizes her to leave her house with him.

4. *Stress abduction:* This group of victims initially agree to leave the house with "offenders" but are stopped when "something goes wrong". Usually what goes wrong is that the offender "exploits" the agreement and rapes the victim, or he brings his friends to have sexual relation with her, or sells her ornaments, or leaves her in the hotel, or at a railway station or bus stand and so forth.

**Motives behind Abduction/Kidnapping**

The following motives may be identified for kidnapping the unmarried girls or abducting the married women:

The unmarried girls and married women may be kidnapped and abducted in the following circumstances:

1. The abduction of girls who lead an unhappy life in their parent's home. A beautiful girl kidnapped from Jharia in her statement refused to go to her parent's house for fear of being killed. Moreover, she expressed her desire to get herself married with a man of position and means. She refused to accept a constable as her husband saying he would better serve as her servant.

2. The abduction of girls whose parents refuse to marry them to the "abductors". A girl research scholar of Patna University left the hostel without any information with a boy of her own choice as she failed to get the consent of her parents.

3. The abduction of young girls with the object of selling them: A gang engaged in selling of kidnapped girls from Assam and Bihar has come to light.
4. The abduction for sexual purposes: A kidnapped girl of Kolkata alleged before the police that she was brought to Patna for working in the house. But she was raped and was asked to entertain VIPs.

**Types of Abductors**

We may classify abductors in four groups on the basis of the news reported in newspapers.

1. *Accesory Abductor:* He "abducts" victim with her consent to marry him.
2. *Opportunist Abductor:* He abducts the victims only for sexual purposes on the enticement for a better life.
3. *Lover Abductor:* He is in love with the victim to the extent that he even abducts her to marry her against her own and her parents wishes.
4. *Fraud abductor:* He abducts the victim to sell her and earn money.

**Types of Abducted Victims**

We may classify the abducted victim in five groups:

1. *Co-operative Victim:* She is a woman who willingly agrees to leave her house with the accused, being very unhappy in father's house.
2. *Accidental Victim:* She is a woman who by chance falls in the hands of a wrong person who abducts her on false pretexts.
3. *Misled Victim:* She is a female who takes the advances of a male seriously.
4. *Corrupt Victim:* She is a female who is in search of pleasure.
5. *Forced Victim:* She is a female who is forcibly abducted against her wishes.

**Suggestions**

Some of the suggestions which need proper attention are as follows:

1. It is desirable that the parents have to be watchful about their wards, both male and female. They must see to it that they keep good company and remain useful engaged.
2. As for the girls, they should be escorted properly in late hours or in desolate areas, they are not to be left to the care of the servants, drivers or even tutors who take liberties with them.
3. Girls and women must enjoy a status of freedom in marriage and position of respect in family and society.
4. Parental control over the children and harmonious relation in the family is necessary for a healthy society. The children both male and female should be equally given due love, affection and respect in the family.
5. Police should be informed about the missing of their wards at the earliest.

Handling the problems of kidnapping/abduction is a difficult task. It can be and ought to be solved through appropriate collective action, the victim, the parents and the police. It is not good blaming the police all the time.

Fourteen

# Homicide

In law, culpable homicide is differentiated from justifiable and excusable homicide (see Gibbons, *Society, Crime and Criminal Careers*, 3rd ed., 1978: 350).

Justifiable homicide is intentional killing sanctioned by law. It is committed on some legal demands, or discharging one's legal responsibility, such as the execution of a legal sentence of death, or the killing of a person in legitimate self-defence, or a police officer's shooting a fleeing dacoit, or a prison officer's killing a prisoner attempting to escape from the jail.

Excusable homicide is one which results accidentally from lawful acts performed by lawful means. It is unintentional killing where no blame is attached; for example, the death of a patient that results accidentally from a surgery by a doctor. *Culpable homicide* is one for which a person is held criminally responsible and is subjected to prosecution and punishment.

Culpable homicide is further divided into three sub-categories: (a) first-degree murder, (b) second-degree murder, and (c) manslaughter. These distinctions rest on the degrees of premeditation and malice aforethought. Premeditation designates 'intent' (to violate the law) formulated prior to the activity, i.e., a decision to commit crime and planning its execution, etc. Malice aforethought does not involve planning, though it involves 'intent to kill' at the time of the act. Thus, for a person to be convicted of murder in the first-degree, both premeditation and malice aforethought have to be established. In second degree murder, only malice aforethought has to be proved. In manslaughter, neither premeditation nor malice aforethought are present. It (manslaughter) is, thus, unintended homicide.

All types of homicides in this chapter are used as a generic term as 'murders'. Although not all homicides are murders, yet if an act is a homicide it states a reason for regarding it as murder and hence as wrong. Calling an act 'murder' presupposes that the act is homicide;

that is the reason why the act is wrong. We could thus say that homicide is morally neutral but not murder.

Official statistics reveal that murder has been on the rise in India during recent years. The figures had gone up from 25,786 in 1984 to 38,577 in 1994, i.e., by 50 per cent (*Crime in India,* 1994:8). Rates also vary by region and by the size of a city, though we cannot say that murder is primarily a city phenomenon. The rates for the rural areas have been higher than the rates for the urban areas. It is rare that murders go unreported and it is also rare that a suspect is not apprehended and charged with murder.

All-India figures of murders in which female victims may be classified on gender basis are not available. No official records are maintained on the incidence of spouse murder. But it is estimated that spousal murders in intra-familial homicides may account for 20 per cent to 30 per cent of all murders and wives killed by their husbands (in comparison to husbands being killed by their wives) make up 68 per cent to 70 per cent of all spousal murders.

Any meaningful study of spousal murder requires to concentrate on four major aspects: the kinds of persons who commit murders, the situations in which murders are committed, the categories of murder, and motivations in murder. We also focused our attention on these and a few other issues. The main concerns of the study of the murder of females were:

* to gain insight into motivations in murder;
* to examine patterns in murders;
* to assess the kinds of men who commit murders;
* to find out the types of women who are usually murdered;
* to study homogeneity-heterogeneity in the offender-victim relationship in murder; and
* to analyze the role of victim in murder.

The data for the present study was collected from prisoners in a jail (all 'lifers' having served one to eight years in jail) and court and police records. In all, 52 cases were studied.

**Offender-victim Relationship**

The offender and the victim were closely related to each other as members of the same family in 92 per cent cases and knew each other as acquaintance in 8 per cent cases. Of the 48 cases in the first category (members of the same family), the victim was related to the murderer as wife in 90 per cent cases, as illegal wife in 4 per cent cases, as daughter-in-law in 4% cases, and as sister-in-law in 2 per cent cases. Thus, a large number of murders by men were murders of their wives. Of the four cases in which the victim was not a member of the murderer's family, one was the landlady (the killer being her servant), one was the offender's old co-tenant (a girl of 19 years of age) and two were colleagues (a teacher in school and a clerk in office).

It could, be said that familial maladjustment in general and marital relations in particular are very crucial in female homicides. Or, what needs to be understood in female murders is adjustment and role performance in family relations. Von Hentig's (*The Criminal and his Victim,* 1948: 392) investigation of murders in Germany in 1930 also brought into light a startling that 62 per cent of the women murdered were killed by their husbands. A similar finding was earlier given by McDonald ("Death Penalty and Homicide" in *American Journal of Sociology*, 1911:16) in his perusal of criminal statistics covering the late 19th and early 20th centuries in several countries. Similar conclusion was made by a study in England and Wales for the years 1885-1905. Out of 487 murders committed by men, 124 were women murdered by their husbands and 115 were mistresses or sweethearts of their assailants. Wolfgang's (*Patterns in Criminal Homicide,* 1958:11) Philadelphia (United States) study during the 1950s also revealed the relationship between gender and murder. He emphasized that homicide is directly related to "relatively close, intimate, personal and direct relationships or primary contacts". His research indicated that primary group relationships, accounted for 65 per cent, of all victim-offender relationships, and that the number of wives, homicidally assaulted by their husbands constituted 41 per cent of all women who were killed. Gibson and Klein's study of homicides occurring between 1957 and 1968 in England (Statistical Report on Murder in England and Wales, 1969) also revealed that wives were usually the most frequent victims.

**Socio-demographic Background of Victim and Murderer**

As regards age, out of 52 victims, 14 per cent were 20 years of age or below at the time of murder, 44 per cent were between 21 and 30 years of age, 27 per cent between 31 and 40 years, and 15 per cent between 41 and 50 years of age. The mean age of the victims was 29.4. Against this, 7 per cent of the murderers were 20 years or below, 52 per cent were between 21 and 30 years, 25 per cent between 31 and 40 years, 10 per cent between 41 and 50 years, 4 per cent between 51 and 60 years and 2 per cent above 60 years of age. The mean age of the murderers was 30.5 years. This indicates that:

(i) three-fifths of the victims (58%) and three-fifths of the murderers (59%) were young, i.e., below 30 years of age, and

(ii) the ratio of middle-aged offenders to middle-aged victims was 1:1.2.

It may be hypothesized that most victims of murders as well as their murderers are young persons (of 18 to 30 years of age) or that young husbands are more likely to kill their wives than older husbands. This does not support Wolfgang's finding that murderers are generally younger than the victims; though it supports Bensing and Schroeder's contention that relatively young persons carrying out most homicides.

The age difference between the murderer and his victim was less than one year in 11 per cent cases, between 1-3 years in 33 per cent cases, between 4-6 years in 31 per cent cases, between 7-9 years in 17 per cent cases and 10 and above years in 8 per cent cases. Thus, the age difference between offenders and victims was very less. On an average, the killers were about 4.5 years older than the victims. A significant fact to remember here is that the murderer in our study was the victim's husband and in Indian society the age difference between husband and wife varies from 2-5 years. The above figures also support Richard Block's (*Homicide in Chicago,* 1973) finding that the homicide offender is young.

*Marital Life*

As regards the marital life, of the 48 victims who were married and members of the offender's family, 9 per cent had enjoyed a married life for less than 1 year, 44 per cent between 1-5 years, 26 per cent between 5-10 years, 14 per cent between 10-15 years, and 7 per cent for more than 15 years. The mean period which the victims had spent with their husbands/in-laws was 6.2 years. About 33 per cent of the victims were married before the age of 18 years, 46 per cent in the age group of 19-22 years and 21 per cent after the age of 23 or more years.

*Children*

Further, 65 per cent of the victims had children and 35 per cent had no children. Of those 31 victims who had children, 31 per cent had one child, 35 per cent had 2 children, 23 per cent had 3 children, and 16 per cent had 4 or more children. The mean number of children was 2.4. The age of the children varied from 1 year to 38 years. Of the total (71) children, the age of 31 per cent of the children was 5 years or less, while 24 per cent of the children belonged to the 6-10 years age-group, 17 per cent to the 11-15 years age-group, 14 per cent to the 16-20 years age-group, 10 per cent to the 21-25 years age-group, and 4 per cent were more than 25 years of age. The mean age of the children was 11 years. Thus, since a little more than half of the victims (53%) had spent one to five years with their husbands/in-laws and a little less than two-fifths (38%) hd one to two children, it may be concluded that—

(i) the rates of murder among women with a marital span of less than 5 years are greater than the rates among women with a marital span of 5-10 years or more than 10 years.

(ii) as the marital span increases, the rate of murder decreases, and

(iii) problems of adjustment of a girl arise not soon after her marriage but after spending several years in the family of procreation.

*Education*

Regarding education, 29 per cent of the murderers were illiterate or had no formal education, 35 per cent were educated up to the primary/middle level, 19 per cent up to the secondary level, 8 per cent up to the higher secondary level, and 9 per cent were graduates/post-graduates or had a technical degree/diploma. Amongst the victims, 40 per cent were illiterate or had no formal education, 31 per cent were educated up to the primary/middle level, 21 per cent up to the high school level and 8 per cent were graduates and/or postgraduates. Thus 7 out of every 10 victims and 6 out of every 10 murderers were either illiterate or less educated. This indicates that educational achievement or level of education is significantly related to murder.

*Caste*

In terms of caste, of the 47 Hindus (five were non-Hindus) 55 per cent belonged to the upper castes, 30 per cent to the intermediate castes, and 15 per cent to the lower castes. The ratio of upper caste to lower caste victims was 3.6:1. It may thus be averred that among lower castes there is no high rates of murder as against the common belief. Further, 60 per cent victims hailed from rural areas and 40 per cent from urban areas, showing thereby that female murder largely tends to be a rural phenomenon.

*Occupation*

In terms of occupation, 39 per cent offenders were cultivators, 17 per cent businessmen (including shopkeepers) 21 per cent servicemen (including teachers), and 13 per cent were self-employed (tailor/ *sari*-printer/nagina-maker/rickshaw-puller/mason/advocate/blacksmith). Of the remaining 10 per cent offenders, two were unemployed and one each was a student, a beggar, and a salesman. Thus, 62 per cent offenders were engaged in occupations of low status. Or, it may be said that homicides of females are more common among low status occupational groups.

*Economic Status*

Finally, analyzing the economic status, it was found that 88 per cent of the murderers were working and earning while 12 per cent were non-earners. Of the 46 earners, 26 per cent were earning up to Rs. 1,000 per month, 48 per cent between Rs. 1,000 and Rs. 2,000, 20 per cent between Rs. 2,000 and Rs. 5,000, and 6 per cent above Rs. 5,000 per month. Nearly 27 per cent of the murderers were the sole bread winners of their families while 73 per cent had co-earners also in their families. Thus, taking the income of all the earning members in the family, 25 per cent were found belonging to lower class (with an income of less than Rs. 1,000 per month), 29 per cent to lower middle class (with an income of Rs. 1,000-2,000), and 46 per cent to middle and upper-middle classes (with an income of Rs. 2,000 and Rs. 6,000 per month). Amongst the victims, only seven women were earning.

These figures reveal that the rates of homicides of women from the lower and lower-middle classes exceed those from women of middle and upper middle economic status. In other words, economic factor is inextricably related to female murder. Our study, thus confirms Bensing and Schroeder's (*Homicide in an Urban Community*, 1972) thesis that low-income families have high rates of murder. It also supports Wolfgang's contention that murderers are largely located in the low stratum of society. Further, it supports our own earlier study on female murderers in India (*Female offenders in India,* 1969) that female murderers generally come from the lower income groups. This makes it necessary to critically examine the link between homicide and lower and lower-middle class adjustment. Scholars like Miller and Bullock (*Urban Homicide in Theory and Fact,* 1952) Wolfgang and Cohen (*Delinquent Boys: The Culture of the Gang,* 1956) have attempted to trace the root of the violence behaviour pattern in what they call 'lower-class sub-culture'. We will examine this theory later on.

Taking all variables together, it may be concluded that:

(1) murderers of females by and large are members of their own families;

(2) they are not-so-young, but are generally illiterate or less educated and moderately poor persons; and

(3) a positive correlation exists between the incidence of homicide and the level of familial adjustment.

Since the last feature makes an analysis of offenders' families essential, we will now attempt to examine the family structure and family relations vis-a-vis murders.

**Family Structure of Murderer**

The family structure pointed out that 37 per cent of the murderers were living in nuclear families, and 63 per cent in joint families. The high incidence of murderers from joint families is probably attributable to the predominance of joint families in the social structure of our society, particularly in rural areas.

It was further found that out of the 48 cases in which victims were members of the killers' families, in 65 per cent cases the murderers were heads of families and in 35 per cent cases they were ordinary members (non-heads). Since the number of murders by heads of families was about two times more than that of non-heads, one must ask if this indicates any relation between murder and the role which the head of the family has to play as leader of the family group.

On the other hand, as far as the status of 48 victims is concerned, 33 per cent of the victims had no young children to bring up in the families, but 67 per cent had small children to look after. Does this not indicate a difficult problem of adjustment in families?

How were relations among members in the families studied? The persistent belief is that if a family is normal, members must love one another and violence must be totally absent. Were then the families of murderers studied abnormal? The respondents did not agree to this contention. Conflicts while common in many families were certainly not abnormally frequent in the homes analyzed. By and large, the families functioned nonviolently. The threat of murder or even physical violence never hung heavy in the air. The murderers interviewed revealed that the victims of their murder had broadly speaking strong feelings for them. That love and threat of murder can coexist in a family is perhaps the most insidious aspect of murderers' family life. Men do hit the people they love. Then what went wrong in the family that led the respondents to commit murders. This is discussed in the following paras on murder motives.

**Motivations of Murder**

The most common homicide situation starts when the parties to the fatal interaction are involved in arguments and altercations, often over matters that might appear relatively trivial to many people. In our study too, quarrels over behaviour with the in-laws, money, children and sundry situational disputes were found to be the precipitating circumstances in many homicides. Petty quarrels resulting from illicit relations, a dislike for the wife, the wife's chronic illness or property conflicts were also found to be the motivating factors in murders.

An in-depth study showed that the main causes of murders were as follows: petty quarrels — 27 per cent, victim's chronic illness 15 per cent, irritating behaviour of wife — 11 per cent, offender's illicit relations — 10 per cent, victim's illicit relations — 5 per cent, fear of victim's revealing offender's secrets — 6 per cent, property conflict — 6 per cent, feeling of revenge — 6 per cent, wife's insistence on visiting parents — 4 per cent and wife's constant demand for money — 10 per cent. Thus, marital maladjustment (58%) because of domestic altercations or wife's chronic illness and sexual infidelity (15%) were the two most important factors in the murder of females.

It was further found that there was no significant relationship between motivation and planning. The planning was associated only with murders committed for revenge. Murders because of petty quarrels or wife's chronic illness or wife's irritating behaviour or irrational demands or illicit relations, etc., were not always planned.

On the basis of this analysis, we can identify the following four types of murders:

(i) Non-malicious emotional murders.

(ii) Non-malicious accidental murders.

(iii) Malicious murders without explicit intention to kill (say, beating with a view to teaching a lesson).

(iv) Malicious murders with premeditated intention to kill.

Of the 52 murders in our study, 27 per cent fall in the first category, 19 per cent in the second category, 31 per cent in the third category, and 23 per cent in the fourth category. This indicates that a large number of murders are committed in the heat of passion or in a state of high emotionalism or in a situation of negligence. Only a small number of offenders kill females in a cool and calculated manner with malice aforethought. Thus, since the real intent to kill is absent in a large number of the cases, it may be pointed out that homicide is the product of a situation characterized by lack of social control.

**Patterns of Murder**

Murders vary not only in terms of causes and relationships between the murderer and the victim but also in terms of operational dimensions like the place and the time of murder, modes of murder, planning in murder, weapon used, help sought, and alcoholic state of mind. We will examine these important dimensions separately.

*Place of Murder*

In 88 per cent of the cases, murders were committed in the homes and in 12 per cent cases outside the homes. The data further showed that there was a direct relationship between the locale and the type of person killed. Primary (43) and secondary (3) kin were mostly killed in their own homes and acquaintances (4) were killed outside their homes. Thus, our finding that a very large number of murders of females are usually committed in home supports Gibson and Klein's thesis (*Murder:* 1957-1968) in their study of homicides occurred between 1957 and 1968 in England that most murders of women occur in their homes. However, our finding is different from that of Wolfgang, Bullock and Pokorny.

*Mode of Killing*

In analyzing the modes of killing, it was found that women were killed by stabbing in 23 per cent cases, by strangulation in 19 per cent cases, by hacking (cutting body in pieces) in 25 per cent cases, by poisoning in 15 per cent cases, by slashing (making cuts with sweeping strokes) in 12 per cent cases, and by shooting, electric shock and burning in 6 per cent cases. Of the 21 cases in which weapons were used in killing, a knife was used in 26 per cent cases, an iron-rod in 23 per cent cases, an axe in 35 per cent cases, and a pistol, gun or sword in 5 per cent cases. Thus, the availability of a licensed weapon has no bearing on murder. It was further found that there was some relationship between the mode of killing and the planned and unplanned nature of murder.

*Planned Murders*

Of the 28 planned murders, 18 per cent were committed by stabbing, 29 per cent by poisoning, 14 per cent by strangulation, 21 per cent by hacking, 7 per cent by shooting and 11 per cent by slashing.

*Unplanned Murders*

Against this, of the 24 per cent unplanned murders, 29 per cent were committed by stabbing, 25 per cent by strangulation, 29 per cent by hacking, and 17 per cent by strangulation and then burning, by electric wire, and by slashing. Thus, there was no great difference in the methods of both planned and unplanned killing.

*Influence of Alcohol*

Only five murders were committed in a state of intoxication and 47 in a sober state of mind. This does not mean that all murderers in the second category were non-alcoholics or all murderers in the first category were necessarily alcoholics. If alcoholism is defined as 'habitual drinking' and is operationalized in terms of physical and psychological dependence of individual on alcohol, it was found that murderers by and large were not alcoholics, although 37 per cent did take alcohol occasionally or once in a while. Thus, we cannot demonstrate any positive correlationship between murder and alcoholism.

*Presence of Accomplices*

Three-fourths of the murders (73%) were committed by the murderers alone while in one-fourth of the cases (27%) someone's help was sought. Of the 14 cases in the latter category (in which the offenders had accomplices), in 12 cases they had only one accomplice and only in two cases did the murderer have two accomplices. Amongst the accomplices, in two cases the accomplice was a member of the murderer's family, in four cases a friend and in one case a brother and his friend. Further, the accomplices were found only in planned murders. The help sought was in terms of killing the victim (9 cases) and in disposing of the body of the victim after the murder (5 cases).

*Element of Planning*

Nearly 54 per cent of the murders were planned and 46 per cent were situational. That is, the latter type of murders were committed in a state of momentary outrage, in a situation of tense interaction with the victims, while the former type of murders were committed in a cool and calculated manner.

**Victim-induced Murders**

Several researchers have hold the view that many victims of murder precipitate their own deaths. This mostly occurs when offenders and victims know each other and their tensions and mutual aggravations reach a point where both indulge in violence. Our study, however, indicated that the number of cases in which victims induced their death through their own menacing actions, was not very high. Only in 15 per cent of the cases, was the first initiative for violence taken by the victim, i.e., a large number of homicides involving women were not victim-precipitated. While more husbands have been found to have provoked their wives, the number of wives provoking their husbands is not large. When our earlier study of female murderers (*Female Offenders in India*, 1969) had shown that in quite a large number of cases, husbands had provoked their wives, our present study of women being murdered by males showed that only 15 per cent wives provoked their husbands. Boudouris's work in Detroit (*Homicide and the Family,* 1971) has also revealed a similar pattern.

A few victim-precipitated cases show the pattern of victim-precipitated murders are described below. The use of scurrilous language by the victim, supplemented by outrageous behaviour, characterizes the most common victim-precipitated homicides. Though these cases exist they are not very large.

*Cases*

In one case, the husband accused his wife of having illicit relations. Once when he was beating her for this, she taunted him that he should kill her if he did not want her in the house. Thus challenged, the husband stabbed her. In the second case, a man (the accused) had married for the second time after paying Rs. 5,000 to have a woman to look after his young children from the first wife. Soon he found that his wife was neglecting the children as well as him (the accused) as well. He tried to argue with her but she always abused him. On one occasion when she started abusing him, he struck with an iron rod and killed her. In the third case, the victim wanted to visit her parents, but the husband (the accused) refused to let her go. On her insistance, he attacked her with an axe. The blow was so fatal that the victim died within a few hours. In the fourth case, the second wife of a husband (the accused) took away ornaments and a lot of cash and gave these to her brother. When the accused went to her house and asked for the money, his brother-in-law started beating him. His wife also started abusing him with a fit of rage, he gave his wife several blows and then struck her with an iron rod. In the fifth case, a husband used to beat his wife regularly; generally the beating was preceded as well as followed by a violent quarrel. One day the wife attacked her husband with a knife. The husband snatched the knife from her hands and stabbed her. In another case, the daughter-in-law and her mother-in-law very frequently quarrelled on petty issues. Both sought the husband's/son's sympathy. The husband tried to pacify both but the quarrels persisted. One night when both started quarrelling in his presence, he physically attacked his wife to calm her down, but the injury was so severe that the wife died in hospital.

## Theories Explaining Violence and Homicide

A number of theories have been advanced to explain violence in general and homicide in particular. Four important theories which have absorbed the attention of scholars in this connection are:

(1) the Instinctive Aggression Theory (bio-psychological view),

(2) the Frustration-Aggression Theory (psychological view),

(3) the Learing Theory (sociological view) and

(4) the Theory of Sub-culture of Violence (sociological view).

We do not consider these theoretical explanations (including the Theory of Sub-culture) adequate explanations for explaining the murders of females in one's own family, particularly of wives.

**Characteristics of Murderer**

Abrahamsen (*The Murdering Mind,* 1973), a psychoanalyst psychologist, has given the following characteristics of a murderer:

(1) hateful impulses,

(2) feelings of distrust, helplessness, fear, insignificance, and loss of self-esteem,

(3) emotional disturbances,

(4) inability to withstand frustration and find sufficient gratification by expressing hostile aggressive feelings,

(5) suggestibility,

(6) a tendency toward transforming identification,

(7) an inability to change persistent egocentricity or self-centredness into a healthy conscience resulting in contempt for authority,

(8) suicidal tendencies with depression, and

(9) a history of a previous antisocial or criminal acts.

An umpteen number of the respondents confessed having the first four attributes, but they denied having the last five characteristics. It is, therefore, difficult to accept the 'personality-type' explanation of Abrahamsen and other psychiatrists of the dynamics of murder. A murderer, in most cases, is a normal individual who acts in an extreme way due to anxiety, fear, anger, or confusion caused by a specific situation. Having said this, it cannot be maintained that we accept the 'emotional-type personality' explanation of a murderer. People who cry at the slightest provocation or who smash things when annoyed are often characterized as 'emotional' people (Newman, G., *Understanding Violence,* 1979). Some studies have referred to the relationship between emotions and aggression, which includes murder. Emotions like fear or rage, etc., erupt as a result of external stimuli though environmental conditions which can lead to a woman's murder cannot be ruled out. However, we do concede that these fear or anxiety or aggression complexes might have developed due to extreme deprivation (of love, sustenance, etc.) at an early age (Kuo, Z.Y., *The Dynamics of Behaviour Development,* 1967).

**Causes of Murder**

A theoretical perspective is needed to explain why a man murders a woman belonging to his own family, particularly his wife. For this, we have to understand the following:

(i) What are the broad expectations from a woman in a specific family setting?

(ii) Why does a woman fail to adjust herself or fail to perform roles according to familial expectations?

(iii) Why does a man (i.e., husband or father-in-law or brother-in-law etc.) react to this failure in a specific way?

(iv) When does the (reacting) man use "murder" as a reaction to woman's failure to familial or individual expectations?

*Context-specific Approach*

To answer these questions, we have to use a 'Context-specific Approach' as proposed by Wegner (*Pacific Sociological Review,* 1975) and used by Dobash and Dobash (*Violence Against Wives,* 1972) in their researches. In this approach, instead of viewing situations, personalities, feelings, etc., in general terms, we view them in specific contexts and specific domains.

With this approach in the background and drawing on contributions from psychology and sociology, our answers to the questions raised above are:

1. The roles and behaviour expectations from a woman vary according to sub-cultural patterns existing in a specific community and a specific family.

2. The failure of a woman to adopt herself to these expectations is circumstancial and partly her personality traits. Thus failure affects her inter-personal relations in the family.

3. A man's reaction to woman's failure and her specific behaviour is the result of his learning, through the process of socialization, a set of beliefs regarding relationship between man and woman and man's authority over woman, and the demonstration of this authority in certain situations.

4. A man's own personality type determines his aggressive ways in enforcing his authority and domination.

5. A passive man with a submissive personality will tolerate woman's failure, but an aggressive man with a domineering personality will react and use violent techniques in enforcing control.

6. The nature of the precipitation in the specific situation determines a man's violent reaction leading to murder.

Thus, in our theoretical explanation, we do not give importance to unfulfilled childhood experiences, or to pathological personalities, or a sub-culture of violence. Our focus is on the social situation (including family structure, family norms, and intra-family relations, man's status in the family), personality characteristics (like impulsiveness, depression, immaturity, etc.) and socio-cultural interpretations given by man to woman's roles, that is, response learned in the process of inter-personal relations.

Cultural attitudes about women and about violence as a means of self-expression and solving problems are at the root of private violence. There is urgent need to bring about a change on this account. Various social factors may be related to different patterns of murder but we need to consider that people have choices as to how they will respond to immediate crisis and stress. Cultural legacy of violence may, in many ways, influence what choices people consider appropriate.

Since our finding is that most of the murders of women are within the family, particularly of wives by husbands, and these murders are not planned and premeditated but are crimes of violence and passion which occur in the heat of inter-personal conflicts and tensions, it may be said that if women adjust in certain situations while dealing with domineering, aggressive and authoritarian males, and if in certain other situations instead of acting as submissive and passive females, they act as efficient and active females, most of the murders would not occur. The level of violence in family (including murder) is the greatest when wife is either too submissive or too dominant in decisions.

Fifteen

# Infanticide

Infanticide is motivated by the necessity of getting rid of an illegitimate child as well as unwelcome offsprings whom the parents cannot afford. Infanticide means murder of an infant or a newly born baby. Infanticide as such has not been defined in the I.P.C. but since it amounts to the killing of a living person, the sections dealing with murder under the penal code is applicable to the offence of infanticide. Those who kill infants or newly born babies cannot claim the benefit of the right of private defence.

## Causes

Infanticide of the female children in India is usually done out of the undermentioned necessity:

(i) Family vanity among the groups of warrior class.

(ii) Inflated dowy demand.

(iii) Heavy expenses required to be incurred by the bride's party during marriages.

(iv) Craze for a male child drives a family to sacrifice a daughter's life on account of superstitions at times under the influence of the miracleman of the community.

## Prevalence

The infanticide of girl babies is widely prevalent in Thar desert area of Rajasthan, particularly among the Bhil Rajput family. The infant is subjected to asphyxial deaths through manual strangulation or through administration of opium. The male-female ratio in this area is 750 females per one thousand males, against All India figure of 929 and Rajasthan figure of 913 females per one thousand males. The figure of Jaisalmer district is 800 female per thousand males and among the Bhatti Rajput family, it is 550 females per one thousand males being the lowest among the Rajputs.

In October 1986, the Central Government ordered an inquiry into the alleged killing of a baby girl in the family of an MLA. A CID enquiry was conducted by two officers, an Additional Superintendent of Police and an Assistant Superintendent of Police. The common thing in both the enquires was that there is truth in the matter but since the Gujjar family in Rajasthan are well-off and carry on money-lending business and, therefore, no one was coming forward to give evidence. In the meantime a Public Interest Litigation (P.I.L.) case was filed before the Rajasthan High Court by Ms Summita Satyarthi, a Human Rights Activist, who pleaded for a direction to be issued for holding a C.B.I. enquiry. Great interest having been shown by the people, a case of murder was registered against the Legislature.

The Kellar community of landless farmers having a strength of about two lakh, the economic condition of the people are so deplorable that it is difficult for any family to foot the bill of marriages of their daughters. However, the people somehow manage the marriage of one daughter but the marriage of two daughters is an impossible task. Therefore, a second daughter on being born, becomes an unwelcome child and is quickly done to death by administering a paste made from poisonous oleander berries. The menfolk dig a pit outside the house, watch the cries of baby and when it is stopped, the dead body is slipped into the pit and buried. There are hardly any families where some or other child is not buried.

According to a *Times of India* news report, from Madurai, a 26 years old woman of Chokknathpuram, who had vowed to carry "Agni Chatti" (firepot) to a nearby temple during the "Panguni Uthiram" festival could not fulfil her vow as her husband declined to give her money for that and in frustration, she doused her three daughters with kerosene and set them on fire. Thereafter she herself attempted to commit suicide. On hearing the cries, the neighbours rushed and retrieved the children and hospitalised them. Only one could survive. It is pertinent to mention that she had a male child as well who was spared.

## Foeticide

In contrast to infanticide, foeticide is the unlawful expulsion of foetus. It is also called "criminal abortion" or "causing miscarriage". When used in the legal sense, it includes both abortion and premature labour. As per medical sense, premature labour means expulsion of a child that has attained viability. The term "abortion" or "miscarriage" signify the expulsion of foetus or ovum at an earlier period. Modern methods of detecting the sex of the foetus through amniocentesis are used nowadays.

**Abortion**

Abortion may be classified into:

(a) natural and

(b) artificial.

*Natural Abortion*

Natural abortions occur due to such reasons as mother's ill-health, local disease, or diseases of the generative organs, shocks, fear, excessive joy, accidental falls, etc. Hence, appropriate care is required in respect of the health of the pregnant woman.

*Artificial Abortion*

Premature evacuation of foetus, whether medically, surgically or through indigenous method is known as artificial abortion. Artificial abortion is a criminal offence punishable under Sections 312-316 of the Indian Penal Code. The Sections run as under:

***Sections 312-316 IPC***

*Sec. 312 Causing Miscarriage*

Whoever voluntarily causes a woman with a child to miscarry, shall, if such miscarriage be not caused in good faith for the purpose of saving the life of the woman, be punished with imprisonment of either description for a term which may extend to three years, or with fine, or with both; and, if the woman be quick with child, shall be punished with imprisonment of either description for a term which may extend to seven years, and shall also be liable to fine.

*Explanation:* A woman who causes herself to miscarry, is within the meaning of this section.

*Sec. 313. Causing Miscarriage without Woman's Consent*

Whoever, commits the offence defined in the last preceding section without the consent of the woman, whether the woman is quick with child or not, shall be punished with imprisonment for life, or with imprisonment of either description for a term which may extend to ten years, and shall be liable to fine.

*Sec. 314. Death caused by act done with intent to cause miscarriage*

Whoever with intent to cause the miscarriage of a woman with child, does any act which caused the death of such woman, shall be punished with imprisonment of either description for a term which may extend to ten years, and shall also be liable to fine.

If Act done without woman's consent, the offender shall be punished either with imprisonment for life, or with punishment mentioned above.

*Explanation*: It is not essential to this offence that the offender should know that the act is likely to cause death.

*Sec. 315. Act done with intent to prevent child being born alive or to cause it to die after birth*

Whoever, before the birth of any child does any act with the intention of thereby preventing that child from being born alive or causing it to die after its birth, shall, if such act not caused in good faith for the purpose of saving the life of the mother be punished with imprisonment of either description for a term which may extend to ten years, or with fine, or with both.

*Sec. 316. Causing death of quick unborn child by act amounting to culpable homicide*

Whoever, does any act under such circumstances, that if he thereby causes death he would be guilty of culpable homicide, and does by such act cause the death of a quick unborn child, shall be punished with imprisonment of either description for a term which may extend to ten years, and shall also be liable to fine.

***Illustration***

A, knowing that he is likely to cause the death of a pregnant woman, does an act which, may cause the death of the woman, this would result in culpable homicide if the woman is, injured but does not die; but the death of an unborn quick child with which she is pregnant is thereby caused, A is guilty of the offence defined in this Section.

## Medical Termination of Pregnancy

*Legislation*

Except for saving the life of the pregnant woman, termination of pregnancy (Bhrun Hatya) was a penal offence in accordance with the provisions of the aforesaid sections of the I.P.C.

After India's independence and with the passage of time, population started growing rapidly with such an alarming speed that it began to be seen that available resources would not be adequate to meet the necessities of the people in the country. Thus, several family planning programmes were evolved and propagated among the people of the country through mass media. It was further thought that a legislation to legalise termination of pregnancy was another means by which the growing population could be checkmated. Thus, Medical Termination of Pregnancy Act (1971) was enacted as a means of population control. According to it (Sec. 3), the objectives of termination of pregnancy are two fold:

*Objectives*

(a) *Therapeutic:* When the continuance of pregnancy is likely to endanger the life of the pregnant woman and could cause grave injuries to her physical and mental health.

(b) *Eugenic:* When there is the risk of the child being born with serious physical or mental handicap. This may occur, if the pregnant woman in the first three months of her pregnancy suffers from:

(a) German measles; chicken pox or small pox, viral infection including viral heptitis, toxoplasmonia or any other disease which would have affected the health of the woman.

(b) The pregnant woman takes certain medicines, whether under medical advice or otherwise which affect the foetus;

(c) The pregnant woman receives radio or any invisible ray therapy; and

(d) Insanity of the either of the two or both spouse.

(c) *Humanitarian:* When the pregnancy is in consequence of sexual assault.

(d) *Social:* When the pregnancy has occurred on account of failure of contraceptive device.

Abortion having become legalized, this act is a blessing for large number of nursing homes who are thriving through such operations.

**Technological Revolution in Reproduction**

Contraceptive means to ensure sex without reproduction. Surrogate motherhood, in vitro fertilisation and artificial insemination are advancements in genetic technology in which reproduction is possible without sex. New techniques have enabled the determination of the abnormalities as well as the sex of the child in advance much before the birth of the child. The prenatal sex-determination is done through amniocentesis, wherein amniotic fluid is drawn through the uterus of a pregnant woman to determine any defect or physical deformity in the child.

Amniocentesis is risky as it constitutes the drawing of amniotic fluid from the uterus. This is the fluid on which the foetus lives until birth. This test is conducted after sixteen weeks pregnancy and if conducted earlier may prove harmful or fatal for the child in which case there can be legal proceedings against the wrong doers.

The determination of sex is also possible through Chorionic Villi Sampling (CVS) by vaginal extraction from eight to sixteen weeks of pregnancy. This method is also dangerous as it causes the pregnant woman to infect and in effect, spontaneous abortions can take place. It may as well result in fatality of the pregnant woman.

The other method of sex determination is through ultrasound scanning which though non-invasive, is unreliable, even at the advanced stage of pregnancy.

**Sex Determination Technology Misuse**

Scientists have developed the genetic technology in order to ascertain in advance if the child in the mother's womb has any deformity. Unscrupulous people in the society are using the know-how to reduce the female population in an organised and systematic manner.

The dangerous form of genetic engineering by selectively aborting the newborn child has been flourishing in the capital city of India as well as in several big and small cities of the state on account of no value being attached to a female child in comparison to the male counterpart. Sex clinics have multiplied and mushroomed throughout the cities and towns. According to a rough estimate around 78,000 female foeticides were aborted after prenatal sex determination test through amniocentesis. In 1983, Bombay had only three sex clinics and over a period of next five years, it had multiplied to 258 private clinics in addition to the sixteen recognised Government clinics. No permit or licence is required to set up a clinic of this type. On account of the coming up of a large number of clinics, there is a competition in the market and the fees charged (which had become between Rs. 150 to Rs. 500) is within the reach of a common man. The popularity of the method has spread to small places in far-flung areas. The samples now can be carried to Mumbai or Delhi or Kolkata or any big city of the country from the nearby places. A survey made by Women's Centre has revealed that out of 8000 abortions checked, 7999 were in respect of females.

One clinic in Mumbai is reported to have advertised that the cost of abortion is cheaper than the amount required for the marriage and payment of dowry. Such statement provoking abortion openly advocate murder of the foetus. What more can be said of such a system. There is a battle being fought between doctors and feminist groups on the availability of medical technology which could assist pre-selection of sex. These organisations have demanded a total ban while the lobby of doctors who perform these tests, on the other hand, oppose the demand on the ground that if the ban is enforced, abortions would be performed by quaks. There is some force in the demand of the doctors also. The whole issue is dependent upon the attitude of the people towards the female child. The rate, the pre-natal sex determination tests are gaining popularity and being used in aborting female foetus, the day is not far when the woman may become an endangered species.

### *MTP Act*

The Medical Termination of Pregnancy Act, 1971 only ensures a legal sanction to a Medical Practitioner to abort a female foetus. Thus, the two together, that is MTPA and Sex-determination Technology have put India on its way to technological and legal femicide. Unregulated technology and the legal Act have created a new problem in bringing a decline in female population.

According to the Provision of Section 3 of the Act, a Registered Medical Practitioner is entitled to abort a foetus within twelve weeks of pregnancy and two of them can abort a pregnancy having a length of 12 to 20 weeks. In either case they will have to take a stand that abortion was necessary in the interest of the health of the woman.

The anguish of a pregnancy by sexual assault is presumed to constitute a grave injury to a woman's mental health. However, the failure of a contraceptive device cannot cause any such damage to the mental health. Assessment of the anticipated risk is rather vague and gives a licence to abort female child with the aid of pre-natal sex determination test. Directly or indirectly the MTP is a licence to kill the foetus as some of its statements lack logic.

Business in abortion became possible and flourishing on account of provisions of Section 5 of the MTP Act, 1971, which is an enabling provision for an emergent situation and permits non-application of provisions of Section 3 and Section 4 of the Act. The Section enables a doctor without any experience in gynaecology and obstetrics to operate after having formed an opinion with due care and attention that termination of pregnancy is immediately necessary to save the life of the pregnant woman. It may be pertinent to mention that while making a provision of the Section, care to provide any safeguard has not been introduced to prevent its misuse. A doctor can now be prosecuted under the I.P.C. only. The Act suffers from the following flaws:

*Flaws in MTP Act*

(i) The Act does not provide any guidelines for calculating the commencement of pregnancy and to assess the period of twelve weeks or twenty weeks. The matter has been left entirely to the wisdom of the doctor.

(ii) The Act does not require that the pregnant woman counter-signs or affixes her signature/thumb impression on the key column of the register containing details regarding the duration of pregnancy. Thus, any evidence, which, otherwise could have been provided, is always missing.

(iii) The evidence is further weakened by the type of consent Form C prescribed under the Central Rules. There is no column that the doctor makes a declaration that he has explained to the pregnant woman the reasons for the termination of her pregnancy.

(iv) As usual, the Act further ensures a cover for the doctor as per Section 8 of the Act which lays down that no suit or proceedings shall lie against the doctor if he has acted in good faith. It is very difficult to prove that the doctor did not exercise reasonable care and lacked good faith.

Initially nearly one dozen doctors in seven states of the country offered to perform these tests which, for the first time was introduced in All India Institute of Medical Sciences, Delhi, primarily to discover genetic disorders in foetus in those cases where the parents had the history of abnormality. Since in course of the determination of the genetic disorder, it was found that the method reveals the sex of the unborn child, it became popular as a method for determination of pre-natal sex of the child. The Medical Termination of Pregnancy Act, 1971, made it a convenient tool for selective abortion.

Consequent upon a widespread resentment against this test, the Maharashtra has taken a lead and the Legislature of Maharashtra Assembly passed the Regulation; "Use of Pre-natal Diagnostic Techniques Act, 1988".

**Pre-natal Diagnostic Techniques Act 1988**

*Features*

(a) Section 3 of the Act prohibits carrying of the pre-natal diagnostic tests by an unregistered genetic centre laboratory or clinic.

(b) Section 4 of the Act lays down the fulfilment of five conditions for the performance of diagnostic tests. The important conditions are that woman should be near about the age of 35 years and she has a history of at least a couple of abortions, family history of mental retardation and/or physical abnormalities.

# Sixteen

# Fate of Prisoners

Accordingly, custodial justice to women has been one of the thrust areas of the activities of the Commission since its inception. The visits to the jails revealed extremely unsatisfactory conditions under which women prisoners live. While the visiting members conveyed to the concerned authorities their general observations about the living condition of women and made specific suggestions about certain hard cases, it was felt that a study should be undertaken to assess the existing conditions in the jails throughout the country.

Observations and Suggestions made by Members Inspecting the Jails

(i) Adequate arrangements for vocational training should be made for women inmates in jail and a programme prepared for rehabilitation of released prisoners. To take an example the visiting Members came across the case of life convict in Assam who was to be released shortly but was very apprehensive of her future since the thought that her husband and society might not accept her. She wanted to acquire some professional skill to be economically independent. She had aptitude for nursing. At the suggestion of the member she was given training in midwifery and was ultimately able to make her by into the profession.

(ii) Courts should ensure that female prisoners are handed over to bona fide guardians after release, so that they may not fall into the hands of imposter guardians who may force them into immoral trafficking the some happens in many cases.

(iii) Mentally ill women should be kept separate from the other women prisoners.

(iv) Certain women prisoners had been kept in custody on the ground of being lunatic despite the fact that they were not actually lunatics. There should therefore, be an objective medical examination of such cases.

(v) The women's wing of Tihar jail was found to be overcrowded by more than four times its capacity. Construction of additional accommodation was suggested to ameliorate the condition of women inmates. It was noted that the women inmates were encouraged to engage themselves in the training of various vocations. Also, a de-addition centre had been set up by the jail authorities. However, revamping of the training programme was suggested so that the inmates were enabled to produce marketable goods and make an earning for themselves for future security.

(vi) In the Jail, Delhi there was a case of a smart girl who had secured the job of a police A.S.I. by impersonation but she was a Karate expert. It was suggested to the Jail authorities to engage her in some fruitful activity like imparting physical training to other prisoners. A similar approach is necessary in like cases.

(vii) In certain prisons, some women inmates were found to suffer from T.B. It was suggested that they should be separated from the others and also given proper medical treatment.

(viii) In the Central Jail in Mumbai the Tata Institute of Social Science was conducting some useful services for the jail inmates in collaboration with the Mumbai Police such as literacy classes, creches for children vocational training counselling, legal guidance, placement on release, etc. This was considered as a good example to be followed.

(ix) The authorities at Sabarmati Central Jail, Ahmedabad expressed the view that the vocational training facilities for male prisoners could not be extended to female inmates as their number was too small. It was suggested that in such cases women inmates could be congregated in one or two suitable jails for making such facilities available or, alternatively provided with such other work as gardening, cooking, etc. and wages paid for the same.

(x) In several jails, regular visits by doctors are not made but they are called only when needed. Also no facilities for lady doctors or nurses exist for women prisoners. It was suggested to the concerned jail authorities that it is desirable that women prisoners are treated only by women doctors, unless the prisoners opt otherwise. However, medical examination should be provided as a matter of routine.

(xi) In the jails visited in Madhya Pradesh, it was found that most of the prisoners were tribal and had their own cultural tradition. The crimes committed by them were not pre-planned and had altogether different background. Therefore, instead of convicting them straightaway under the provisions of Criminal Procedure Code, a lenient view should be taken in the context of their socio-economic environment. It was as suggested that suitable training should be given to Adivasi women prisoners in bidi making sericultre and other related industries to which they are traditionally accustomed.

(xii) Women prisoners convicted under TADA were generally found to be young school and college-going girls. It was suggested that they should be provided with facilities to continue their studies and persistently motivated to return to the mainstream of life.

**Existing Conditions in Jails**

The personal visits of Members to the jails convinced the Commission that there was a serious shortfall in the delivery of services to women who are in custody in jails. The Commission therefore decided to issue a questionnaire to all the States and Union Territories calling for data/information in respect of facilities available to women inmates with regard to diet accommodation medical aid sanitation, education vocational training, legal aid, recreational opportunities, provisions for children accompanying prisoners, visitorial facilities ventilation of grievances, etc.

The information received from all over the country is being processed in the Commission and an analysis thereof will be presented before the Export Committee with a view to formulating recommendations bearing on the conditions of women in custody and norms therefore.

The Commission also thought it fit that some immediate suggestions should be preferred it the Ministry of Home affairs, Government of India, for adoption in order to secure custodial justice for women behind the bar. While drawing up these suggestions, consideration was given also to the aspect of gender justice in the realm of criminal law a administration after taking a stock of the recommendations made by various commissions and committees on the subject, notable among which is the Report of the National Expert Committee on Women prisoners headed by justice Krishna Iyer as well as that of All India Committee for Jail Reforms and also various findings of the Supreme Court of India on the subject.

The suggestions were want for immediate implementation as these are supposed not to entail any substantial strain on the governmental exchequer and are implementable as a short-term measure. These are given below.

(1)Women shall not be arrested between sunset and sunrise and shall not be arrested expect in the presence of women. This will necessitate amendment of section 46 Cr. P.C. 1973.

(2)In all cases of bailable offences, bail on her bond shall be granted forthwith by the police themselves. As far as possible in non-bailable cases also, bail should be granted unless special circumstances warrant a different course, in which case, the arrested woman shall be remanded to judicial custody with utmost expedition.

(3)On arrest, the police should immediately obtain from the arrestee the name a relative or friend to whom the intimation of her arrest should be promptly given.

(4)If consideration of arrestee's own safety and freedom from ensnarement by anti-social elements demand detention in public institutions, bail shall be refused to the women in her own interest unless she is specifically states her willingness to be thus released even after being altered to the above consideration.

(5)The person of a women shall not be searched except by a women authorised by law, and in a manner strictly in accordance with the requirement of decency. Whether in custody or in transit, the arrested woman must always be guarded by a woman police or female surrogate. A relative may be permitted to accompany the female arrestee.

(6)Whenever a woman is to be examined by the police or other investigative agency as a witness it should be done only at her residence; nor should she be summoned to the police or investigative station unless she expresses her preference to be examined at the station.

(7)No female prisoner shall be subjected to any form of

corporal punishment or use of handcuffs fetters or isolation as a form of disciplining.

(8)When women are examined in court as accused or as witnesses, due courtesy and decency shall be shown. If circumstances so demand in the interest of modesty and privacy of a woman, the trial may be held in camera or the woman may be examined on commission through women advocates.

Exclusive Custody for Women:

(1)There should be police stations exclusive for women and exclusive lockups under the control of women police. This will necessitate amendment of prison Act and police Act. Separated space for female arrestees in every police lockup and complete segregation of women prisoners in jail and other custody should be maintained.

(2)Where such facility is not available, a female arrestee may be lodged in a special home or institution designated under any law for the time being in force to receive women. At no, time shall a woman arrestee be left unguarded by a woman guard or surrogate.

In all places of police custody, basic amenities such as living space, water, toilet, food medical examination and care, and provisions to meet the special needs of women shall be provided.

(3)As far as possible each state should have at least one or more separate jail for women.

(4)There should be separate custodial facilities for convicts and under trial women. Separate institutions or reception centres where undertrial and remanded women may be kept, should be set up in larger cities, district headquarters, and in female-crime-endemic areas. Where convicts and undertrials are currently housed in one institution they must be kept apart in separate wings until independent facilities are set up.

Visitorial Provision in Custody:

(1)Additional provision should be made in the existing legislation conferring visitorial rights on recognised institutions or individuals, institutional and individual accountability for lapses and excesses should also be provided for.

(2)Information on women in custody should be made available

to recognised social organisations and individuals on request. Persons and institutions accredited as visitors should be allowed as of right free access to police stations and records.

(3)Visiting Committees to jails should be constituted in consultation with professional bodies and university department of laws, criminologists, social workers and social scientists from the neighbouring area. Visitors should be nominated on the bases of merit, public spiritedness activist record and actual time likely to be made available to the visitorial function.

A woman DIG should be appointed at state headquarters preferably from the prison service to specifically look after the work relating to women prisoners and women prison staff.

**Autonomous Prisons for Women**

Women superintendents of separate prisons for women (currently six in number) should be made fully autonomous in functioning.

**Prisoners Councils**

Prisoners Councils or Bandi Sabhas should be set up in all prisons to help airing prisoners grievances and difficulties.

**Socio-legal Counselling**

(1) Socio-legal counselling cells should be set up in every prison for women inmates.

(2) In exceptional circumstances when a woman arrestee is taken to a police lock-up the police should immediately give intimation to the nearest Legal Aid Committee or recognized legal service or body which must render all necessary legal services at State expense.

(3) Magistrates shall inform women when first produced of their right to legal aid at state expense and direct the provision of necessary services. They shall also explain the nature and scope of the proceedings against her and her rights in it.

(4) Legal aid and counselling through professional bodies assisted by para-legal and social workers should be institutionalised in respect of every prison and custodial institution.

Law schools and schools of social work should be encouraged and permitted to render socio-legal counselling service to the inmates.

(5) In the disposition of women offenders courts should mandatorally call for and give due regard to the probation officers report and to the report of medical/psychiatric examination. Where probation officers are not available, probation investigation should be entrusted to recognized and accredited institutions and individuals.

**Released Prisoners' Aid Society**

(1) Released Prisoners' Aid Societies should operate in every district to provide a single-window assistance towards rehabilitation and mainstreaming of the released women prisoners.

(2) Before a female prisoner is released, her relatives should be informed and where no relative exists or shows up the released prisoner should be sent to her destination with a female escort.

(3) Appropriate assistance should be rendered to every female prisoner on release whether during or after completion of sentence. For this purpose a centre for assisting released prisoners should be set up to serve a cluster of prisons and custodial institutions on an area-wise basis. Even without the centre the prison authorities should take necessary steps to arrange the rehabilitation of the released prisoner either through the family, the relief centre or a voluntary organisation.

(4) Aftercare and short-stay homes for women prisoners may be established in every state to serve those prisoners who are homeless or rejected by their families.

Children Accompanying Women in Police Custody/Jail Custody:

(1) When arresting a women, proper arrangements for the protection and care of her accompanying children should be the responsibility of the state. Children who need to be custodialized jointly with their mothers should enjoy rights justly needed, while in custody in terms of food, living space, health, clothing and visitation.

(2) In the disposition of women to custody or otherwise, the magistrate must enquire and direct that suitable for the welfare of their children be made in a manner that protects the rights of children. While sentencing women to imprisonment or any form of custodialisation suitable orders should be made for the custody and welfare of their children.

(3) Expectant mothers in custody should be shown special consideration by way of medical and nutritional care, education in child rearing and mother craft.

**Women's Assistance Police Unit**

(1) Women's Assistance Police Unit contacting cadre of men and women police with specific task of crime prevention work and assistance to women should be set up in each district.

(2) In endemic female crime areas, or wherever otherwise desirable exclusive police station or booths and counters within police stations, shall be set up to deal with women needing protection of or coming in conflict with law. Such booths and police stations should be managed by an integrated cadre of men and women police specially trained and sensitized to deal with women.

On 3rd February, 1993, the Commission organised in New Delhi a conference of Inspectors General of Prisons from all over the country with a view to obtaining their views on the diverse issues relating to custodial justice as well as gender justice in the realm of criminal law administration.

The Conference discussed at length a host of issues arising out of the topic of custodial justice to women as well as gender justice in the realm of criminal law administration. It was felt that the issues deserve a more thorough probe in the light of desirability as well as implement ability of the various suggestions emerging out of the Conference.

Moreover, the suggestions were also desired to be screened and reviewed by the Expert Committee on Custodial Justice in order that light may be shed from all angles of views and a consensus arrived at. Accordingly a sub-committee of eight persons out of the participants of the Conference was appointed to interact with the Expert Committee on Custodial Justice to women on all the significant suggestions and in particular about the suggested amendments to the laws in force in the realm. This culminated in formulation of recommendations by the Commission for amendment of the code of Criminal Procedure.

# Seventeen

# Violence in Rural Belts

Before the advent of the Aryans, women had a high status in the family and in society under the matriarchal system that was then practised. Then came the patriarchal system, taking the men to a superior status and leading to men the subordination of women and the beginning of domestic violence.

**Lifestyle of Rural Population**

In order to understand the nature of domestic violence in rural areas, we must study the lifestyle of the rural population. The Indian rural economy is based on agriculture. Most of the farmers are marginal farmers, owning even less than ten acres of land. Most of them cultivate only one crop. They cannot look after their land properly. When they face economic problems like a daughter's marriage or a death in the family, they are forced to sell their land.

Marginal farmers, landless labourers, scheduled caste communities, self-employed workers whose occupation is connected with agriculture, form more than 90 per cent of the population in rural areas. Every member of the family, whether old or young, male or female has to work hard for his/her living. Although some superficial changes have occurred in their work habits like the use of fertilisers, chemicals, machines and modern communication systems, they do not commensurate with their economic conditions. The society continues to be a traditional one, characterized by relatively slow rate of social change. Child marriages are common. People are aware of the law against polygamy, but they find the loopholes in it. They do not consider women to be humans but beasts of burden.This reduces their self-image and esteem.

They are brought up since childhood to cherish values like patience and tolerance supposed to be inherent qualities of women. This encourages the men to suppress and torture them knowing fully well that they won't retaliate.

*Dowry System*

The dowry system is prevalent among the higher castes and rich families in rural areas, now the middle and lower middle class also tend to taking dowry to establish their status in society. In the poor class, the dowry amounts to a few hundred rupees, wedding clothes for the bridegroom and some utensils. However, this amount is also too much for the bride's father who earns his bread on daily wages. If the bride's father cannot keep the promises made to the bridegroom's father before the ceremony, this creates problems for the daughter with her husband's family. She faces domestic violence. She cannot disclose her problems to her parents. The parents also believe that a married daughter should not complain against her in-laws or her husband. Moving cases like the ones described below raise a pertinent question in our mind — who to blame and how to put an end to this slaughter.

In one case a newly-married pregnant daughter sent a letter to her father requesting him to send the promised dowry amount of Rs. 15,000 which had not been given and gifts for her first pregnancy. Her father could not manage the amount and one day the girl was found dead in the garbage tank behind the house. Her elder sister who is married, came to register the case in our centre. She told us that her sister's husband and other members of his family had tied her hands, legs and mouth, had given her electric shocks and had thrown her body into the tank. Her father registered a complaint with the police, saying that their daughter had been murdered by her husband for money.

Who is responsible for the death of a young, innocent and pregnant girl? Her parents? Her in-laws? Or she herself? Or Society? We have observed many cases of women facing violence, being driven away from home with their children, or committing suicide, simply because their parents could not fulfil the promises given to the bridegroom's parents.

In many cases, girls are punished either by the husband or his family. The nature of these punishments is beyond human imagination. One husband forced his wife to stand on one leg. When she could not, he beat her brutally. Locking up of girls in a room without food or water is very common. In one case, a father-in-law said his daughter-in-law was dead, when she had actually been locked up in a dark lumber room at the top of the house. At midnight, her mother-in-law would give her a small piece of bread and a cup of water. One day, a cricket ball fell into the room and the children trying to retrieve it saw the dreadful figure of the woman. They told their parents that they had seen a female goblin. Their parents complained about it at the police station. A young police officer raided the house suddenly and released the young girl. She stayed at Manaswini shelter home for a year. She earns her living now, but is very weak and has very poor eyesight due to continuous weeping. Punishments like thrusting hands into boiling water or oil, forcing women to stand for hours together with a mill-stone on the head, are very common.

*Marriage*

The average age at which girls are married in rural areas is 13-14 years. According to tradition, a daughter must be married before puberty. Usually, a newly-married girl knows nothing of sexual relations and when she cannot co-operate with her husbands' advances and naturally she is harassed by him. A repulse towards sexual relations develops in her at times leading to her husband's second marriage. In many cases, the newly-married girls escape to their parents' home where they receive no sympathy and are forced to return. Being of a tender and excitable age and unable to cope with constant nagging and violence, many girls commit suicide.

In rural areas, a man does not go by personal factors in his choice of a wife. He is attracted to easy money which he can get with his bride's dowry having availed of all benefits, he no longer likes his wife. He beats her and harasses her. She is not given enough food, or is given left overs. Finally, she is driven out of the house with her girl child. In many cases, the husband takes written permission from his wife for a second marriage — through violent methods. Legally, it has no value.

Women in rural areas accept polygamy as a natural phenomenon of man's personality and do not object to a second marriage. But both wives cannot live together peacefully. One of them suffers all her life. Very few women file suits in the court against their husbands.

Addiction to liquor is one of the main causes of domestic violence. Women in villages say that liquor is their rival. Intoxication makes a man brutal and savage, and he behaves inhumanly towards his wife. Some men behave badly only under intoxication, which

**Violence: Types and Perpetrators**

Now let us look at the various types of violence.

1.Physical harassment, beating with the hand or a stick, kicking.

2.Dragging the woman by the hair.

3.Scorching her on various parts of the body.

4.Sometimes she is not given food and is imprisoned in an isolated room.

5.Abusing her and using foul language. Actually to insult a woman and demean her by foul language is very common in this area.

6.Taunting for dowry makes her conscious of her secondary status. "Your father is a beggar," "You are a fool," "Your relatives are like animals" — this type of language is very common and if a woman expresses resentment, she'll be definitely a victim of violence. The perpetrators of verbal violence hardly consider it as violence. The taunting of a woman on her lack of looks or household skills may drive the woman to commit suicide many a time.

The perpetrators of violence:

1.In most of the cases the married woman is harassed by her husband, then her in-laws.

2.In case of unmarried girls her own father, brother and mother also make her a victim of violence.

**The Common Attitude and Reaction**

The woman prefers to be silent during the early stage of violence. She generally reacts through speech and rarely by resorting to violence. Rarely does she decide to take help from the police or the court. Immediate relief is what she looks for in the situation of violence, so that she can be somewhat at ease. She always looks for help from her parental family. When she gets moral support, she feels that she is empowered and then she struggles against domestic violence. This attitude is mostly seen in labour class women, whereas middle or upper class women expect somebody else to fight for them. The women of all classes endure violence for the sake of their children.

**Support Structures**

In resorting to counselling the woman finds the much needed relief and gains confidence by seeing a way out of her desperate situation. Counselling of both parties also plays a good role in the process of her struggle for existence. At times when a woman takes help from the some organization, Panch, the police or the court, one has to take into account the expense, time and energy involved. And if they fail to understand her problem from her angle she gets frustrated. Women's issues from a feminist perspective. It is a bitter truth that even her paternal relatives also do not understand her reality and help her half-heartedly.

It is our general experience that nobody is sincerely interested in helping the woman, not even her own paternal relatives. Once in a while, even if they want to teach a lesson to the cruel in-laws, after some time they do not pursue the matter or they make a compromise. Nowadays it is often maintained that I.P.C. Section 498-A provides help to women victims and if this section is applied properly by the police, court and lawyers it can be useful. But bitter reality faced by the organisation is corruption at all levels of the state machinery. The case takes such a peculiar turn that the woman is placed in a position where she becomes the accused and she has to defend herself from false allegations. And in such circumstances all our efforts are in vain and even one experience of failure affects the image of an organisation whereas when the work is done in the right way, accompanies a feeling of victory.

Believing that an organisation would prove more effective than an individual 'Astitva' organization was founded. Soon it was realized that the state machinery does not help positively. When they feel that a strong group is supporting the woman, that time they have to take an interest in her case but their interest is not genuine. Actually, without the help of police and court the organisational efforts can sometimes get hopeful results also. The District Level Committee against Violence Against Women, Free Legal Aid Centres or the Lok Adalats are also some support structures set up to help the women against violence. They too have not succeeded because of limited resources, lack of time, proper knowledge of the root causes and of co-ordination. No one tends to understand the problem from a feminist perspective. Even the language of the law, the procedure of the case in the court, the police and the persons who are handling the case all come from the patriarchal value-based society. This is the reality which is very disappointing. Yet we feel that if we can respond to the problems of the woman properly and give her moral support in her struggle, that itself is an achievement. And this optimistic attitude encourages us to continue our work in the field.

To create an environment against violence in the society, awareness generation programmes are employed. They include leaflet distribution, camps, seminars, street plays and songs. The Nari Mukti Din is also celebrated on the 8th March and 25th November every year, this is the International Day against Violence against Women. These programmes have difficulties of funds, time and commitment and other resources.

Even though no support structure gets 100 per cent success they should not be ignored, may they be the police or the court they are needed in many a case. Media too has its importance as it can play a good role in educating society even though at times the messages may create confusion and contradiction resulting in an adverse effect.

# Eighteen

## Fundamental Rights

As the universality and pervasiveness of violence against women cuts across geographical, cultural and ethnic boundaries, it also persists despite social changes. Difference being of cultural and temporally specific manifestations, and rarely of presence or absence of this violence.

A telling illustration of pervasiveness of violence against women through the ages is of the Indian society and its transition from traditional to modern Indian women have done us proud and have also been revered down the ages.

India probably is the only nation in the world which exclusively enshrines female deities in artistically built temples. The Meenakshi temple at Madurai, Ambabai temple at Kolhapur and the Shantadurga and Mahalaxmi temples at Goa are ample proof of the Hindu reverence for female deities. India has also been proud of women's extraordinary ventures in the field of welfare, politics, art, literature and of late, sports. However, these women who forged themselves undauntedly in a male dominated milieu are exceptions. These women established their identity due to their special upbringing, push of circumstances, familial factors and the motivation of freedom fighters and reformers. India boasted of a woman prime minister. Currently too, we have women who have made a mark for themselves in fields hitherto reserved exclusively for men, for example P.T. Usha the sportswoman and Kiran Bedi, the Deputy Commissioner of Police.

The truth, however, which stares us in the face, indicates clearly the pitiable condition of Indian womanhood trapped in the web of socio-cultural factors such as superstitions and blind faith perpetuated by a male dominated society. The saga of the Indian woman is riddled with cruel, inhuman and pathetic attacks on her physical, emotional, social, political, and even spiritual growth. Her struggle for survival continues from the womb to the tomb without respite.

**Women's Rights**

In order to state and analyse the various types of violence tampling her human rights beginning with the female foetus and going on till old age, the following rights have been discussed — the right to life, liberty and security of the person, right to education, right to work, the right to be free from torture and the right to knowledge.

***(i) Right to Life***

*Female Abortion and Infanticide*

The struggle for survival continues throughout the woman's life from womb to tomb. The advent of amniocentesis in India has given yet another sound blow to this struggle. Prior to the Maharashtra Regulation of Use of Prenatal Diagnostic Techniques Act of 1988, both the municipal and governmental hospitals as well as private practitioners were conducting abortions of female foetuses. Although the Act is a deterrent, private practitioners have continued to conduct abortions with a sex bias. They are safeguarded by the Medical Termination of Pregnancy Act of 1971 which has legalised abortion under specific conditions such as the danger of the health of the mother and/or the child. The Government of India has implicitly sanctioned female foeticide because, apart from Maharashtra and Goa, no other state has passed legislation against female foeticide following amniocentesis. The dire need of such a law at a national level has often been discussed at various fora but, as yet, there is no universal law banning sex specific abortion. In fact, amniocentesis is propagated through advertisements which influence the psychology of parents. There are advertisements in Delhi such as "Pay Rs. 500 now or Rs. 5 lakhs later (dowry)." It is estimated that between 1978 and 1983 as many as 78,000 female foetuses in India have been aborted.

In certain states, such as Gujarat, Rajasthan, U.P. and Tamil Nadu, female infants in some communities are murdered as soon as they are born. They are drowned in a basin of milk, poisoned by opium applied to the breasts of mothers, strangled to death or sacrificed at an altar to a god. Four out of ten of those killed are murdered with a wet towel. It is pitiable that the mother herself is asked to do these things. No questions are asked.

In the Bhatti community in Jaisalmer, Rajasthan, the sex ratio is

550 women to 1000 men, the all-India ratio being 929 women to 1000 men. There has been no *barat* for decades in this community. Rajendra Singh, a Congressman of Bharatpur, Rajasthan had made a statement that 34 girls in his community had been reportedly murdered soon after birth (*India Today* — October 1988).

### (ii) Right to Education and Knowledge

Girls' education is generally neglected despite the constitutional provision for compulsory education for all upto the age of 14 years. The percentage of girls attending school varies from state to state, being sometimes ranging between 20-50 per cent.

Female literacy in India is 24.8 per cent as compared to the male literacy of 46.9 per cent. The right to education is indirectly related to violence against women, as it has been observed that education contributes to women's assertion of other rights such as decision-making. There is a direct relation between education of women and adoption of small family norm according to researchers in family planning.

### (iii) Right to be Free from Torture

The Indian woman is a slave to the so-called institutionalised cultural shackles where she is relegated to right from birth. Her mobility is restricted within the four walls of the kitchen, her self expression is monitored and her thoughts influenced by others in her milieu. She is the victim of suspicion by her brothers, parents, husband and in-laws. The following illustration will suffice to prove the point. In Dharavi, a large slum in Mumbai, a young man bashed the head of his sister because he suspected her of having an affair with a young man in the neighbourhood. The brother intended to kill his sister but she survived and now is a severely handicapped person totally dependent on him. In marital conflict cases, suspicion of the wife is a common reason. Some wives are brutally beaten, tortured and thrown out of their homes due to the husband's suspicion.

### Gender Bias and Exploitation at Work

Women take on additional responsibility of supplementary family income due to economic constraints and demands of improved lifestyles. Lower class women have, of course, always been working. In this area too, women do not have the freedom to regulate their lives. Research by Dr. Pramila Kapur indicates that earning women from the middle and upper middle classes have no control over their income. They are expected to hand over their salary to their in-laws and forfeit all their rights over it. Coping with the homefront and office the alcoholic husbands squandering away their wives, earnings and the suspicions about the woman's character further aggravate the situation. There was a case of a lady doctor who was given only Rs. 2 daily for her expenses by her in-laws. The male dominance is all-pervading and there are implicit assumptions that the wife should have a lesser designation at the work place and earn a lower salary than her husband. Gender bias at work expects a woman executive to "look like a woman, behave like a lady, think like a man and work like a dog" ("Gender Bias" *Times of India*, 2.8.1993). Junior women lawyers report molestation by male lawyers. Molestations at the work place are reported by a few bold women while others suffer in silence.

Countless cases both in rural as well as urban areas are recorded. Dalit women fall a prey to the lust of the land owners and the other affluent individuals in the rural areas. There are cases of the anganwadi workers being abused sexually or otherwise by the male senior officers. In Mumbai, recently there were two reported cases of women lecturers being harassed by their seniors because of their refusal to satisfy the sexual demands of higher-ups. The case of the air-hostess molested by a senior minister is still fresh in our minds. Discrimination is still prevalent in the matter of wages paid to male and female casual labourers. In the earthquake-affected region of Latur, women were paid Rs. 8 per day for casual labour while men were paid Rs. 20.

Most women have no freedom to select their careers. Elders in the family, neighbours and friends influence young women to take up stereotyped jobs hitherto reserved for women such as nursing and teaching. In the cities the scenario is different. We do observe women gradually coming out of homes. And yet, they have to work doubly hard to prove their efficiency to keep their status.

At an interview of women executives on TV it was stated that in order to keep their positions and climb the career ladder, they needed to be consistent, persevering, professional, confident, analytical, objective in interpersonal relationships, patient and continuously strive for knowledge and efficiency. The demands on male executives are not so numerous nor strong.

**Early Marriage and Motherhood**

In the matter of marriage too, women have no choice. Most marriages are arranged by the families of the groom and bride. In the cities parents of a few communities in the upper middle and upper classes give the freedom to their daughters to select their marriage partners. Even though there are restrictions based on religion, caste and community.

In spite of the Child Marriage Restraint Act passed in the early part of this century, infants are being married in their cradles, in Rajasthan. Early marriage, frequent pregnancies and deliveries take their toll and 13 per cent of deaths before the woman reaches her 25th year are due to complications in child birth. Maternal mortality is the main cause of death among women in the reproductive stage. It is estimated that maternal mortality in India is 500 per 100,000 live births. The danger of death is the greatest when the mother is below 20 years and above 35 years. The average Indian woman becomes pregnant 8 times, produces 6-7 children out of which 4 survive. It seems as if 8 per cent of her reproductive life is gone for pregnancy and lactation (Dr. Shanti Ghosh. *The Girl Child in India*, 1993).

The process of arranging the marriage and the ceremony itself is a humiliatory experience for the prospective bride. In Maharashtra the groom and his family are invited to tea party by the bride's parents. The bride is to be asked to prepare snacks and tea and serve them to their guests. Her culinary and other skills are praised by her parents in order to impress the parents of the potential groom. The girl is asked questions about her education, hobbies, friends and other matters and thus the party ends. The boy is rarely asked any questions. The matter of dowry is finalised at such meetings. The humiliation for a girl is worsened when she is rejected.

**Dowry Deaths**

Among the cases of violence against women, the problem of dowry is the most brutal and oft-repeated. It is estimated that a bride is burnt every two days in India, thus giving India the unenviable reputation of being the country with an unbeaten record of bride burning.

*The Statistics*

The Dowry Prohibition Act of 1961, amended in 1986, was meant to be a deterrent to this evil custom. The reality, however, was different. The number of dowry deaths increased from 1912 in 1987 to 5157 in 1991. It is estimated that one woman is burnt to death every five days in India for not bringing 'adequate' dowry.

*Reasons for Non-Redressal by Parents*

It is difficult to estimate the exact figures in relation to dowry harassment and death because many cases are not reported. Women suffer in silence as they are conditioned to do so from childhood. Parents of the bride who is burnt to death, at times, do not pursue the matter in the court. Some of the reasons for such behaviour are as follows:

1. When the girls reach marriageable age the parents in their desire to fulfil their duties and also to lighten their burdens marry their daughters accepting all conditions of the grooms party. They are forced to borrow money from the moneylender, sell their property such as land in order to 'marry off ' their daughter. As a consequence, they are steeped in debt. They, therefore, are financially too weak to legally pursue the matter of their daughter's death and thus do not seek any redressal.

2. Parents thus resign themselves to fate feeling that it is futile to aggravate the matter as their daughter will not come back to life. They are also worried about the marriage of their other daughters, if any.

3. Being emotionally and physically exhausted in the nexus formed, at times, between the bridegroom's family, lawyers and the police, parents surrender.

4. In case of dying declarations taken in suspicious circumstances generally in cases of deaths due to burns, most women tend to state that their burns are due to an accident or that they have attempted suicide. This is due to the following reasons:

(i) The victim's husband's family threatens her that if she tells the truth, her parents' family will be murdered.

(ii) The dying woman is worried about her children's upbringing and future, in case, her husband is convicted.

(iii) She is weary of the stigma which her children may have to suffer if their father is convicted.

(iv) She is also apprehensive that if she survives, her husband and in-laws may again try to murder her.

(v) She is afraid that if she lives, her life would be hell as she accused her in-laws of murder. Generally parents also disown their daughters in such cases.

A girl in India is brought up to be obedient, docile, patient and tolerant and self-sacrificing. In the urban areas girls from the middle and upper middle classes are educated and, at times, given occupational training. Some of them take up jobs before marriage. All this freedom ends with the marriage, which symbolically represents the *lakshman rekha.*

*Justifications for Claiming Dowry*

1. Most men assume obtaining dowry is their 'birth right'. The groom's parents justify dowry by stating that they have made tremendous financial sacrifices in order to educate their son. Therefore, they expect to recover the expenses by obtaining dowry from the bride.

2. The groom and his parents believe that the bride will be an eternal economic burden on them. They therefore demand dowry to make up for her lifetime expenses.

3. The myth that dowry is considered a monopoly of the affluent classes is not true because the lower classes in the process of identifying with the rich have imbibed some of the unethical customs.

4. There is an impression that only the Hindus demand dowry, in reality except for Zoroastrians, all other religious groups have the custom of dowry. However, there are some sections in each religious group which do not believe in dowry this differs from family and individual beliefs.

5. It is the mother-in-law who demands dowry. We have often heard that woman is her own enemy. In our experiences and observations we find that this is not true. In the 54 cases of dowry harassment studied by the students placed in Sakhya, the Anti-Dowry Guidance Cell, only in 8 cases was the mother-in-law exclusively responsible for demanding dowry and harassing the

daughter-in-law. Mothers-in-law are made to do the dirty job representing the wishes of the family, unlike common impression of their villainous role in perpetrating the crime. Their acts are rationalized due to the following reasons:

(i) Her family coaxes her to demand dowry, stating that since she is elderly and a woman, the bride's family will not reject her demands. This is true in most cases as elderly women are still respected in most homes.

(ii) The mother-in-law demands dowry so that she, in turn, can give it to her daughter. Who then is the cause of dowry? Only the mother-in-law?

(iii) The mother-in-law, in most cases, has herself been exploited, suppressed and victimised as a young daughter-in-law. She, therefore, nurtures hostility against those who harassed her and displaces these feelings onto her daughter-in-law. The dynamics can be understood in the theory postulated by Paulo Freire, namely, that the oppressed internalise the qualities and behaviour of the oppressor.

6. Girls in their desire to take maximum assets and riches at their marriage time which would result in their happiness also welcome taking dowry to their new homes. We cannot generalise because most girls are so conditioned as to adjust to any type of life.

7. Giving large sums of money and expensive presents need not be a ticket to a happy married life. Girls have been harassed regardless of the quantum of dowry.

*The Virtual Reality of Dowry*

1. Dowry is not a one shot affair. It is an unending ritual taking its toll at every festival and celebration throughout married life.

2. Most people are vaguely aware of the law against dowry. They are, therefore, doubly careful in camouflaging their demands. They suggest that the bride's parents present a 'Honda' or a 'Maruti' car to the groom so that he can return home from work early enough to take his wife out in the evening!

3. Most brides suffer harassment in silence for many years. They do so as they are conditioned to believe that after a girl's marriage her permanent place is with her husband and in-laws. Moreover they fear that their parents would have to suffer social ostracism. There have been incidents of young unmarried girls committing suicide to protect their parents from the burden of dowry.

4. Men who do not take dowry are not thought much of their community. It is felt that they might have some shortcoming in them which could be the reason for their no dowry marriage.

5. In dowry death cases (mostly due to burns) most women give a false dying declaration stating that the burns are due to an accident or that they have attempted suicide. Appreciations of the future for their children and parents make them prevent their in-laws and husband from being punished by giving false declaration.

**Wife Battering**

Wife beating is generally accepted as a cultural phenomenon. Most men take it upon themselves to beat their wives to 'improve them'. Women too tolerate it as a part of life. It is perceived as a token of the husband's affection. The police too, especially of the lower ranks, all view it as a societal norm. The legislation against physical and mental torture (Sec. 498 A) is of recent origin. Unfortunately, there are lapses in its implementation.

Mental torture of the wife is equally injurious. It may be even more devasting than the physical assaults. It is manifested in the following forms — taunting the wife, insulting her in the presence of the children, guests and domestic help, ignoring her completely and cutting off communication with her. In a case of harassing daugher-in-law, a home visit was paid to conduct a family interview. The wife was not permitted to participate in the interview saying that she was stupid and that he was the spokesman of the family. Insistence to interview was thoroughly criticized saying that 'Women libbers wreck families'. In another case a marital conflict the working wife stated that her husband locked up all the kitchen gadgets such as the mixer, peeler and pressure cooker so that she had to spend more time in the kitchen and consequently report late for work. This case has now been solved.

*Why the wives suffer?*

The harassed wives suffer in silence because of the following reasons:

(a)They have been conditioned to obey their husbands.

(b)Culturally it is assumed that the wife will silently bear the assaults.

(c)They have no support as such. Their parental family and other relatives refuse to accept them back and bear the burden of supporting them and the children (if any) for the rest of their lives.

(d)They are ignorant of the provision in the law to safeguard their rights, as well as of shelter homes run by welfare organisations and the government.

(e)Even if they are aware of seeking redressal through law, they are brainwashed to keep the *Khandan ki Izzat* unblemished.

Rape by the husband is not as yet a cognisable offence in India. Women are conditioned to play a submissive role especially in the matter of sexual relations. Most husbands feel a sense of exclusive possession over their wives. Hence in sexual relations, the wife's consent is rarely taken. Cases have been reported to deviant sexual behaviour of the husband, for example, beating the wife prior to the sexual intercourse, burning her with cigarette butts or thrusting hard objects in her vagina. Refusal to give in to the insatiable sexual desire of the husband is interpreted as the result of her extramarital relations. She is therefore, 'duly punished'.

There was a case of murder of a young housewife in Mumbai. She had been married for eight months. Her husband was impotent but this was not revealed to her prior to their marriage. In his efforts to cure his impotency, the husband forced her to have sexual relations with his friends in his presence. She was also victimized by her brother-in-law and father-in-law. On one occasion when she strongly resisted her father-in-law's advances, he strangled her and then threw her out of their sixteenth floor apartment. But for the intervention of a passerby nurse, this case would have been registered as suicide because the in-laws made a statement to the police that the woman was mentally deranged. Cases of cruelty by the husband and his relatives have increased from 11603 in 1989 to 15949 in 1991 (*Social Welfare,* Vol. XXXIX, no. 11-12 Feb.-Mar. 1993).

Consumption of liquor is one of the prime causes of domestic violence and misery in the family. Liquor, foreign and indigenous is freely available in most Indian states. The hard-earned money of both the husband and wife is devoured by alcohol. Consequently, the wives resort to taking up extra jobs and hiding their income. Deaths' due to the consumption of alcohol are increasing but there is no statistical data available. It is estimated that the number of deaths due to spurious liquor exceeds the deaths due to communal riots. Many cases, however go unreported. The death of the husband due to liquor consumption places heavy burdens on the wife. She has to shoulder the entire responsibility of supporting her family if she has no grown-up children. At times, men have been blinded as a result of spurious liquor thus leaving the family in unending miseries.

## Family Planning and Women

### *Passive Role of Women*

The average Indian woman has no choice in relation to important events in her life such as marriage, parenthood, family planning, participation in community activities and divorce. "We have mouths but we use them only for crying", a young woman said in a camp conducted for rural women. The family, community and society in general, assume that women have to be told, nay ordered, to behave in accordance with the norms of the family community and society. The in-laws, especially the mother-in-law, play a strong part in the matter of the number of children that the couple has. The wife is often blamed, ostracised and even divorced for her inability to produce sons or in case of sterility. The small family norm has not been effective. Despite India's acceptance of family planning in 1952 as a national issue. There are, of course, regional differences. In the family planning programme it is the woman who is at the receiving end. Men are still reluctant to undergo vasectomy or to use condoms. Women are forced to undergo sterilization despite their ill health and protests. They are not involved neither in the selection of family planning methods nor in the matter of family size. On the other hand they have to suffer all the pain.

Women, especially from the low and middle income groups suffer from ill-health and malnutrition and are the worst suffers from contraceptive services. Women with loops inserted complain of heavy bleeding and backache. Lack of adequate follow-up services is a deterrent to the acceptance of loops and other contraceptive devices or methods. The Indian Council of Medical Research (ICMR) intended to recruit 20,000 women for experimenting with NORPLANT through the medical college hospital even though a case registered against NORPLANT was still pending in the court (Karkal, July 1992). Men do not want to face any inconvenience and leave that for the woman 'a traditional beast of burden'.

Inadequate medical information supplied to patients, both men and women causes the break up of the family. To illustrate when a man undergoes vasectomy he has to be advised to get his semen tested periodically to ensure that it is free of sperms. In the interim period the couple has to be advised to utilise other contraceptive methods or devices. In some cases that is not done. When pregnancy occurs, the husband accuses his wife of infidelity and throws her out of the house thus causing family break-ups.

Voluntary efforts in the medical field have been geared mostly to women. While one appreciates the concern of the voluntary sector in relation to women and family planning, one wonders why similar efforts are not directed towards the males. Women from the low income groups have no privacy in their homes which prevents them from utilising devices such as the diaphram and jelly. Dr. Billing's ovulation method, though very sound, feasible and scientifically tested also cannot be utilised by all women. This method also requires that women have some privacy to test the vaginal mucous.

By and large, women in slums find it very difficult to stick to the schedule of oral pills. There have been cases when women have forgotten to take the pill for a few days and then have swallowed a whole lot of pills to make up the deficit. Most women do not know that a thorough medical examination is essential prior to the acceptance of this method nor are they aware of the positive and negative effects of the pills.

It is stated that one-fifth of 132 sterilisation camps surveyed by the ICMR had no life-saving drugs, as a result of which there were 180 deaths in Maharashtra, 92 in U.P., 86 in Gujarat, 82 in Kerala, 76 in Orissa and 66 in Andhra Pradesh from 1985 to 1987 (*Times of India,* 27th July, 1989).

In amniocentesis too women are not the ones to take a decision. Most of them are harassed for producing daughters and the choice of amniocentesis is imposed on them. Some are brainwashed to such an extent that they opt for an abortion. In a survey of 100 women at a Delhi clinic who underwent abortion following amniocentesis, most women said that they were taunted continuously by their in-laws for having given birth to a daughter ("Licence to Kill" *Grassroot Action*, 3rd Issue, April 1990).

The eldest male in the family is still the decision-maker in relation to familial issues with a few exceptions. It is only in minor matters such as those relating to the kitchen that the women can have their say.

*Lack of Awareness of Methods of Family Planning*

Eventhough T.V. has invaded all homes in the length and breadth of the country breaking all information barriers, how many utilise this opportunity? Interests of the rural women are limited to film songs and films. This leaves them ignorant about the functioning of their bodies, especially the reproductive system. Lack of sex education and the consequent faculty attitude towards sex and sexuality increases morbidity in women. Most women are ignorant of the types of contraceptives available, their advantages and disadvantages. An incident related by an institution working in the area of family planning in Tamil Nadu illustrates how women were taken for granted in this programme. The institution spread the word regarding the loop, motivated women in rural areas and inserted loops in a large number of women. It soon observed that the number of women coming for loop insertion decreased day by day. Exploration of this phenomenon revealed the rumour taking rounds that one or two women had large worms due to the loop. Investigations revealed that the loop inserted in these women had fallen out and was viewed as a large worm. One of the reasons for such miscommunication is the fact that the doctors had not explained the process of loop insertion to the women concerned. In the survey mentioned earlier, most women who underwent amniocentesis did not know the names of these tests nor their harmful effects.

**Legislations for Protection of Women's Rights**

Women are not aware of their legal rights nor are they aware of the political situation and its effects on the masses. In a study in Bihar it was found that most women knew about the right of inheritance to paternal property. The least known rights were the (MTP) Medical Termination of Pregnancy Act (among the rural and urban women of Gaya). Minimum Wages Act and Child Marriage Restraint Act (among Women of Bhojpur) and Widow Remarriage Act (among urban women of Madhubani) (Sachidananda Sinha, 1984). There is no question of assertion of their rights in respect of these laws. If women are ignorant of the laws passed in their interest.

## Role of Women in Gram Panchayats

The Government of India has recently passed legislation reserving 30 per cent of the seats for women in the gram panchayat (GP) and Zilla Parishad (ZP). Orientation programmes for these women at the ZP level are organised by voluntary organisations. In one such programme many of the participants lacked knowledge of the philosophy of reservations for women, the procedures of GP and ZP and their role therein. Some admitted that their husbands represent them at the meetings of GP or ZP. Those who were not educated said that when resolutions are passed at the meetings of GP, papers are sent to the homes of these women members for their thumb impression. Most women representatives do not take an active role in decision-making. They are merely 'nodders' at these meetings. One representative of a GP was beaten up for taking an active role in one of the meetings. She expressed her opinion on an issue very effectively and was applauded by all including her husband who was present at this meeting. When the couple returned home, the husband beat her mercilessly and asked her not to open her mouth henceforth. Some of these women are being monitored by their husbands and are forced to stand for the election of GP and ZP.

## Women's Organisations in Mumbai

The following chart depicts a picture of some women's organisations in Mumbai and their main area of work.

| | *Name of the Organisation* | *Focal Point/Objectives* |
|---|---|---|
| 1. | Majlis | Legislation for women and its implications. |
| 2. | Stree Hitakarni | Health and its implications for women. |
| 3. | Prerana | Problems of prostitutes and their children. |
| 4. | Sakhya | Eradication of dowry and management of marital conflicts. |
| 5. | Stree Mukti Sanghatana | Women's problems in general, i.e., |
| 6. | Maitrini | Status of women in terms of employ- |
| 7. | Mahila Dakshata Samiti | ment, rights, violence against women, |
| 8. | Women's Forum | services available, etc. |
| 9. | Swadhar | |

There are numerous other women's organizations spread all over India. SEWA of Ahmedabad concentrated on forming trade unions of women handcart-pullers has now expanded its field to women's self-employment as a whole. Similarly, Saheli in Delhi, Sathin in Rajasthan, Stree Adhar Kendra in Pune are some other organisations working towards the improvement of women's status. All these organisations have shifted from a welfare approach to a development one. The improvement of women being their major thrust.

**National Commission for Women**

*Functions covered by the Commission*

The NCW was set up on 31st January 1992 as per the National Commission for Women Act 1990. The mandate of the commission covers a wide range of functions which are summarised as under:

(i) Investigate and examine the legal safeguards provided for women under the Constitution and other laws and recommend to government measures for their effective implementation.

(ii) Review the existing provisions of the Constitution and other laws affecting women and recommend amendments to meet any lacunae, inadequacies or shortcomings in such laws.

(iii) Look into complaints and take suo moto notice of matters relating to deprivation of women's rights and take up the issue with appropriate authorities.

(iv) Take up studies/research on socio-economic issues.

(v) Participate and advise on the planning process of socio-economic development of women and evaluate the progress made.

(vi) Inspect jails, remand homes where women are kept under custody and seek remedial action where necessary.

While investigating cases of violation of safeguards for women and complaints relating to deprivation of women's rights the Commission has the powers of a civil court trying a suit. The Commission can summon any person and examine the person under oath.

In order to carry out the functions effectively, eleven expert committees have been set up on women- related issues to tender advice and suggest appropriate measures, for corrective action. A complaints and pre-litigation cell to resolve conflicts outside the legal proceedings is functioning with the active collaboration of counsellors deputed by NGOs.

As an autonomous statutory body, the Commission is working relentlessly towards its goal and has adopted a holistic multipronged approach towards empowerment of women, taking up cudgels against legal, social, cultural as well as political barriers to their advancement. A number of bills have been proposed, which include the Marriage Bill, 1994 Compulsory Regulations of Marriage, Domestic Violence, etc.

**Recommendations**

A number of important recommendations have been made by the National Commission for Women which include inter alia the following:

(i) GPC be amended to provide that women should normally not be remanded to police custody;

(ii) Bail be relaxed in three cases — where the accused is a woman, is ill, or is a juvenile;

(iii) Speedy investigations and speedy trials should take place in respect of women undertrials;

(iv) More women should be appointed in the police departments;

(v) The investigating officers should not be authorized to publish the name of the victim;

(vi) Mandatory training programmes on gender sensitization of the police and all those responsible for administration of justice should be organized regularly;

(vii) The Legal Services Authority Act should be amended to incorporate provision for holding Parivarik Mahila Lok Adalats to ensure speedy justice to women;

(viii) Sex education be included in the school curricula for adolescent girls and boys;

(ix) A fund (statutory or otherwise) should be created for rehabilitation of rape victims. The sources of fund could be fine/penalty imposed on the accused, donations from charitable trusts and contributions from government and local bodies. Further vocational training/skill development centres-cum-production units should be set up by NGOs and local bodies for the benefit of victims of abuse and violence;

(x) Community awareness and advocacy campaigns should be conducted for parents and local community members on the importance of girls' education and related needs; and

(xi) Support forums should be set up to analyse policies and develop strategies for amending laws related to women and to promote an agenda for the betterment of women.

## Central Social Welfare Board

*Programmes and Schemes*

The Central Social Welfare Board established in 1953 and subsequently registered as a charitable company in the mid-sixties, has been serving the cause of women, children and other underprivileged groups through NGOs. In keeping with its objectives, the Central Social Welfare Board provides financial support and assistance for several need-based programmes which facilitate the socio-economic empowerment of women. These include Condensed Course of Education, Vocational Training Courses, Awareness Generation Camps, Voluntary Action Bureaus and Family Counselling Centres. The latter two schemes offer preventive and rehabilitative services to women who are victims of family violence and atrocities. These programmes are providing focal points for evolving social consciousness in respect of violence against women, and are helping them by adopting a "conciliatory approach".

The Voluntary Actions Bureau and Family Counselling Centres run by NGOs with financial support from Central Social Welfare Board follow a policy which leads to better integration of women within the family, rather than a policy which would lead to disintegration of the family as an institution. The family continues to be the basic social unit, with common interests and enjoys the advantage of a common front and can be a catalyst of change for the betterment of all its members.

***Work Done by Women's Organisations***

The chart above depicts the area(s) of work selected by different women's organisations. However, all of them adopt different strategies in relation to their objectives. The main ones are as follows:

*(i) Micro Level Intervention*

This involves dealing with individual cases in the setting of their families and immediate environment. It includes dealing with various types of groups, for example, groups of dowry-affected women.

The micro level is linked with the meso, exo and macro levels. The women's issues (or any other for that matter) are linked with other sub-systems of society, for example, education and health. It is important that the organisations working towards the empowerment of women study the impact of the micro-level system on women's issues and devise strategies to handle it. Issues such as the ineffective educational systems which is not geared to the consistent involvement of the girl child. The atrocious onslaught of contraceptives on women in the family welfare planning programme are raised.

*(ii) Macro Level Intervention*

Unless our efforts are not geared towards changes at the macro level they will go waste. The policy-makers have to be galvanised into action. Changes in the age-old laws, machinery for their implementation, projects for women and their functioning have to be scrutinised and geared to women's overall development. On the whole, most of the women's organisations have been working on the above mentioned lines. The establishment of the National Women's Commission followed by the state level commission is a big step towards the establishment of separate identities for women. These commissions operate at macro level but do take up individual cases if they involve a larger issue, for example rape. The National Commission in its attempt to review the law against rape and to effect changes in it has consulted women's organizations in various parts of India on this issue before final submission of its recommendations to the Central Government.

The problem of alcoholism has driven the village women of Tamil Nadu and Maharashtra to wage a war against this evil. There are distilleries galore in slums and villages. For ages together women have suffered the demonic attacks of alcohol on their families' health, economy and happiness in general. These women have organised themselves and forced the closure of distilleries in their vicinity. They have approached the state government to enact legislation accordingly. Thus, their power lies informing groups of like-minded women fighting for their causes.

*(iii) International Linkages*

Collaboration with international women's organisations is indispensable to effect global change in the status of women. They are one of the most powerful means to effective change in women's status. The Nairobi conference had set the ball rolling, here women all over the world unite once in two years to share their experiences and interventional strategies. The India-Canada conference on violence against women held in December 1993 was also an attempt in the same direction.

*(iv) Seeking Implementation through Collaboration with Government Machinery*

The Government on its part, makes efforts to stem violence against women. The Judiciary and the police system do make all the possible efforts towards this goal. The setting up of family courts and the enactment of Sec. 498A are the concrete forms of these efforts. The role of a women's organisation is that of a vigilant group to see to the proper implementation of these legal provisions. A few years ago, women's organisations in Mumbai observed that cases of mental cruelty against women were not registered by the Police under Sec. 498A. A recent development in the process of women's improvement is the collaboration with the police. The College of Social Work, Nirmala Niketan, initiated students, placement in police stations in 1983, so as to sensitize the police to the social issues and to their role therein so as to effect good police-public relations. The common issues highlighted are those related to the status of women, prostitution, drugs, AIDS, street children and dowry. Accordingly, we give these inputs in the training of the police at various levels at different training centres. Similarly social work intervention in the area of women police constables (WPC) has also been initiated. Regular workshops are conducted for male police constables and officers and for WPCs. Small surveys are also conducted on the functioning of the police and reports are regularly submitted to the Commissioner of Police. The Tata Institute of Social Sciences has instituted a special cell for women and children in the office of the Commissioner of Police as well as in one police station in Mumbai. Sakhya, a voluntary organisation has been granted permission to work in three police stations in Mumbai.

The widespread and rampant atrocities against women prompted the State Women's Commission to plan women's security cells in each of the 72 police stations in Mumbai. The Commission called a meeting of all women's organisations and explained the rationale for the Mahila Suraksha Samiti (Women's Security Cells) inviting volunteers to work through the police stations. The members of this Samiti will act as vigilant groups to ensure that the police deal justly in relation to women's issues, for example, dying declarations. The law states that a police officer and a Special Executive Magistrate be present to note the dying declarations of women dying under suspicious circumstances, the presence of relatives being prohibited. However, we find that this is not adhered to and the woman's in-laws force her to tell lies, thus rendering all laws ineffective.

**Mobilization of Public Awareness, Regarding Women's Status**

The status and self esteem of women needs to be drastically uplifted and given their due share in all spheres.

There is a dire need to create awareness among different groups regarding the status of women, gender bias and injustice against women generally. The perceptions of youth regarding marriage, women's status and roles in the family need to be revised and changed. Young boys and girls need to develop skills to strengthen the bond of marriage and family life. Young women should learn to assert themselves in their families of origin and matrimony. They should be empowered to take firm decisions in relation to the selection of marriage partners, type of wedding, refusal to give dowry, number of children, type of contraceptives and other familial and non-familial matters. Men, too, need to realise the dignity of women and to appreciate their contribution in various fields.

In a workshop with a group of young girls and boys between the ages of 16 to 22 years belonging to the lower middle class with the above mentioned objectives, there was a question related to their reasons for marriage. The answers of all the boys indicated that they needed a wife to work at home. Their responses were as follows:

"My mother is too old to do housework and hence I need a wife."

"My parents can't work on our farm any more. Therefore, I want to marry so that my wife can take over from them." "I am the only earning member in my family, and my income is insufficient to support six family members. I, therefore, want to marry a working woman."

It was indeed sad to note that none of them said that they need a companion for life to share their joys and sorrows, to enjoy life's bounty together and to jointly achieve their goals in life. The girls had a more positive bent of mind and were emphatic in their decision to marry someone to share their joys and sorrows. In the subsequent session there was a mutual confrontation and the boys later stated that no one had earlier explained to them the significance of marriage.

Family life including sex education should be introduced in schools beginning with the nursery. The objective of such an education should be to impart scientific facts about sex and sexuality, roles and responsibilities in the family and to shape attitudes conducive to a happy family life without a gender bias.

Women's organisations are also becoming vigilant about the portrayals of women in the audio-visual media. Except for a few art serials, the woman in most commercial movies is portrayed as a sex bomb, a cantankerous wife/mother-in-law or an obedient and dutiful wife. Remarks about violence against women need to be scrutinized. A film named *Damini* portrays the courage of a woman who raises her voice against rape and the unjust judicial system. However, there are two sentences uttered by the barrister in the movie which are shocking. Regarding a gang rape of a married domestic worker by the employer's son and his friends, he says: *Ladkon ne jo kuch kiya utni badi baat nahi hai. Jawani me to yeh sub kuch hota hi raheta hai.*" (There is nothing objectionable in what the boys have done. Such things keep happening in youth). Unfortunately this has gone unnoticed except for the letter to the Editors of Newspapers written by the author. One would have expected the PTAs of schools, women's organizations and the union of domestic workers to raise a hue and cry. Education of the masses in relation to violence against women could be imparted in the context of human rights.

**Conclusion**

The focus on women as an exploited, victimised and marginalised group is a recent development in the world. It has been now recognised that despite all their rights being violated, women have been suffering in silence. In India, the concept of Seeta/Savitri (dutiful wives) is imbibed in a girl's mind from the early stages of her life. A vigorous multi-pronged and multi-professional effort is needed to establish the woman as a human being in her own right. It is time to dispel myths, superstitions and misconceptions about woman and her duties and adopt a rational attitude towards the woman as a human being and not a beast of burden.

Nineteen

# Constitutional Cover

Our Constitution makers could foresee the social problems associated with the emancipation of women. They had seen prevailing gender inequality during their time and had visualised that the sex-equality was crucial for the development of the country. In order to do away with the inequality and to provide reasonable opportunities and create awareness for the exercise of human rights and claim, it was necessary to promote with special care, educational and economic interests not only of men but women too and to provide necessary protection from social injustice and exploitation. The Constitution of India provides the following:

(i)Right to equality (Article 14, 15 and 16).

(ii)Right against exploitation (Article 23).

(iii)Directive Principles of State Policy (Articles 38, 39(a) & (d), 42 and 44)

(iv)Fundamental Duties (Article 51A Q (e))

(v)Elections (Article 325)

Besides the above, the Preamble, which incorporates the chief goal enshrined in the Constitution reflects the spirit of equality. A look into the Preamble will enable us to locate the ideal incorporated into the Constitution.

**I. The Preamble of the Constitution**

The Preamble of the Constitution of India, has been expressed in the following words:

"We the people of India having solemnly resolved to constitute India into a Sovereign Socialist Secular Democratic Republic and to secure to all citizens:

Justice, social, economic and political;

Liberty of thought, expression, belief, faith and worship;

Equality of status and of opportunity; and to promote among them all,

Fraternity, assuring the dignity of the individual, (unity and integrity of the nation);

In our Constituent Assembly, this twenty-sixth day of November, 1949 do hereby adopt, enact and give to ourselves this Constitution."

The expression appearing in the Preamble of our Constitution was then described by Pandit Jawaharlal Nehru in the Objective Resolution which he moved in the Constituent Assembly in its first session and the Assembly adopted the same unanimously. But Nehru's Resolution itself had taken shape out of what had already been said by Mahatma Gandhi in 1931 when Mahatmaji was standing on the deck of a ship taking him to London in the capacity of the spokesman and representative of Nationalist India to the Second Round Table Conference. When asked by a correspondent at that time as to what Constitution he would bring back if he could help it, Mahatma Gandhi offered the following reply:

"I shall strive for a Constitution which will release India from all that dom and patronage and give her, if need be, the right to sin. I shall work for an India, in which the poorest shall feel that it is their country in whose making they have an effective voice; an India where there shall not be high class and low class of people; an India in which all communities shall live in perfect harmony; there can be no room in such an India for the curse of untouchability or the curse of intoxicating drinks or drugs. Women shall enjoy the same right as men. Since we shall be at the pace with all the rest of the world neither exploiting nor being exploited by any of them. We shall have the smallest army imaginable. All interests not to be in conflict with the interests of the millions of dumb that will be respected, whether foreign or indigenous. This is the India of my dream."

The opening words of the Preamble emphasise on the ultimate authority of the people from whom the Constitution emerges. There is no sex discrimination. The words "We the People of India" includes both males and females.

*Explanation*

The Preamble outlines four objectives of the Indian Republic, viz. justice, liberty, equality and faternity. Justice implies a harmonious reconcilement of individual conduct with the general welfare of the society. The essence of justice lies in the attainment of the common good. It embraces as the preamble proclaims the entire social, economic and political spheres of human activity.

It is in the interest of the society to ensure the maximum liberty of thought and action of the individual consistent with the circumstances and social conditions. 'Liberty' in the Preamble, signifies not only the absence of any arbitrary restraint on the freedom of individual's action but also for the creation of conditions which would provide for the necessary ingredient required for the proper development of the personality of the individual. Since society consists of individuals, social progress depends on the progress of individuals.

The two words 'liberty' and 'equality' are complimentary. Equality does not mean that all human beings are mentally and physically equal. It signifies equality of status and equal opportunity.

It is the spirit of brotherhood that is emphasised by the expression 'fraternity'. In a country like ours with diverse religion, language, culture and social system, unity can be achieved through the spirit of faternity. Fraternity ensures two things, viz. the dignity of the individual and unity and integrity of the country.

## II. Fundamental Rights

Fundamental Rights, receives its treatment under Articles 12 to 35 of the Constitution and includes such principles as right to equality, right to freedom, right against exploitation, right to religion, right to culture and education, saving of certain laws and right to constitutional remedies.

### *1. Right to Equality*

*Art 14. Equality Before Law*

"The State shall not deny to any person equality before law or equal protection of laws within the territory of India."

*Notes:* The Constitution of India guarantees equality before law or equal protection of law to every person irrespective of the fact that he is, or he is not the citizen of India. Both the phrases aim to establish what is called the equality of status and of opportunities as envisaged in the Preamble. Article 14 of the Constitution prevents any arbitrary discrimination.

Interpreting the scope of this Article, the Supreme Court of India held as under:

(I) In considering the fundamental right of equality of opportunity, a technical pendantic or doctrinaire approach should not be made and the doctrine should not be involved even if different scales of pay, service conditions, leave, etc. are introduced in different or dissimilar posts.

(II) Article 14 forbids hostile discrimination but not reasonable classification. Thus, where persons belonging to a particular class in view of their special attributes, qualities, mode of recruitment and the like are differently treated in public interests to advance and boost members belonging to backward classes, such a classification shall be outside the scope of discrimination having a close nexus with the object sought to be achieved so that in such a case, Article 14 will be completely out of the way.

(III) Article 14 certainly applies where equals are treated differently without any reasonable basis.

(IV) Where equals and unequals are treated differently, Article 14 would have no application.

(V) Even if there be one class of service having several categories with different attributes and incidents, such a category becomes a separate class by itself and no difference or discrimination between such category and the general members of the other class would amount to any discrimination or to denial of equality of opportunity.

(VI) In order to judge whether a separate category has been carved out of a class of service, the following circumstances have generally to be examined:

(i) the nature, the mode and the manner of recruitment of a particular category from the very start;

(ii) the classification of the particular category;

(iii) the terms and conditions of service of the members of the category;

(iv) the nature and character of the posts and promotional avenues;

(v) the specific attributes that the particular category possesses which are not to be found in other classes and the like."

It is rather difficult to lay down a rule of universal application but the circumstances mentioned above may be taken as illustrative guidelines for determining the question.

In its struggle for social and political freedom, mankind has always tried to move forward to the idea of equality for all. The urge for equality and liberty has been the moving force of many resolutions. The Charter of the United Nations records the determination of the member Nations to reaffirm their faith in the equal rights of men and women.

However, fulfilment of complete equality between men and women in all spheres of life has always been proved to be a distant dream. The laws of a country can at best assure to its citizens only a limited measure of equality. The Constitution makers gave only political and legal equality and the status of a fundamental right. Aspects like economic and social equality were included within the scope of Directive Principles of the State Policy.

*Article 15*

Article 15 of the Constitution ensures prohibition of discrimination on grounds of religion, race, caste, sex or place of birth. Stated in words, it stands as follows:

(1)The State shall not discriminate against any citizen on grounds only of religion, race, caste, sex, place of birth or any of them.

(2)No citizen shall, on grounds only of religion, race, caste, sex, place of birth or any of them be subject to any disability, liability, restriction or conditions with regard to—

(a)access to shops, public restaurants, hotels and places of public entertainment; or

(b)the use of wells, tanks, bathing ghats, roads and places of public resort maintained wholly or partly out of state funds or dedicated to the use of general public.

(3)Nothing in this Article shall prevent the State from making any provision for women.

3[(4)Nothing in this Article or in Clause (2) of Article 29 shall prevent the State from making any special provision for the advancement of any socially and economically backward classes of citizen or for the Scheduled Castes and Scheduled Tribes.]

Article 15 guarantees non-discrimination on special grounds, that is religion, race, caste, sex, place of birth or any of them. But, this right is available to citizens only.

Article 15(1) is conferred on a citizen as an individual and is a guarantee against his being subjected to discrimination in the matters of rights, privileges and immunities pertaining to him by virtue of his status as a citizen.

The significance of Article 15 is that it is a guarantee against every form of discrimination by the state on the basis of religion, race, caste or sex. Article 15 strikes at the root of provincialism by prohibiting discrimination based upon one's place of birth. It is also in conformity with the ideal of a single citizenship which the Constitution establishes for the whole of the country.

Article 15, however, has provided a couple of exceptions in its application. Article 15(3) allows the state to make any special provision for women and children. Article 15(4) permits the state to make any special provision for the advancement of socially and educationally backward classes or for the Scheduled Caste or Scheduled Tribes. The treatment meted out to women and children is in the larger and longer range interest of the community. Article 15(e) was included in the Constitution as a result of the First Consitutional Amendment in 1951.

*Article 16*

This Article guarantees equality of opportunity in matters of public employment. It is stated in the following words:

(I) There shall be equality of opportunity for all citizens in matters relating to employment or appointment to any office under the state.

(II) No citizen shall, on grounds only of religion, race, caste, sex, descent, place of birth, residence or any of them be ineligible for, or discriminated against in respect of any employment or office under the state.

(III) Nothing in this Article shall prevent Parliament from making any law prescribing, in regard to a class or classes of employment to an office (under the Government of, or any local or other authority within a state or Union Territory, any requirement as to residence within that State or Union Territory) prior to such employment or appointment.

(IV) Nothing in this Article shall prevent the state from making provision for the reservation of posts in favour of any backward class of citizen which, in the opinion of the state is not adequately represented in the services under the state.

(V) Nothing in this Article shall affect the operation of any law which provides that the incumbent of any office in connection with the affairs of any religious or denominational institution or any member of the Governing body thereof shall be a person professing a peculiar religion or belonging to a particular denomination.

*Notes:* Under Article 16(1), the general rule laid down is that there shall be equal opportunity for all citizens in matters of public appointment under the State, thereby the universality of Indian citizenship is emphasised.

Article 16(2) prohibits discrimination to any citizen in respect of appointment on grounds of religion, caste, race, sex, descent, place of birth or residence, should that appointment be under the State.

Articles 16(3) to 16(5) are in the nature of exceptions. According to Article 16(3), residence, qualifications may be made necessary in case of appointments under the State for particular positions. The discretion, however, does not rest with the state but within the powers of the Parliament. Article 16(4) empowers the state Government to make reservation of positions in public employment for any backward class. The state is empowered to declare a class of people as backward class. The exceptions embodied in Article 16(5) seek to take out of the scope of the general principle, the management of the affairs of any religious or denominational institutions under any special law providing for the same.

What Article 15(1) and 16(2) prohibit is that discrimination should not be made only on the ground of sex. However, these Articles do not prohibit the state from making discrimination on the ground of sex coupled with other considerations. In case titled "*Yusuf Aziz* Vs. *State of Bombay* and *Hussainbhoy Laljea,*" sex was held to be a permissible classification. While dealing with this aspect of the matter, the Supreme Court remarked as under:

"Article 14 is general and must be read with the other provisions which set out the ambit of fundamental rights. Sex is a sound classification and although there can be no discrimination in general on that ground, the Constitution itself makes special provisions in respect of women and children. The two Articles when read together validate the impugned chance in Sec. 497 I.P.C."

Justice Krishna Iyer in the case titled *Ms. C.B. Muthamma* Vs. *Union of India* expressed somewhat similar views in the following words:

"We do not mean to universalise or dogmatise that men and women are equal in all occupations and all situations and do not exclude the need programatise where the requirement of particular employment, the sensitivities of sex or the peculiarities of social sectors or the handicaps of either sex may compel sensitivity. But save, where the differentiation is demonstrable, the rule of equality must govern."

An example of violation of Article 14 is the case *Air India* Vs. *Nargesh Mirza,* where the Supreme Court observed that having taken the air hostess in service and after having utilised her services for four years, to terminate her services by the management in the event of her becoming pregnant amounts to compelling the poor air hostess not to have any children and thus interfere with and divert the ordinary course of human nature. The termination of the services of an air hostess under such circumstances is not only a callous and cruel act but an open insult to Indian womanhood, the most sacrosant and cherished institution. Such a course of action is extremely detestable and abhorant to the notion of a civilised society. Apart from being grossly unethical, it smacks of a deep rooted sense of an utter selfishness at the cost of all human values. Such a provision, therefore is not only manifestly unreasonable and arbitrary but contains the quality of unfairness and is, therefore, clearly violative of Article 14.

The Supreme Court while dealing with a rule barring married women from working in a particular firm criticised validity of the rule in the following words:

"We are not impressed by these reasons for retaining a rule of this type ... Nor do we think that because the work has to be done as a team, it cannot be done by married women. We also feel that there is nothing to show that married women would be more likely to be absent than unmarried women or widows. If it is the presence of children which would account for greater absentation of married women, that would be so with the widows having children. The fact that the work has to be carried out by the workers as a team and presence of all these workmen, is in our opinion no disqualification. So far as married women or widows are entitled to such leave as the rule of the Respondent's Firm provide and they would be availing themselves of these facilities."

***2. Right Against Exploitation***

The following expression constitute the relevant portion in Article 23 of the Constitution.

"*Prohibition of traffic in human beings and forced labour*"

I.Traffic in human beings and 'begar' and other similar forms of forced labour are prohibited and any contravention of this provision shall be an offence punishable in accordance with law.

II.Nothing in this Article shall prevent the State from imposing compulsory service for public purposes and in imposing such service, the State shall not make any discrimination on grounds only of religion, race, caste or class or any of them."

While comparing Article 23 to the 13th Amendment of the Constitution of America which abolished slavery, it may be seen that in our country, at the time of adoption of the Constitution, there was no such practice like slavery in India but there existed large scale exploitation of forced bonded labour practiced by upper caste people upon the unprivileged section of the society. There existed a practice under which people mortgaged their labour to the upper caste masters in lieu of the interest that would accrue on the principal amount taken as loan and this bondage could continue from generations to generations. The labour working under this situation had no right to seek employment without his master's approval and consent. His dependence on his master or landlord was so severe that it virtually amounted to slavery.

According to the practice of devdasi women or girls were either sold or dedicated to temples in the name of gods, where they could become an object of lust and instrument of sexual exploitation so long as their youth lasted. The practice of *devdasi, jogan* and other similar practices in Southern, Western part of the country and some of the temples in Orissa particularly bordering Andhra Pradesh were rampant and are still existing.

The ideal of human dignity pervades the entire Constitution and has been expressed in explicit terms in the form of this Article. The expression 'Traffic in Human Beings' means disposal by way of sale or hire or otherwise of human beings more or less in the same manner as man does with the disposable articles.

The trafficking in women and girls in the male dominated society has been treated as the evil practice since old times. Medieval feudalism brought down the position of women to a very low mark. Prostitution became rampant and flesh trade established itself with agents and pimps and the dignity of women had gone down to the lowest ebb. To counter this, the Parliament enacted "The Suppression of Immoral Traffic in Women and Girls Act, 1956." This Act was renamed as "Immoral Traffic (Prevention) Act, 1956" and was substituted by Act No. 44 of 1986 with effect from Jan 26, 1987. The Act was enacted by the Parliament in persuance of the ratification by India of the International Convention of the Suppression of Traffic in persons and of the prostitution by others, signed in New York in 1950 on May 9. (Detailed study of this problem is being dealt with in the Chapter on Prostitution.)

### *3. Cultural and Educational Rights*

Under Articles 29 and 30, certain cultural and educational rights are guaranteed.

*Article 29: Protection of interests of minorities*

(I) Any section of the citizen residing in the territory of India or any part thereof having a distinct language, script or culture of its own, shall have the right to conserve the same.

(II) No citizen shall be denied admission into any educational institution maintained by the State or receiving aid out of State funds on grounds only of religion, race, caste, language or any of them.

Thus sex is a prohibited ground of discrimination under Article 15 and Article 16, but not under Article 29. Courts, however, have come to settle down with an interpretation which means that sex as a basis of classification may be a suspect but cannot altogether be prohibited. Special laws for women can be made in different kinds of cases notwithstanding the fact whether they are favourable or unfavourable to women. It has only to be seen in such a situation that such orders may not only be reasonable but also seem to be reasonable. The following cases are cited by way of example:

(1)In the case titled *Anjali Roy* Vs. *The State*, the fact involved was that after opening of a college exclusively for women, girl students were denied admission into another college which was a co-educational institution. Accordingly one Anjali Roy was denied admission in the co-educational college under the orders of the Director of Public Instruction of the Government of West Bengal. The petitioner challenged the orders of the D.P.I. as arbitrary malafide and unreasonable. The Hon'ble High Court of Kolkata dismissed the Writ Petition holding that the order prohibiting the admission of the girl students to the former co-educational institution was with the intention to make the girl students to take admission in women's college so that the same could be popular and well established and thus, become a self-sufficient. This was thus, a special provision as contemplated by Article 15(3) for the benefit of women and in consequence the provisions of Article 15(1) was not available for this. It was further held that Article 15(1) was of wider implications as compared to Article 29(2) and prohibited discrimination on the ground of sex on all matters and so it included discrimination in matters of admission into educational institutions with the result that Article 15(1) should control Article 29(2).

(2)In the case titled "*University of Madras* Vs. *Santhabai and another*. The High Court of Madras took a different view to deny admission to *Santhabai* in a newly opened college. The Court held the view that the University of Madras is not a 'State' as defined in Article 12 of the Constitution and thus its regulation will not be subject to prohibition of Article 15(1) of the Constitution of India. Another point is that admissions are regulated within the ambit of Article 29(2) and the regulation of the University required that colleges should have the necessary infrastructure to provide essential facilities for women before they could be admitted. This fact is not discriminatory on ground of sex.

So far as the scope of Article 15(3) is concerned, the High Court expressed that notwithstanding Article 15(1), it was lawful for the state to establish educational institutions solely for women and the exclusion of men students from such institutions does not contravene Article 15(1). The cumulative effect of Article 15(3) and 29(2) is that while male students have no right to get admission in women's college, the women's right to admission to other colleges is a matter within the regulation of authorities. Article 29(2) contains the controlling provisions where the question relating to admission to colleges involves.

The scope of Article 29(2) came up for detailed interpretation before the Apex Court in two cases, both of which were appeals against the judgement and order of Madras High Court relating to admission to Educational Institutions maintained by the state. The Supreme Court, after a threadbare discussion, observed as follows:

"It will be noticed that while Cl. (1) protects the language, script or culture of a section of the citizen, Cl. (2) guarantees the fundamental right of an individual, who is citizen. The right to get admission into any educational institution of the type appearing in Cl. (2) is a right which an individual has as a citizen and not by virtue of belonging to any community or class of citizen. The right of the citizen is not to be denied to him on grounds only of sex, religion, race, caste, or language or any of them. If a citizen, who seeks admission into any such educational institution but does not possess the requisite academic qualifications and on this account is denied admission on that ground only, certainly he cannot be held to complain of any infraction of his fundamental rights under the Constitution within the framework of this Article. In the event of his having the required academic qualifications if he is refused admission only on grounds of religion, race, caste, language or any of them, then it amounts to clear violation of his fundamental rights."

The State, contended that Article 46, charged the state with promoting with special care, the educational and special interests of the weaker section of the people and in particular of the SC/ST and with protecting them from social justice and all forms of exploitation. But, the court rejected this argument holding that this was a Directive Principle—a non-justiciable right—and it could not over-ride a Fundamental Right which was justiciable. It was the duty of the court to enforce a Fundamental Right.

The passing of the 42nd Amendment of the Constitution of India in 1976, Sec. 3, w.e.f. January 1, 1977 ensured the Supremacy of the Parliament and gave primacy to Directive Principles over the Fundamental rights. In view of the passing away of this Amendment, the aforesaid argument of the Court has little force.

***4. The Right to Constitutional Remedy***

The declaration of Fundamental Rights becomes infructuous unless there is an effective instrument for enforcement of the right. Article 32 of the Constitution provides a remedy for the enforcement of the fundamental rights. The remedy is in the forms of specific writs mentioned in the Article. Hence, if there is an aggrieved person who seeks a remedy from the court through a particular writ, the nature of the remedy itself is clear both to the aggrieved person and to the court.

The writs mentioned in the Constitution are:

*(1) Habeas Corpus*

This is a Latin term which literally means "You May Have The Body". The Writ was regarded in English as a foundation of the human freedom and the British citizen insisted upon this privilege wherever he wanted whether for business or for colonisation. This is how it found a place in the Constitution of the United States when the British colonies in America won their independence and established a new State under the Constitution.

In India, the power to issue a writ vests only in Supreme Court and the High Court. The Writ is a direction of the court to a person who is detaining another, commanding him to bring the body of the person in his custody at a specified time to a specified place for a specified purpose.

The writ has only one purpose, that is, to set at liberty a person who is confined without legal jurisdiction; to secure release from confinement of a person detained unlawfully. The writ, in accordance with circumstances can be issued against the State and its authorities as well as private individual or organisation.

*(2) Mandamus*

This is a Latin expression and means "We Order". The Writ of Mandamus is an order of the Supreme Court or the High Court commanding a person or a body to do that which is his or its duty to do so. For instance an appointing authority is obliged to issue a letter of appointment to a candidate if all the formalities of selection is over and the candidate is declared fit for appointment to the post. But despite the fulfilment of such condition, if the officer or the authority concerned refuses or fails to issue the appointment letter, the aggrieved person has a right to seek the remedy through a Writ of Mandamus.

*(3) Prohibition*

A Writ of Prohibition is issued primarily to prevent a lower court from exceeding its jurisdiction, or acting contrary to the rules of natural justice. For instance, a judge may be restrained from adjudication upon a case wherein he is personally interested. The Writ of Prohibition is a counterpart of the Writ of Certiorari and an aggrieved person may make an application to the issue of both the Writs, that is 'Prohibition' and 'Certiorari'.

*(4) Certiorari*

It is a Writ which orders the removal of a suit from any court to another which is superior to the first. It may be used before a trial commences to prevent an excess or abuse of jurisdiction and to transfer the case for trial before a higher court. It may be invoked after trial as well in order to quash an order which has been made without jurisdiction or in defiance of the Rules of Natural Justice.

*(5) Quo Warranto*

An application for Writ of Quo Warranto seeks an order from the Supreme Court or High Court to restrain a person from acting in an office to which he is not entitled. It may also seek the office to be declared as vacant. What the court has to do is to determine where there has been unsurpation of an office of a public nature. For instance, a member of a Municipal Corporation may, through an application of Writ of Quo Warranto, challenge the authority of the Mayor, if he is of opinion that the Mayor was not properly elected.

The High Court can issue Writ under provisions of Articles 226 and 227 of the Constitution.

*Article 226. Powers of High courts to issue Writs*

(1)Notwithstanding anything in Article 32, every High Court shall have power, throughout the territories in relation to which it exercises jurisdiction to issue to any person or authority, including in appropriate cases, any Government, within those territories, directions, orders or Writs, including Writs in the nature of habeas corpus, mandamus, prohibition, quo warranto and certiorari, or any of them, for the enforcement of any of the rights conferred in Part III and for any other purpose.

(2)The power conferred by Clause (1) to issue directions, orders or Writs to any Government authority or person may also be exercised by any High Court exercising jurisdiction in relation to the territories within which the cause of action, wholly or in part, arises for the exercise of such power, notwithstanding that the seat of such Government or authority or the residence is not within those territories.

(3)Where any party against whom an interim order, whether by way of injunction or stay or in any other manner, is made on, or in any proceeding relating to, a petition under Clause (1), without

(a)furnishing to such party copies of such petition and all documents in support of the plea for such interim order; and

(b)giving such party an opportunity of being heard, makes an application to the High Court for the vacation of such order and furnishes a copy of such application to the party in whose favour such order has been made or to the counsel of such party, the High Court shall dispose of the application within a period of four weeks from the date on which the copy of such application is so furnished, whichever is later, or where the High Court is closed, on the last day of that period, before the expiry of the next day afterwards on which the High Court is open, and if the application is not so disposed of, the interim order, shall on the expiry of that period, or as the case may be, the expiry of the said next day, stand vacated.

(4)The power conferred on a High Court by this Article shall not be in derogation of the power conferred on the Supreme Court by Clause (2) of Article 32.

*Article 227. Power of Superintendence over all courts by the High Court*

(1)Every High Court shall have superintendence over all courts and tribunals throughout the territories in relation to which it exercises jurisdiction.

(2)Without prejudice to the generality of the foregoing provisions, the High Court may:

(a)call for returns from such courts;

(b)make and issue general rules and prescribe forms for regulating the practice and proceedings of such courts; and

(c)prescribe forms in which books, entries and accounts shall be kept by the officers of any such courts.

(3)The High Court may also settle tables of fees to be allowed to the sheriff and all clerks and officers of such courts and to attorneys, advocates and pleaders practising therein.

Providing that any rules made, forms prescribed or tables settled under Clause (2) or Clause (3) shall not be inconsistent with the provision of any law for the time being in force, and shall require the previous approval of the Governor.

(4)Nothing in this Article shall be deemed to confer on a High Court powers to superintendence over any court or tribunal constituted by or under any law relating to the Armed Forces.

**III. Directive Principles of the State Policy**

The Directive Principles of State Policy constitute the third part of the Constitution and are unique and novel in so far as they depict the ambitions and aspirations of the fathers of the Constitution. It was laid down that these provisions are not enforceable in any court but they are fundamental in the governance of the country and it was the duty of the State to apply these principles in making laws.

*Article 39. Certain Principles of Policy to be followed by the State*

The State shall, in particular, direct the policy towards securing:

(a)that the citizens, men and women, equally have the right to an adequate means of livelihood;

(b)that the ownership and control of the material resources of the community are so distributed as best to subserve the common good;

(c)that the operation of the economic system does not result in the concentration of wealth and means of production to the common detriment;

(d)that there is equal pay for equal work for both men and women;

(e)that the health and strength of workers, men and women, and the tender age of children are not abused and the citizens are not forced by economic necessity to enter a vocation unsuited to their age of strength;

(f)that the children are given opportunities and facilities to develop in a healthy manner and in conditions of freedom and dignity and that childhood and youth are protected against exploitation and against moral and material abandonment.

The picture, so far as it relates to the Constitutional Provision of equal pay for equal work for both, men and women is concerned is very grim. According to the "Report of the Committee on the Status of Women", wage discrimination is very much practised in the form of fixing lower wage rate for women as compared to their male counterparts. The minimum wages fixed for non-skilled male workers is Rs. 7 to 9 per day for 8 hours a day whereas the wages for women for the same type of work and for the same period is Rs. 4 to 7 per day.

A case came up for consideration before the Supreme Court which involved the question of equal pay for equal work for both men and women. The facts of the case was that Andrey D'Costa, a confidential lady stenographer of the company was being paid remuneration at the rate less favourable than her male colleague doing the same work. The company opposed it by saying that she was not doing the same work. The Supreme Court held that the discrimination between the male and female stenographer of the company was only on the ground of sex and the act does not permit the management to pay to a section of its employees doing the same work or a work of similar nature lesser pay contrary to the provisions of Section 4(1) of Equal Remuneration Act, 1976 (No. 25 of 1976).

*Article 42. Provision for just and humane conditions of work and maternity relief.*

The State shall make a provision for securing just and humane conditions of work and for maternity relief.

*Article 44. Uniform Civil Code for the Citizen*

The State shall endeavour to secure for the citizens a uniform Civil Code throughout the territory of India.

The passing of a Uniform Civil Code is not an easy proposition in a country where the population is composed of diverse religious and ethnic groups and different customs and rituals are being practised by each of them. The passing of the Hindu Marriage Act (1955) and the Hindu Succession Act (1956) are examples of such efforts. However, on the question of giving maintenance to Shah Bano by the Supreme Court in accordance with Sec. 125 of Cr. P.C. (Act 2 of 1974) generated sufficient opposition from a section of the society and the Government of India was pressurised to make a separate Act for Muslim women. Nevertheless, the courts in our country are granting maintenance applying Sec. 125 Cr. P.C. to Muslim women in appropriate cases.

**Cases of Conversion to Islam and its Misuse**

The absence of a Uniform Civil Code in India puts Muslim women to disadvantage as according to Shariat, a Muslim male can marry and keep up to four wives as against the Hindus, Parsis, and Christian, etc. Thus, converting to Islam to gain a new spouse is being practised by a few Hindus. The following cases are being cited by way of example.

(1)JM, a businessman married to N are having three children out of this wedlock, over a period of fifteen years, changed his religion and embraced Islam. He took a Muslim alias and married a girl friend S and when confronted by N ended the matter saying that his relationship with S was perfectly justified and legitimate as both had embraced Islam. And after three months of his conversion, JM declared through an oath his decision to become a Hindu.

(2)The case of RK, whose marriage to VK dates back to the year 1978 was equally expedient. From the very beginning of the marriage VK alleged harassment by her in-laws over the question of dowry. One day RK brought home another woman 'A' and legitimised their relationship through conversion to Islam and weeks later reconverted to Hinduism in a temple.

Thus, the convenience afforded by the Islamic personal law to opportunistic Hindu men with bigamy in their mind is misused to gain a new spouse as well as to escape payment of maintenance. The thing becomes all the more difficult for the discarded wife as the onus to prove bigamy is on the complainant and where can she get evidence to prove this. Thus, such misuse of religion and conversions should be stopped. Having a Uniform Civil Code can go a long way in propagating this.

Twenty

# Status under Law

One of the directive principles of state policy prescribes that the state should direct its policy towards securing equal pay for equal work for both men and women. Although the directive principles are fundamental in the governance of the country and are to be applied in enacting legislation, they are not judicially enforceable. In this context, one of the provisions of the Constitution is of special significance. After having laid down that the state shall not discriminate against any citizen on grounds of sex, among other things, it provides that nothing in this article shall prevent the state from making any special provision for women and children. So there is a Constitutional provision in India permitting the state to discriminate in favour of women, if such discrimination is found necessary.

Child marriage, especially of the female infant, was common; widow marriage was prohibited, even if she succeeded in escaping from the funeral pyre of her deceased husband where she was expected to be burnt alive; a divorce was generally looked down upon and her remarriage was socially disapproved. If some of these attitudes still persist it is not because legislation has lagged behind, but because law has not succeeded in playing its role of social engineering and changing certain deeply-rooted social attitudes. During the last two decades a number of laws were adopted with a view to ensuring equality of status and opportunity for women. But it appears that in practice this equality eludes the Indian woman's grasp.

In what follows an attempt is made to examine some of the more important legislation enacted by the Central legislature in India to ameliorate certain unhappy conditions in which women, particularly Hindu women, found themselves. Occasionally, there is talk about ameliorating the conditions of Muslim women, but political consideration stand in the way of doing anything substantial towards that end. Muslim personal laws are considered to be part of the religion of Islam and government generally considers it necessary not to interfere directly in matters regarded as religious.

With a view to preventing child marriages, especially the giving away of infant girls in marriage, the Child Marriage Restraint Act was passed in 1929 declaring it an offence for a man to marry a girl under fifteen years of age. Any person who performs a marriage where the bridegroom is below 18 years or the bride below 15 years commits an offence, as also parents or guardians of the bridegroom or the bride.

This socially motivated legislation has been made relatively ineffective by stating that a marriage celebrated in violation of the stipulation regarding age would nevertheless be valid. The same restrictions regarding marriageable age are found in the Hindu Marriage Act, 1955. There is a Dowry Prohibition Act also in the Indian statute book which prohibits the giving or taking dowry. But this again is ineffective in practice mainly because any dowry given may be construed as "presents" which are not prohibited by law if made at the time of marriage. In the case of both these statutes the teeth of the legislation are practically blunted both by loopholes within the law and by the resistance of social structures and attitudes to change. Certain conservative section of the community regard child marriage a good, if not a proper, thing and would prefer to pay a fine rather than keep their infant sons and daughters unmarried.' A large number of young men and their parents consider dowry a legitimate stepping stone to higher rungs in the social ladder, and possibly a passport to domestic comfort if not happiness.

Two years before the adoption of the Hindu Marriage Act, which inter alia provided of or divorce, the Special Marriage Act, 1954 was enacted. There is a provision in the Special Marriage Act for obtaining a decree of divorce by mutual consent, provided the parties have lived separately for a year and three years have elapsed since the date of marriage. Apart from the common grounds on which either party to the marriage may obtain dissolution of a marriage performed or registered under the Act, the wife may sue the husband for divorce on the ground that he has committed rape, sodomy or bestiality. Persons married under the Act with the result that they would now be governed by its provisions.

Those who marry under the Act or whose marriages are registered under it are, in matters of inheritance, governed by the Indian Succession Act, 1925. When a man to whom the Indian Succession Act applies dies leaving a widow and lineal descendants, the widow is entitled to one third of the property of the deceased and the lineal descendants to two-thirds. Under the Act, in the case of Christians, a widow in the absence of lineal descendants will get the entire property of the husband, provided its value does not exceed Rs. 5,000. If it does, she will receive Rs. 5,000 and a share in what remains along with the kindred of the deceased according to the specific rules laid down in the Act. Some persons, especially women, prefer to be married under the Special Marriage Act because of its beneficial provisions regarding divorce and interstate succession. We shall advert to this later.

It may be said in general that the right of a wife to obtain a divorce in India is much more restricted than that of the husband under customary law; however, in certain Hindu communities, as also among most tribal groups, it is possible for the husband and the wife to obtain divorce without resource course to court.

They are only required to follow some customary practice, like making a declaration before the elders of the community or the headman of the tribe that they no longer desire their marital relationship to continue. It is well known that among Muslims, while the husband can unilaterally and without assigning any reason divorce his wife by pronouncing *talaq* (that is by uttering the words, "I divorce you") three times, the wife has to get a judicial pronouncement of divorce on specified grounds.

It is, however, possible for the wife to have the power of divorce delegated too her by the husband at the time of entering into the marriage contract. For instance, it may be stipulated that if he takes a second wife, she should have the option of repudiating her marriage. Such delegation is, however, uncommon. Considering the fact that the Constitution makes provision for equality of the sexes, it may be desirable to give judicial recognition to *fasaq* by means of which a Muslim wife may unilaterally repudiate her marriage. An opportunity for such recognition was lost when the Kerala High Court in 1975 ruled that the right of Muslim women to obtain divorce is exclusively governed by the Dissolution of Muslim Marriages Act, 1939 and that it is not permissible to go beyond it.

The divorce provisions of the Hindu Marriage Act, 1955 maintain equality of the sexes in the matter of grounds for divorce. The Act applies to Hindus, Buddhists, Jains and Sikhs. In the provisions of the Indian Divorce Act, which applies to Christians there is some discrimination between the sexes in the matter of grounds for divorce. A single isolated act of adultery on the part of the wife is a valid ground for granting a divorce on the petition of the husband but, if a wife has to be successful in her petition for divorce, she has generally to prove against her husband not only adultery, but also an additional ground such as desertion or cruelty.

Commission or rape, sodomy or bestiality by the husband can also be ground for obtaining a decree of divorce. This Act was modeled after English enactments for matrimonial reliefs adopted about the middle of the last century. Over a hundred years later, the United kingdom prescribed by legislation a single valid ground for divorce, that is, irretrievable breakdown of marriage.

If in 1869 the idea was that Indian Christians would do well to follow in the footsteps of the British in obtaining matrimonial reliefs, is there any valid reason to assume that they should be governed by rules different from those applicable to the British after the passage of a century. If irretrievable breakdown of marriage is made the only ground for judicial declaration of divorce applicable to all communities and religious groups in India there will be equality of treatment not only between men and women but also between various religious groups.

Perhaps one has to wait for the adoption of a uniform civil code for such unification of laws. In the meantime, the Indian Divorce Act could be amended making grounds for divorce identical for both men and women, preferably adopting the provision regarding irretrievable breakdown of marriage as the sole ground of divorce as laid down in the (British) Divorce Referm Act. 1969.

During the pendency of a suit under the Indian Divorce Act, a wife may apply for alimony and the court may grant an amount not exceeding one-fifth of the husband's average net income. While passing a decree for divorce or judicial separation, the court may order the husband to pay a lump sum or make periodical payments for life to the wife, taking into account her fortune, the means of the husband and the conduct of the parties.

There are similar provisions for the benefit of the wife in the Parsi Marriage and Divorce Act, 1936. The spirit of equality envisaged in the Constitution finds clear expression in the Hindu Marriage Act, 1955. It makes provision for the grant of expenses of matrimonial suits and a monthly allowance for the support of either spouse during the pendency of legal proceedings, provided the spouse applying for the expenses and allowances has not sufficient income to support himself or herself.

The Act also has a provision for making an order for permanent alimony or maintenance in favour of either of the spouses. On remarriage the spouse loses his or her right to maintenance. Further, if the recipient of the alimony is the wife, she is required to remain chaste; if maintenance is granted to the husband, he is enjoined from having sexual relations with any other woman.

In spite of the provisions for divorce contained in the Act of 1955, it is not often that recourse is to them : this is because Hindu social values in general are opposed to the concept of divorce. As Kapadia puts it, "the principle of divorce is alien to the social pattern" with the result that "the norm accepted by law has not been accepted in practice". Whereas prior to 1955, divorce was considered absolute anathema by women of the higher castes, after the passing of the Act, it is the women of the upper classes and higher castes as well as the rich and educated in urban areas who petition the courts for divorce. Probably, the illiterate women in the rural areas do not even know that there are legal provisions for divorce apart from those enshrined in the customary law of certain communities or tribes.

Marriage under the Special Marriage Act has the effect of making the provisions of the Indian Succession Act applicable to the parties. These provisions were more beneficial to women, be they Hindus, Muslims Indian Christians of Pondicherry or Indian Christians in those areas of Kerala which formerly comprised the princely states of Travancore and Cochin, provided they were not governed by matrilineal custom. Before the adoption of the Hindu succession Act in 1956, when a woman succeeded to the divided property of a deceased Hindu male, she took only a limited interest. A woman was denied her legal capacity in a Hindu joint family.

The Hindu Succession Act, 1956, which applies to Hindus, Buddhists, Jains and Sikhs determines the their on the basis of consanguinity or affinity without any discrimination on the ground of sex. It gives a woman full ownership in the property inherited or acquired by her. The widow, the mother and the daughter now not only inherit property along with the son but also take an equal share with him. A Parsi woman takes only half the share that her brother gets in their father's property. A similar half share is the lot of Muslim women as well. Though the Indian Succession Act is generally applicable to Christians, there are various regions in the country where the Act is not applied.

There are also certain Christian Communities to which it not made applicable. Certain tribal Christian communities and those who follow matriliny are outside the purview of the Act. As the Act is not extended to the Union Territory of Pondicherry, Indian Christians in the territory are governed by traditional Hindu law (that is, Hindu law as it was in force in the region before certain changes were effected by the Indian Parliament in 1955 and 1956) in the matter of inheritance with all the disadvantages and disabilities which that law imposed on women.

In the erstwhile princely states of Travancore and Cochin, there are in operation local enactment relating to succession among Christians which appear to discriminate against women. Under the Travancore Christian Succession Regulation, 1916 the share of the widow in the estate of the husband is a life interest, terminable on her death or remarriage, except where she gets the whole estate in the absence of certain specified relatives of her deceased husband.

Under the Cochin Christian Succession Act, 1921 the widow gets share equal to two-thirds of the share of a son if the deceased is survived by a son or lineal descendants of a son. The Travancore Regulation seems to discriminate against daughters who can take only one-fourth of the value of the share of a son or Rs. 5,000 whichever is less. The Regulation does not apply to the small body of Indian Christians in the taluk of Neyyattinkara of the erstwhile princely state who follow Marumakkathayam (matrilineal descent).

The Roman Catholic Christians of the Latin rite and certain non-Catholic Christens living in a few southern taluks of Travancore follow their customary usage, and among them male and female heirs of an intestate share equally in his property. Under the Travancore Regulation, the maternal relatives are excluded from succeeding to the intestate if there are paternal relatives surviving him, whereas in the Cochin Act no maternal relatives are included among the heirs.

The areas where these two enactments are still in force are remarkable for a high female literacy rate and a large number of highly educated women. Nevertheless the fact remains that these women, if they happen to .be Christians to whom these enactments apply, have a right to only a quarter of the share of a brother in the property of their deceased father. Would these educated women and their literate sisters think of reverting to matriliny which was once prevalent in these areas? At the moment they do not appear to be eager to effect any change.

The Hindu Minority and guardianship Act, 1956 also bestowed a few additional rights on Hindu women. It provides that though the father may appoint by will a guardian for his minor children, any such appointment will not take effect during the lifetime of the mother if she survives the father. It will take effect only on her death, provided she has not appointed a guardian by her own will. A Hindu mother is entitled to act as the natural guardian of her minor children if the father ceases to be a Hindu or renounces the world by becoming a hermit or ascetic. The Hindu widow and the Hindu mother, entitled to act as natural guardians of their minor children, are empowered under the Act to appoint guardians for them by will.

In 1956 substantial changes were effected in the law of adoption applicable to Hindus. The Hindu Adoption and Maintenance Act, 1956 has invested the Hindu woman with certain rights of adoption which she had not enjoyed before. Previously an adoption could only be to a male but, under the Act, a woman is competent to adopt to herself a son or a daughter.

Again, under the Act, a married man cannot, except under certain special circumstances, make an adoption without the consent of his wife. Under the earlier law her consent was immaterial but under the present law, her consent is unnecessary only when she has renounced the world or has ceased to be Hindu or has been judicially declared to be of unsound mind. A Hindu woman who is not of unsound mind and who is not a minor is now competent to adopt a son as well as a daughter, provided she is a spinster, divorcee, or widow or one whose husband has finally renounced the world or has ceased to be a Hindu or has been judicially declared to be of unsound mind. In general, during coverture it is only the husband who can adopt. If the woman wants to adopt a son, she should not have a Hindu son, son's son or son's son's son living at the time of the adopted should be younger to her by at least twenty one years.

If she intends adopting a daughter, an essential condition is hat she should have no Hindu daughter or son's daughter living at the time of the adoption. Corresponding requirements have also to be observed by the man who wishes to adopt a son or daughter.

The wife has a right to maintenance for life. She may not forfeit this right even if she lives separately from her husband on certain specific grounds such as the husband's cruelty, desertion, keeping a concubine or having another wife, his suffering from a virulent form of leprosy, his conversion to another religion or any other cause justifying her living separately. She, however, forfeits her right to maintenance if she is unchaste or ceases to be a Hindu.

The Factories Act, 1948 empowers state governments to prohibit employment of women in dangerous operations. A few enactments lay down the general rule that women should not be permitted to work between 7 p.m and 6 a.m., but this rule is relaxable in certain circumstances. Provisions for maternity benefits for women have been incorporated in the Employees, State Insurance Act, 1948 and a number of state enactments. While maternity benefit in coal mines is governed by the Maternity Benefit Act, 1961 women workers in factories and plantations are entitled to maternity leave according to the maternity benefit enactments of different states. Both the Factories Act, 1948 and the Plantations Labour Act, 1951 make it obligatory for factories and plantation employing not less than fifty women to provide creches. In spite of these statutory benefits and the Constitutional directive regarding equal pay for equal work, women agricultural labourers generally get 10 to 60 per cent less in wages than men for the same work. It is not infrequent that, when the husband becomes a "bonded labourer" for the landlord or the labour contractor, the wife also becomes similarly "bonded" with the not unusual result that she is made vulnerable exploitation including trafficking for immoral purposes.

Only 13 per cent of Indian women, according to the 1971 Census, may be regarded as workers, i.e. those who are engaged in some form of economic activity. About 80 per cent of these working women are engaged in agriculture. Only 12 per cent of the total employees in central and state administrative services and public sector undertakings are women. This may not be unrelated to their education or lack of it.

Only 18 per cent of India women are literate. Though one of the directive principles of the Constitution requires the state to provide free and compulsory education for all children under 14 years of age the directive is generally followed with callous disregard of its spirits and its significance for the country. Coupled with the general apathy to women's education, this indifference to put in practice a Constitutional directive results in greater social and economic deprivation for girls than for boys.

At the primary school level while 97 out of 100 boys attend school, the corresponding figure for girls is 62. Further, out of 100 girls who enter the first grade only 26 go up to the fifth grade. It is only about 2 per cent of women who are able to benefit by the opportunities provided for higher education. In 1971-72, 36 girls only were under instruction at various levels of education compared to a hundred boys. If in 1971 about 18 per cent of women were literate, this may appear to compare well with only 8 per cent literacy for women on the eve of independence in 1947, but an increase of 10 per cent in the not too short span of about three decades is hardly something that should make us complacent.

There are certain other types of social legislation which seek to protect interests and benefits that are of special concern to women. The Suppression of Immoral Traffic in Women and Girls Act. 1956, as its title indicates, is intended to protect helpless women and girls from a typical mode of exploitation not altogether unknown in the country. The same year saw the enactment of another piece of social legislation: the Women's and Children's institutions (Licensing) Act, 1956. This was later on superseded by the Orphanages and Other Charitable Homes (Supervision and Control) Act, 1960.

The object of the enactment was to regulate the activities of these institutions and to prescribe a proper standard to which the treatment and the training of the inmates should conform. Such a measure was found necessary because, while there are many good and properly-managed charitable institutions, there are many others run with the objective of exploitation as their main and sustaining inspiration.

The Medical Termination of Pregnancy Act, 1971 may also be mentioned in the context of social legislation relative to women. The enactment seeks, among other things, to protect women's interests. It has a few provisions which, it is clear, were enacted with the sufferings of women in the legislator's mind. It provides that a pregnancy may be terminated where the length of the pregnancy does not exceed twenty weeks, if two medical practitioners are of the opinion that the continuance of the pregnancy would involve a risk to the life of the pregnant woman or of grave injury to her physical or mental health. Two explanations are offered in the enactment itself of what constitutes grave injury to the mental health of the pregnant woman. The first explanation reads: when any pregnancy is alleged by the pregnant woman to have been caused by rape, the anguish caused by such pregnancy shall be presumed to constitute a grave injury to the mental health of the pregnant woman.

In this case the "anguish" is perhaps palpable. The second explanation is more intriguing in that "anguish" is given an extended application. It states:

Where a pregnancy occurs as a result of failure of any device or method used by any married woman or her husband for the purpose of limiting the number of children, the anguish caused by such unwanted pregnancy may be presumed to constitute a grave injury to the mental health of the pregnant woman. Though the promotional slant of the government's family planning programme may be perceptible in this explanation, it is evident that Parliament cannot be blamed for any lack of solicitude for the largest minority in the country.

This solicitude may be even more evident in another provision of the Act which stipulates that in determining whether the continuance of a pregnancy would involve grave risk to the health of a pregnant woman, account may be taken of her actual or reasonably foreseeable environment. This enactment has been hailed as "a major landmark in India's social legislation", and "a far-reaching measure assuring the women of India freedom from undesirable and unwanted pregnancies.

From a study of the ameliorative legal provisions relating to women and the actual situation in which they find themselves, it is clear that something more than legislation is required. Perhaps that first thing to be attempted is to make women aware of their rights, however this is done. It is also necessary to change the attitudes of both men and women, of society in general, to social objectives sought to be achieved by legislation. A radical change in the attitudes of women induced by an awareness of their rights, which are constitutionally guaranteed and legally protected will be the first step in the complex process of transforming the social structure so that women may enjoy full equality with men in every sphere of life.

Convention on the elimination of all forms of discrimination against women

*The States Parties to the Present Convention*

Noting that the Charter of the United Nations reaffirms faith in fundamental human rights, in the dignity and worth of the human person and in the equal rights of men and women,

Noting that the Universal Declaration of Human Rights affirms the principle of the inadmissibility of discrimination and proclaims that all human beings are born free and equal in dignity and rights and that everyone is entitled to all the rights and freedoms set forth therein, without distinction of any kind including distinction based on sex,

Noting that the States Parties to the International Covenants of Human Rights have the obligation to ensure the equal rights of men and women to enjoy all economic, social cultural, civil and political rights,

Considering the international conventions concluded under the auspices of the United Nations and the specialized agencies promoting equality of rights of men and women,

Noting also the resolutions, declarations and recommendations adopted by the United Nations and the specialized agencies promoting equality of rights of men and women,

Concerned, however, that despite these various instruments, extensive discrimination against women continues to exist,

Recalling that discrimination against women violates the principles of equality of rights and respect for human dignity, is an obstacle to the participation of women, on equal terms with men, in the political, social, economic and cultural life of their countries, hampers the growth of the prosperity of society and the family and makes more difficult the full development of the potentialities of women in the service of their countries and of humanity,

Concerned that in situations of poverty women have the least access to food, health, education, training and opportunities for employment and other needs,

Convinced that the establishment of the new international economic order based on equity and justice will contribute significantly towards the promotion of equality between men and women,

Emphasizing that the eradication of apartheid, all forms of racism, racial discrimination, colonialism, neo-colonialism, aggression, foreign occupation and domination and interference in the internal affairs of States is essential to the full enjoyment of the rights of men and women,

Affirming that the strengthening of international peace and security, the relaxation of international tension, mutual cooperation among all States irrespective of their social and economic systems, general and complete disarmament, in particular nuclear disarmament under strict and effective international control, the affirmation of the principles of justice, equality and mutual benefit in relations, among countries and the realization of the right of peoples under alien and colonial domination and foreign occupation to self-determination and independence, as well as respect for national sovereignty and territorial integrity, will promote social progress and development and as a consequence, will contribute to the attainment of full equality between men and women,

Convinced that the full and complete development of a country, the welfare of the world and the cause of peace require the maximum participation of women of equal terms with men in all fields,

Bearing in mind the great contribution of women to the welfare of the family and to the development of society, so far not fully recognized, the social significance of maternity and the role of both parents in the family and in the upbringing of children, and aware that the role of women in procreation should not be a basis for discrimination but that the upbringing of children requires a sharing of responsibility between men and women and society as a whole,

Aware that a change in the traditional role of men as well as the role of women in society and in the family is needed to achieve full equality between men and women,

Determined to implement the principles set forth in the Declaration on the Elimination of Discrimination against Women and, for that purpose, to adept the measures required for the elimination of such discrimination in all its forms and manifestations,

Have agreed on the following

Article I

For the purposes of the present Convention, the term "discrimination against women" shall mean any distinction, exclusion or restriction made on the basis of sex which has the effect or purpose of impairing or nullifying the recognition, enjoyment or exercise by women, irrespective of their marital status, on a basis of equality of men and women, of human rights and fundamental freedoms in the political, economic, social, cultural, civil or any other field.

Article 2 States Parties condemn discrimination against women in all its forms, agree to pursue by all appropriate means and without delay a policy of eliminating discrimination against women and, to this end, undertake:

(a)To embody the principle of the equality of men and women in their national constitutions or other appropriate legislation if not yet incorporated therein and to ensure, through law and other appropriate means, the practical realization of this principle;

(b)To adopt appropriate legislative and other measures, including sanctions where appropriate, prohibiting all discrimination against women;

(c)To establish legal protection of the rights of women on an equal basis with men and to ensure through competent national tribunals and other public institutions the effective protection of women against any act of discrimination;

(d)To refrain from engaging in any act or practice of discrimination against women and to ensure that public authorities and institutions shall act in conformity with this obligation;

(e)To take all appropriate measures to eliminate discrimination against women by any person, organization or enterprise;

(f)To take all appropriate measures, including legislation, to modify or abolish existing laws, regulations, customs and practices which constitute discrimination against women;

(g)To repeal all national penal provisions which constitute discrimination against women.

Article 3: States Parties shall take in all fields, in particular in the political, social, economic and cultural fields, all appropriate measures, including legislation, to ensure the full development and advancement of women, for the purpose of guaranteeing them the exercise and enjoyment of human rights and fundamental freedoms on a basis of equality with men.

Article 4

1.Adoption by States Parties of temporary special measures aimed at accelerating de fact equality between men and women shall not be considered discrimination as defined in the present Convention, but shall in no way entail as a consequence, the maintenance of unequal or separate standards; these measures shall be discontinued when the objectives of equality of opportunity and treatment have been achieved.

2.Adoption by States Parties of special measures, including those measures contained in the present Convention, aimed at protecting maternity shall not be considered discriminatory.

Article 5: States Parties shall take all appropriate measures:

(a)To modify the social and cultural patterns of conduct of men and women, with a view to achieving the elimination of prejudices and customary and all other practices which are based on the idea of the inferiority or the superiority of either of the sexes or on stereotyped roles for men and women;

(b)To ensure that family education includes a proper understanding of maternity as a social function and the recognition of the common responsibility of men and women in the upbringing and development of their children, it being understood that the interest of the children is the primordial consideration in all cases.

Article 6: States Parties shall take all appropriate measures, including legislation, to suppress all forms of traffic in women and exploitation of prostitution of women.

Article 7: States Parties shall take all appropriate measures to eliminate discrimination against women in the political and public life of the country and, in particular, shall ensure to women, on equal terms with men, the right:

(a)To vote in all elections and public referenda and to be eligible for election to all publicly elected bodies;

(b)To participate in the formulation of government policy and the implementation thereof and to hold public office and perform all public functions at all levels of government;

(c)To participate in non-governmental organizations and associations concerned with the public and political life of the country.

Article 8: States Parties shall take all appropriate measures to ensure to women, on equal terms with men and without any discrimination, the opportunity to represent their Governments at the international level and to participate in the work of international organizations.

Article 9

1.States Parties shall grant women equal rights with men to acquire, change or retain their nationality. They shall ensure in particular that neither marriage to an alien nor change of nationality by the husband during marriage shall automatically change the nationality of the wife, render her stateless or force upon her the nationality of the husband.

2.States Parties shall grant women equal rights with men with respect to the nationality of their children.

Article 10 States Parties shall take all appropriate measures to eliminate discrimination against women in order to ensure to them equal rights with men in the field of education and in particular to ensure, on a basis of equality of men and women

(a)The same conditions for career and vocational guidance, for access to studies and for the achievement of diplomas in educational establishments of all categories in rural as well as in urban areas; this equality shall be ensured in pre-school, general, technical, professional and higher technical education, as well as in all types of vocational training;

(b)Access to the same curricula, the same examinations, teaching staff with qualifications of the same standard and school premises and equipment of the same quality;

(c)The elimination of any stereotyped concept of the roles of men and women at all levels and in all forms of education by encouraging coeducation and other types of education which will help to achieve this aim and, in particular, by the revision of textbooks and school programmes and the adaptation of teaching methods;

(d)The same opportunities to benefit from scholarships and other study grants;

(e)The same opportunities for access to programmes of continuing education, including adult and functional literacy programmes, particularly those aimed at reducing, at the earliest possible time, any gap in education existing between men and women;

(f)The reduction of female student dropout rates and the organization of programmes for girls and women who have left school prematurely;

(g)The same opportunities to participate actively in sports and physical education;

(h)Access to specific educational information to help to ensure the health and well-being of families, including information and advice on family planning.

Article 11 1. States Parties shall take all appropriate measures to eliminate discrimination against women in the field of employment in order to ensure, on a basis of equality of men and women the same rights in particular;

(a)The right to work as a right of all human beings.

(b)The right to the same employment opportunities, including the application of the same criteria for selection in matters of employment;

(c)The right to free choice of profession and employment, the right to promotion, job security and all benefits and conditions of service and the right to receive vocational training and retraining, including apprenticeships, advanced vocational training and recurrent training;

(d)The right to equal remuneration, including benefits, and to equal treatment in respect of work of equal value, as well as equality of treatment in the evaluation of the quality of work;

(e)The right to social security, particularly in cases of retirement, unemployment, sickness, invalidity and old age and other incapacity to work, as well as right to paid leave;

(f)The right to protection of health and to safety in working conditions, including the safeguarding of the function of reproduction.

2. In order to prevent discrimination against women on the grounds of marriage or maternity and to ensure their effective right to work, States Parties shall take appropriate measures:

(a)To prohibit, subject to the imposition of sanctions, dismissal on the grounds of pregnancy or of maternity leave and discrimination in dismissals on the basis of marital status;

(b)To introduce maternity leave with pay or with comparable social benefits without loss of former employment, seniority or social allowances;

(c)To encourage the provision of the necessary supporting social services to enable parents to combine family obligations with work responsibilities and participation in public life, in particular through promoting the establishment and development of a network of child-care facilities;

(d)To provide special protection to women during pregnancy in types of work proved to be harmful to them.

3. Protective legislation relating to matters covered in this Article shall be reviewed periodically in the light of scientific and technological knowledge and shall be revised, repealed or extended as necessary.

Article 12

1.States Parties shall take all appropriate measures to eliminate discrimination against women in the field of health care in order to ensure, on a basis of equality of men and women, access to health care services, including those related to family planning.

2.Notwithstanding the provisions of paragraph 1 of this Article, States Parties shall ensure to women appropriate services in connection with pregnancy, confinement and the post-natal period, granting free services where necessary, as well as adequate nutrition during pregnancy and lactation.

Article 13 States Parties shall take all appropriate measures to eliminate discrimination against women in other areas of economic and social life in order to ensure, on a basis of equality of men and women, the same rights, in particular:

(a)The right to family benefits;

(b)The right to bank loans, mortgages and other forms of financial credit;

(c)The right to participate in recreational activities, sports and all aspects of cultural life.

Article 14

1.States Parties shall take into account the particular problems faced by rural women and the significant roles which rural women play in the economic survival of their families, including their work in the non-monetized sectors of the economy, and shall take all appropriate measures to ensure the application of the provisions of the present convention to women in rural areas.

2.States Parties shall take all appropriate measures to eliminate discrimination against women in rural areas in order to ensure, on a basis of equality of men and women, that they participate in and benefit from rural development and, in particular, shall ensure to such women the right:

(a)To participate in the elaboration and implementation of development planning at all levels;

(b)To have access to adequate health care facilities, including information, counselling and services in family planning;

(c)To benefit directly from social security programmes;

(d)To obtain all types of training and education, formal and non-formal, including that relating to functional literacy, as well as, inter alia, the benefit of all community and extension services, in order to increase their technical proficiency;

(e)To organize self-help groups and co-operatives in order to obtain equal access to economic opportunities through employment or self-employment;

(f)To participate in all community activities;

(g)To have access to agricultural credit and loans, marketing facilities, appropriate technology and equal treatment in land and agrarian reform as well as in land resettlement schemes;

(h)To enjoy adequate living conditions, particularly in relation to housing, sanitation, electricity and water supply, transport and communications.

Article 15

1.States Parties shall accord to women equality with men before the law.

2.States Parties shall accord to women, in civil matters, a legal capacity identical to that of men and the same opportunities to exercise that capacity. In particular, they shall give women equal rights to conclude contracts and to administer property and shall treat them equally in all stages of procedure in courts and tribunals.

3.States Parties agree that all contracts and all other private instruments of any kind with a legal effect which is directed at restricting the legal capacity of women shall be deemed null and void.

4.States Parties shall accord to men and women the same rights with regard to the law relating to the movement of persons and the freedom to choose their residence and domicile.

Article 16

1.States Parties shall take all appropriate measures to eliminate discrimination against women in all matters relating to marriage and family relations and in particular shall ensure, on a basis of equality of men and women:

(a)The same right to enter into marriage;

(b)The same right freely to choose a spouse and to enter into marriage only with their free and full consent;

(c)The same rights and responsibilities during marriage and at its dissolution;

(d)The same rights and responsibilities as parents, irrespective of their marital status, in matters relating to their children; in all cases the interests of the children shall be paramount;

(e)The same rights to decide freely and responsibly on the number and spacing of their children and to have access to the information, education and means to enable them to exercise these rights;

(f)The same rights and responsibilities with regard to guardianship, wardship, trusteeship and adoption of children, or similar institutions where these concepts exist in national legislation; in all cases the interests of the children shall be paramount;

(g)The same personal rights as husband and wife, including the right to choose a family name, a profession and an occupation;

(h)The same rights for both spouses in respect of the ownership, acquisition, management, administration, enjoyment and disposition of property, whether free of charge or for a valuable consideration.

2.The betrothal and the marriage of a child shall have no legal effect, and all necessary action, including legislation, shall be taken to specify a minimum age for marriage and to make the registration of marriages in an official registry compulsory.

Article 17

1.For the purpose of considering the progress made in the implementation of the present Convention, there shall be established a Committee on the Elimination of Discrimination against Women (hereinafter referred to as the Committee) consisting, at the time of entry into force of the Convention, of eighteen and, after ratification of or accession to the Convention by the thirty-fifth State Party, of twenty-three experts of high moral standing and competence in the field covered by the Convention. The experts shall be elected by States Parties from among their nationals and shall serve in their personal capacity, consideration being given to equitable geographical distribution and to the representation of the different forms of civilization as well as the principal legal systems.

2.The members of the Committee shall be elected by secret ballot from a list of persons nominated by States Parties. Each Party may nominate one person from among its own nationals.

3.The initial election shall be held six months after the date of the entry into force of the present Convention. At least three months before the date of each election, the Secretary General of the United Nations shall address a letter to the States Parties inviting them to submit their nominations within two months. The Secretary General shall prepare a list in alphabetical order of all persons thus nominated, indicating the States Parties which have nominated them, and shall submit it to the States Parties.

4.Elections of the members of the Committee shall be held at a meeting of States Parties convened by the Secretary General at United Nations Headquarters. At that meeting, for which two thirds of the States Parties shall constitute a quorum, the persons elected to the Committee shall be those nominees who obtain the largest number of votes and an absolute majority of the votes of the representatives of States Parties present and voting.

5.The members of the Committee shall be elected for a term of four years. However, the terms of nine of the members elected at the first election shall expire at the end of two years; immediately after the first election the names of these nine members shall be chosen by lot by the Chairman of the Committee.

6.The election of the five additional members of the Committee shall be held in accordance with the provisions of paragraphs 2,3 and 4 of this article, following the thirty-fifth ratification or accession. The terms of two of the additional members elected on this occasion shall expire at the end of two years, the names of these two members having been chosen by lot by the Chairman of the Committee.

7.For the filling of casual vacancies, the State Party whose expert has ceased to function as a member of the Committee shall appoint another expert from among its nationals, subject to the approval of the Committee.

8.The members of the Committee shall, with the approval of the General Assembly, receive emoluments from United Nations resources on such terms and conditions as the Assembly may decide, having regard to the importance of the Committee's responsibilities.

9.The Secretary-General of the United Nations shall provide the necessary staff and facilities for the effective performance of the functions of the Committee under the present Convention.

Article 18

1.States Parties undertake to submit to the Secretary General of the United Nations, for consideration by the Committee, a report on the legislative, judicial, administrative or other measures which they have adopted to give effect to the provisions of the present Convention and on the progress made in this respect:

(a)Within one year after the entry into force for the State concerned;

(b)Thereafter at least every four years and further whenever the Committee so requests.

2.Reports may indicate factors and difficulties affecting the degree of fulfilment of obligations under the present Convention.

Article 19

1.The Committee shall adopt its own rules of procedure.

2.The Committee shall elect its officers for a term of two years.

Article 20

1.The Committee shall normally meet for a period of not more than two weeks annually in order to consider the reports submitted in accordance with article 1 S of the present Convention.

2.The meetings of the Committee shall normally be held at United Nations Headquarters or at any other convenient place as determined by the Committee. .

Article 21

1.The Committee shall, through the Economic and Social Council, report annually to the General Assembly of the United Nations on its activities and may make suggestions and general recommendations based on the examination of reports and information received from the States Parties. Such suggestions and general recommendations shall be included in the report of the Committee together with comments, if any, from States Parties.

2.The Secretary General of the United Nations shall transmit the reports of the Committee to the Commission on the status of Women for its information.

Article 22

The specialized agencies shall be entitled to be represented at the consideration of the implementation of such provisions of the present Convention as fall within the scope of their activities. The committee may invite the specialized agencies to submit reports on the implementation of the Convention in areas falling within the scope of their activities.

Article 23 Nothing in the present Convention shall affect any provisions that are more conducive to the achievement of equality between men and women which may be contained:

(a)In the legislation of a State Party; or

(b)In any other international convention, treaty or agreement in force for that State.

Article 24 States Parties undertake to adopt all necessary measures at the national level aimed at achieving the full realization of the rights recognized in the present Convention.

Article 25

1.The present Convention shall be open for signature by all States.

2.The Secretary-General of the United Nations is designated as the depositary of the present Convention.

3.The present Convention is subject to ratification. Instruments of ratification shall be deposited with the Secretary-General of the United Nations.

4.The present Convention shall be open to accession by all States. Accession shall be effected by the deposit of an instrument of accession with the Secretary General of the United Nations.

Article 26

1.A request for the revision of the present Convention may be made at any time by any State Party by means of a notification in writing addressed to the Secretary-General of the United Nations.

2.The General Assembly of the United Nations shall decide upon the steps, if any, to be taken in respect of such a request.

Article 27

1.The present Convention shall enter into force on the thirtieth day after the deposit with the Secretary General of the United Nations of the twentieth instrument of ratification or accession.

2.For each State ratifying the present Convention or acceding to it after the deposit of the twentieth instrument of ratification or accession, the Convention shall enter into force on the thirtieth day after the date of the deposit of its own instrument of ratification or accession.

Article 28

1.The Secretary General of the United Nations shall receive and circulate to all States the text of reservations made by States at the time of ratification or accession.

2.A reservation incompatible with the object and purpose of the present Convention shall not be permitted.

3.Reservations may be withdrawn at any time by notification to this effect addressed to the Secretary-General of the United Nations, who shall then inform all States thereof. Such notification shall take effect on the date on which it is received.

Article 29

1.Any dispute between two or more States Parties concerning the interpretation or application of the present Convention which is not settled by negotiation shall, at the request of one of them, be submitted to arbitration. If within six months from the date of the request for arbitration, the Parties are unable to agree on the organization of the arbitration, any one of those parties may refer the dispute to the International Court of Justice by request in conformity with the statute of the Court.

2.Each State Party may at the time of signature or ratification of the present Convention or accession thereto declare that it does not consider itself bound by paragraph 1 of this article. The other States Parties shall not be bound by that paragraph with respect to any State Party which has made such a reservation.

3.Any State Party which has made a reservation in accordance with paragraph 2 of this article may at any time withdraw that reservation by notification to the Secretary General of the United Nations.

Article 30 The present Convention, the Arabic, Chinese. English, French, Russian and Spanish texts of which are equally authentic, shall be deposited with the Secretary-General of the United Nations.

In Witness Whereof the undersigned, duly authorized, have signed the present Convention.

Declaration on the Elimination of Discrimination against Women

The General Assembly,

Considering that the peoples of the United Nations have, in the Charter, reaffirmed their faith in fundamental human rights, in the dignity and worth of the human person and in the equal rights of men and women,

Considering that the Universal Declaration on Human Rights asserts the principle of non-discrimination and proclaims that all human beings are born free and equal in dignity and rights and that everyone is entitled to all the rights and freedoms set forth therein without distinction of any kind, including any distinction as to sex,

Taking into account the resolutions, declarations, conventions and recommendations of the United Nations and the specialized agencies designed to eliminate all forms of discrimination and to promote equal rights for men and women,

Concerned that, despite the Charter of the United Nations the Universal Declaration of Human Rights, the International Covenants on Human Rights and other instruments of the United Nations and the specialized agencies and despite the progress made in the matter of equality of rights, there continues to exist considerable discrimination against women,

Considering that discrimination against women is incompatible with human dignity and with the welfare of the family and of society, prevents their participation, on equal terms with men, in the political, social, economic and cultural life of their countries and is an obstacle to the full development of the potentialities of women in the service of their countries and of humanity,

Bearing in mind the great contribution made by women to social, political, economic and cultural life and the part they play in the family and particularly in the rearing of children,

Convinced that the full and complete development of a country, the welfare of the world and the cause of peace require the maximum participation of women as well as men in all fields,

Considering that it is necessary to ensure the universal recognition in law and in fact of the principle of equality of men and women, Solemnly proclaims this declaration:

Article 1 Discrimination against women, denying or limiting as it does their equality of rights with men, is fundamentally unjust and constitutes an offence against human dignity.

Article 2 All appropriate measures shall be taken to abolish existing laws, customs, regulations and practices which are discriminatory against women, and to establish adequate legal protection for equal rights of men and women, in particular

(a)The principle of equality of rights shall be embodied in the constitution or otherwise guaranteed by law;

(b)The international instruments of the United Nations and the specialized agencies relating to the elimination of discrimination against women shall be ratified or acceded to and fully implemented as soon as practicable.

Article 3 All appropriate measures shall be taken to educate public opinion and to direct national aspirations towards the eradication of prejudice and the abolition of customary and all other practices which are based on the idea of the inferiority of women.

Article 4 All appropriate measures shall be taken to ensure to women on equal terms with men, without any discrimination:

(a)The right to vote in all elections and be eligible for election to all publicly elected oodles;

(b)The right to vote in all public referenda;

(c)The right to hold public office and to exercise all public functions.

Such rights shall be guaranteed by legislation.

Article 5 Women shall have the same rights as men to acquire, change or retain their nationality. Marriage to an alien shall not automatically affect the nationality of the wife either by rendering her stateless or by forcing upon her the nationality of her husband.

Article 6

1.Without prejudice to the safeguarding of the unity and the harmony of the family, which remains the basic unit of any society, all appropriate measures, particularly legislative measures, shall be taken to ensure to women, married, or unmarried, equal rights with men in field of civil law, and in particular:

(a)The right to acquire, administer, enjoy, dispose of and inherit property, including property acquired during marriage;

(b)The right to equality in legal capacity and the exercise thereof;

(c)The same rights as men and with regard to the law on the movement of persons.

2.All appropriate measures shall be taken to ensure the principle of equality of status of the husband and wife, and in particular:

(a)Women shall have the same right as men to free choice of a spouse and to enter into marriage only with their free and full consent;

(b)Women shall have equal rights with men during marriage and at its dissolution. In all cases the interest of the children shall be paramount;

(c)Parents shall have equal rights and duties in matters relating to their children. In all cases the interest of the children shall be paramount.

3.Child marriage and the betrothal of young girls before puberty shall be prohibited, and effective action, including legislation, shall be taken to specify a minimum age for marriage and to make the registration of marriages in an official registry compulsory.

Article 7 All provisions of penal codes which constitute discrimination against women shall be repealed.

Article 8 All appropriate measures, including legislation, shall be taken to combat all forms of traffic in women and exploitation of prostitution of women.

Article 9 All appropriate measures shall be taken to ensure to girls and women, married or unmarried, equal rights with men in education at all levels, and in particular:

(a) Equal conditions of access to, and study in educational institutions of all types, including universities and vocational, technical and professional schools;

(b)The same choice of curricula, the same examinations, teaching staff with qualifications of the same standard, and school premises and equipment of the same quality, whether the institutions are co-educational or not;

(c)Equal opportunities to benefit from scholarships and other study grants;

(d)Equal opportunities for access to programmes of continuing education, including adult literacy programmes;

(e)Access to educational information to help in ensuring the health and well-being of families.

Article 10

1.All appropriate measures shall be taken to ensure to women, married or unmarried, equal rights with men in the field of economic and social life, and in particular:

(a)The right, without discrimination on grounds of marital status or any other grounds, to receive vocational training, to work, to free choice of profession and employment, and to professional and vocational advancement;

(b)The right to equal remuneration with men and to equality of treatment in respect of work of equal value;

(c)The right to leave with pay, retirement privileges and provision for security in respect of unemployment, sickness, old age or other incapacity to work;

(d)The right to receive family allowances on equal terms with men.

2.In order to prevent discrimination against women on account of marriage or maternity and to ensure their effective right to work, measures shall be taken to prevent their dismissal in the event of marriage or maternity and to provide paid maternity leave, with the guarantee of returning to former employment, and to provide the necessary social services, including child-care facilities.

Recommendation on consent to marriage, minimum age for marriage and registration of marriages

The General Assembly, recognizing that the family group should be strengthened because it is the basic unit of every society, and that men and women of full age have the right to marry and to found a family, that they are entitled to equal rights as to marriage and that marriage shall be entered into only with the free and full consent of the intending spouses, in accordance with the provisions of article 16 of the Universal Declaration of Human Rights, Recalling its resolution 843(IX) of 17 December 1954,

Recalling further article 2 of the Supplementary Convention on the Abolition of Slavery, the Slave Trade, and Institutions and Practices Similar to Slavery of 1956, which makes certain provisions concerning the age of marriage, consent to marriage and registration of marriages,

Recalling also that Article 13, paragraph lb. of the Charter of the United Nations provides that the General Assembly shall make recommendations for the purpose of assisting in the realization of human rights and fundamental freedoms for all without distinction as to race, sex, language or religion,

Recalling likewise that, under Article 64 of the Charter, the Economic and Social Council may make arrangements with the Members of the United Nations to obtain reports on the steps taken to give effect to its own recommendations and to recommendations on matters falling within its competence made by the General Assembly,

1.Recommends, that, where not already provided by existing legislative or other measures, each Member State should take the necessary steps, in accordance with its constitutional processes and its traditional and religious practices, to adopt such legislative or other measures as may be appropriate to give effect to the following principles:

Principle I

(a)No marriage shall be legally entered into without the full and free consent of both the parties, such consent to be expressed by them in person, after due publicity and in the presence of the authority competent to solemnize the marriage and of witnesses, as prescribed by law,

(b)Marriage by proxy shall be permitted only when the competent authorities are satisfied that each party has, before a competent authority and in such manner as may be prescribed by law, fully and freely expressed consent before witnesses and not withdrawn such consent.

Principle II

Member States shall take legislative action to specify a minimum age for marriage, which in any case shall not be less than fifteen years of age; no marriage shall be legally entered into by any person under this age, except where a competent authority has granted a dispensation as to age, for serious reasons, in the interest of the intending spouses.

Principle III

All marriages shall be registered in an appropriate official register by the competent authority.

2.Recommends that each Member State should bring the Recommendations on Consent to Marriage, Minimum Age for Marriage and Registration of Marriages contained in the present resolution before the authorities competent to enact legislation or to take other action at the earliest practicable moment and, if possible, not later than eighteen months after the adoption of the Recommendation;

3.Recommends that Member States should inform the Secretary General, as soon as possible after the action referred to in paragraph 2 above, of the measures taken under the present Recommendation to bring it before the competent authority or authorities, with particulars regarding the authority or authorities considered as competent;

4.Recommends further that Member States should report to the Secretary General at the end of three years, and thereafter at intervals of five years, on their law and practice with regard to the matters dealt within the present Recommendation, showing the extent to which effect has been given or is proposed to be given to the provisions of the Recommendation and such modifications as have been found or may be found necessary in adapting or applying it;

5.Requests the Secretary General to prepare for the Commission on the Status of Women a document containing the reports received from Governments concerning methods of implementing the three basic principles of the present Recommendation;

6.Invites the Commission on the Status of Women to examine the reports received from Member States pursuant to the present Recommendation and to report thereon to the Economic and Social Council with such recommendations as it may deem fitting.

# Twenty One

# Legal Protection

Fundamental rights which every man or woman should be entitled to by virtue of having been born as a human being constitute what are called Human Rights. Human Rights propagate the concept of non-discrimination and equality. Whereas women represent more than half of the world's population and are engaged in work that contributes immensely to the life and wealth of nations, they are subjected to gender discrimination at work, in their homes, and in every sphere of human activity. This situation will have to change one day, else this exploitation and subjugation will continue thus adversely effecting the social fabric in time to come.

In the recent Dravidian and Aryan cultures, women had free access to educational opportunities and discrimination on the basis of sex was unknown. Women rose to high positions during Dravidian and Aryan culture in different disciplines and *brahmaradinis* like Gargi challenged great men and scholars in learned discourses on equal grounds. This was the status of women in the ancient times. Woman was the *sahadharmi* equal partner in the performance of *dharm*, the righteous duties in life.

It has been said by various scholars that only when women are educated and respected will the world emerge prosperous. This world may be as small as the family or as large as the nation — it implies for all. The subjugation of women started in the Smriti period. Manu and Yagna Valkya subscribed a subordinate social role to women. The degradation of women's position was reflected in customs relating to marriage, religion and property where socio-economic freedom was denied to them. They were expected to be under the "protective control" of the father, husband and son. This deterioration continued during the medieval and British periods.

Apart from the Dravidian and Aryan civilization where women were respected, the past of Indian women is the story of subjugation. During India's 5000 years of civilization, its history has to a great extent been "his" story. Women by and large led circumscribed lives. The nineteenth century was one of social reformers who highlighted the problems faced by women — the horrors of *devdasis*, child marriage, child widows and female exclusion, they included Raja Ram Mohun Roy, Ishwar Chandra Vidya Sagar and enlightened Westerners such as Macaulay, William Bentinck and Marcus Puller. A few Indian women writers in the latter part of the nineteenth century and beginning of twentieth century wrote about women and their experiences. But these have been largely about educated women, the elite, the Brahmins, or about women who participated in the political struggle.

The freedom movement brought in a new dimension to this struggle. Gandhiji with his foresight comprehended that only with the active participation of women, could every Indian home be turned into a bastion of the freedom struggle. The manner in which hundreds and thousands of women shed their veils and left their sheltered homes to come into the street to fight side by side in the struggle with their brothers and often put to shame their menfolk was a landmark in the political and social history of India.

The twentieth century, particularly after Independence saw the Indian women bring in a number of achievements to their credit. In all fields of higher learning — engineering, nuclear physics, computer sciences, administration, management, the arts and humanities — women have proved equal to men and have won laurels. It may be a reason to be proud but we cannot ignore the fact that even now 75 per cent of India's over 400 million women are illiterate, invisible and unaware of the going on in the universe. So immersed are they in their daily chores that they have no time to think of what is happening in the world. They are voiceless and subjected to myriad forms of class, caste and gender oppression. Responsible for the pathetic situation of women are the deep-rooted societal and religious traditions. The arbitrary division of male and female roles in society initiate sex-based discrimination and deprivation. Women, by and large have little access to productive resources and control over family income. Ranging from the exclusion of women from development programmes, sex discrimination is seen in wage discrimination and also perpetrates violence against women. A number of laws have been enacted to protect and promote the rights/interests of women, some of which are:

## Pre-Independence Laws Protecting Women's Rights

In the pre-Independence colonial era, the few laws relating to crimes against women were mainly those relating to rape, causing miscarriage, assault on women's modesty, kidnapping/abduction, etc. and offences relating to marriage (all non cognisable). Social legislation for protection of women was even less and was limited to — Sati prohibition, maintenance laws or some laws enabling widow remarriage, etc. Laws relating to property, adoption, divorce, etc. were heavily subscribed by males keeping their interests in mind furthering the inferior or subordinate position of women in society and confirming their superiority over them in all respects.

## Post-Independence Laws Protecting Women's Rights

The post-Independence period witnessed a spate of enactments — criminal, civil and social — besides amendments to some old laws to protect and improve the status of women which came about as a result of the provision in our Constitution on equality in all respects and spheres and non-discrimination on any ground, and even special protection to women and children as part of state policy. The new-found political and social awakening and agitations and movements for women's causes, to which both men and women contributed, gave further impetus to this process of legislation aimed at implementing the philosophy behind the Constitution. (The only exception to this policy would appear to be the Muslim Womens' Protection of Rights on Divorce Act, 1986, apparently an instance of misconceived and miscalculated political opportunism).

These enactments can be divided into two broad categories— those directly relating to checking of violence against women and preventing their exploitation and those aimed at improving their legal and social status.

The first category included the laws relating to domestic violence, which for the first time took cognisance of the concept of mental cruelty besides physical violence, changes in rape laws, laws relating to dowry prohibition and prevention of immoral traffic, 'Sati' indecent representation of women, etc., with some changes in evidence and procedural laws to facilitate their implementation.

The second category included laws relating to woman's/ daughter's share in property, adoption laws, changes in divorce laws, etc. In the criminal laws, the emphasis was mainly on stringent punishments and more helpful procedures. The second category of laws were pursued through institutions of family courts, legal aid bureaus, etc.

*Lacunae and Loopholes in Laws*

Expected to remove various legal lacunae and hurdles, criminal laws were made to provide effective deterrence to violence against women, while those falling in the category of social legislation were meant to work as catalysts for social change. In practice, however, none of the two expectations have been fulfilled. Deterrence in law remains confined to the status book with symbolic convictions and a large majority of cases remaining undisposed of in courts for years together while crimes against women have been showing a continuously increasing trend. Social legislation being relegated to paper only, without any proper awareness about their provisions, either amongst the people or the police. The laws themselves are to be blamed for this ineffective trend in their implementation despite intentions of their framers to the contrary. Often badly conceived and poorly drafted these legislations have many lacunae and loopholes thus exposing inadequacies of the criminal justice system and procedures and lack of public awareness. Generally found missing is the acceptability or support sometimes even positive antipathy — due to the absence of any efforts for public education, either about their provisions or their purpose.

**Dowry Prohibition Act**

With the noble objective of putting a stop to the practice of dowry which had degenerated into one of the worst instruments of exploitation and even extortion, particularly in Hindu society, the Act was brought about in 1961 and was amended twice in 1984 and 1986 to streamline its provisions and make the penalties more deterrent, but continues to be one of the most ineffective laws. Despite the efforts through amendments to remove some of the earlier lacunae several major anomalies still remain. Most of the cases registered fall under the category of Sections (u/s) 4 or 6 of the Act (usually along with Sec. 498-A, IPC) for demand of dowry and harassment or non-return of Dowry/Istridhan by the husband/in-laws reported after the marriage has run aground. A few cases included belong to u/s 3 of the Act for dowry giving and taking before or at the time of marriage even though the Section was specifically amended in 1984 to provide for a stringent minimum punishment of 5 years' imprisonment and

Rs. 15,000 or amount of value of dowry (whichever is more) as fine.

*Objectives of the Act*

The basic objective behind this enactment and subsequent amendments which followed the alarming increase in reported cases of bride burning for dowry in the late seventies and early eighties, was to prevent extortion of dowry.

*Lacunae of the Act*

Even the definition of dowry "any property or valuable security given or agreed to be given" (Sec. 2) emphasizes on 'giving' rather than on the 'demand' or 'extortion' aspect. Demand of dowry is specifically punishable u/s 4 but the validity of this section is under a question mark in view of judgements of two High Courts, Calcutta (*Shankar Pd. Shaw and ors. vs State & ors* - 1991 Cr. : L.J. 639 Calcutta H.C.) and Allahabad (Ramesh Chand vs. State of U.P. - 1992 (3) RCR 511), both holding that in view of the very definition of 'dowry' which has 'giving' or agreement to give as its basic ingredients, mere demand cannot be termed as an offence unless there was 'giving' or 'agreement to give'. The Calcutta High Court had, accordingly even suggested a change in the definition of "dowry u/s 2 of the Act in the light of sub clause (6) u/s 498-A of the Penal Code" if demand for dowry or extortion was proposed to be brought under its ambit. Even otherwise, u/s 3 which makes giving or taking of dowry an offence, both the 'giver' and the 'taker' are placed on a par although the giver, in most of the cases, is a helpless victim of extortion under the evil social custom rather than a willful or conscious offender. Despite all the enactments it is not surprising that only a few cases are reported under this section before or at the time of marriage, even while dowry continues to be given and taken extensively and even openly and spread through the fabric of society.

Difficulties also arise because of other provisions. The term "in connection with marriage" and "in consideration for marriage" used earlier need further clarification. That the demand or payment was "in connection with the marriage", particularly in cases of 'extended' dowry demands/payments after the marriage for example, in the garb of customary gifts/presents on occasions of marriages in the natal or marital families, child births, birthdays and other religious or social festivals/occasions, or on grounds of financing foreign education trips, purchase of house or setting up or expanding of business by the husband, etc. is often difficult to prove especially when they are not 'agreed to be given' at the time of marriage. Section 3(3) while exempting the presents given or taken at the time of marriage to the bride/bridegroom if they are: (i) given without any demand with entry in lists as per rules, (ii) of customary nature and not excessive to the financial status of the giver, provide further loopholes for enforcement because of the impracticability and vagueness of these conditions.

Having been obviously made to save customary gifts given voluntarily and within their means by the parents and other persons of the bride's party out of love and consideration for the daughter from coming under its ambit, this provision excludes from its scope any gifts given before or after the marriage (e.g. on the occasion of *Tika, Sagai* or other ceremonies or child birth etc.) even though they may also be given voluntarily as part of tradition/custom. Even this limited provision is exploited to cover forcible demand or extortion of dowry since the desire of parents of girls, keen to somehow or the other fulfil their filial and social obligation of marrying off their daughter ovrrules the complain of demand of dowry. They do not, in any way, wish to jeopardize the marriage itself or prevent the likelihood of future proposals coming their way, thus putting the girls in worse trouble. Regarding the condition of preparation of lists of dowry gifts, there is a provision framed in this connection by the Central Government (Dowry Prohibition Maintenance of Lists of Presents to the Bride and Bridegroom Rules, 1985) which requires these lists to be prepared and signed by the bride and the bridegroom. As the lists are required to be prepared at the time of or soon after the marriage with full details about the presents and the givers this provision is impractical. Most of the giving and taking of presents at the time of the marriage is done by the parents of the bride and not by the bridegroom who should be the proper persons to be fixed with this responsibility.

Unless made mandatory the inhibitions and apprehensions on the part of parents of the bride in asking for such lists to be prepared or signed by the bridegroom will hamper the very objective of this provision. Under the present social ethos in the Hindu society, no such system has generally prevailed so far (unlike the Muslim community where preparation of such lists, particularly for jewellery and other costly presents, is considered to be a normal and acceptable convention). By making it mandatory with specific rsponsibility, particularly of the receiver (parents of the bridegroom even for gifts received on behalf of the bride) this new practice will be effective in its objective. Provision for mandatory filing of a copy of the lists with the area 'Dowry Prohibition Officer' or 'Marriage Registration Officer' could even be considered.

Due to the aforesaid lacunae, this Act does not curb the practice of giving, taking or demand of dowry before or at the time of marriage or even afterwards. It is not taken recourse to as long as the marriage works or the girl is prepared to suffer quietly. Recourse to this Act is sought in case of breakdown of marriaged or death of the girl by violence, with a large majority of cases being registered u/s 6 of the Act often along with sections 498-A/406, IPC) for return of dowry/ Istridhan.

The 'matrimonial home' after the marriage concept poses difficulties in seeking redressal after breakdown of marriage. Under this Section (Sec. 6) for non/return of dowry/Istridhan articles since the proceedings can be initiated only at the place where the dowry/ Istridhan was given or was due to be transferred to the wife, normally the matrimonial home after the marriage. Since the wife, after the breakdown of the marriage (when only such complaints are normally filed) is generally not staying in the matrimonial home and usually shifts to another place either to stay with her parents or take up a job, etc. she is hardly in a position to pursue the case in the court at the place of her matrimonial home.

Similar lacunae exist in provision (b) under sec. 6(3) of the Act which provides for the property to "be held in trust" for the children of the woman who dies from unnatural causes within seven years of her marriage, pending its transfer to the children (normally when they attain the age of majority). Due to this provision the aggressor husband or in-laws merrily continue to hold the property and enjoy the fruits of their crime on the pretext of keeping the property "in trust" and indulge in other malpractices, thus further perpetrating such crimes.

Therefore, in spite of the protection provided to "the person aggrieved by the offence" (which would include the "giver") u/s 7(3) of the Act, saving such a person from prosecution on the basis of his statement and shifting the onus of proof on the accused u/s 8-A in case of offence u/s 3 or 4, there has been no case under the Act, which has ended in conviction in Delhi, Mumbai and Bangalore up to the time of the study and the all-India rate of conviction had also been only about 5 per cent (between 28 per cent and 36 per cent of decided cases) from 1988-1991, according to *Crime in India* published by NCRB (cases under this Act were not published separately before 1988).

*Provisions of Dowry Prohibition Act*

Section 8-B(1) of the Act provides for appointment of Dowry Prohibition Officers and Section 8-B(4) for constitution of Advisory Boards comprising social workers of the area for advising and assisting such officers. The Dowry Prohibition Officers are to be responsible (u/s 8-B(2)) for compliance with provisions of the Act, preventing demand or taking of dowry and collecting evidence for prosecution of the offenders. They may, for this purpose, be conferred with requisite police powers (Sec. 8-B(3)). Rules for functioning of such officers are to be framed by the State Government u/s 10(2) of the Act. These provisions introduced under 1984 amendments, were deliberately meant to involve the social workers of the area in enforcement of the Act rather than depending on the police alone for curbing the evil of dowry. The few officers who have been appointed do not generally perform any duties with regard to prevention of demand or giving or taking of dowry in the absence of rules which should have been framed by the Central or State Governments for their functioning. Similarly there is absence of Advisory Committees and no area social workers have been appointed at most places nor have any rules been framed for their constitution.

It appears that while the Act was framed and later modified twice with a lot of fanfare under pressure from women's groups and other social workers, not much effort has gone into ensuring its proper enforcement therafter, as is evident from this lack of even basic follow up action in these matters.

Due to the Acts being masterminded by men who form the majority of law makers, there are many places which have been deliberately left untouched so as to give vent to their plans and furtherance of social norms whilst ignoring their misgivings.

*Suggestions for Effective Implementation*

(a)An amendment in definition of dowry so as to bring about a clear-cut picture of demand and giving aspect of dowry. In fact, subjecting the daughter-in-law to threats, harassment or cruelty to coerce her if she does not get 'extended' dowry after the marriage, amounts to 'extortion' which should be treated as an aggravated form of 'dowry demand' carrying a higher punishment. Section 498-A IPC, which covers such cases at present is hardly adequate to deal with this type of crime. A lot of cases where the daughter-in-law is threatened with grievious hurt or death by burning etc. if she does not get further dowry or property, would squarely make out offences u/s 386 or 387 of IPC, punishable with imprisonment up to ten years or seven years respectively, besides fine as against a punishment of up to two years only (with a minimum punishment of 6 months) u/s 4 of Dowry Prohibition Act and three years only u/s 498-A IPC.

(b)Clarification is needed on the term "in connection with the marriage". It should either be deleted entirely or an 'explanation' added to the section. The demand from or giving of any property or valuable security by the party of the bride to the party of the bridegroom 'without any consideration' other than consideration of marriage itself, should be considered as being "in connection with the marriage". The onus for proving any such other consideration being on the receiver/the person demanding such consideration.

(c)Unless and until active initiative or connivance on the part of the given in the transaction is proved, culpability of the "giver" should be limited.

(d)It should be made mandatory for the bridegrooms party to prepare a list of presents to the bride or the bridegroom covered under Section 3 of Dowry Prohibition Act failing which they should be held fully responsible. Incomplete or false lists being made offences. Such lists should be prepared at the time of or within one month of the marriage, signed by both the parties (bride's/ bridegroom's) and a copy thereof given to the bride's parents/ guardians.

(e)The value of gifts should commensurate with the economic standing of the bride's parents. A maximum limit should be prescribed for such gifts. They should be limited to a prescribed proportion of the gross annual income/wealth in case of those assessed for Income or Wealth Tax and a maximum prescribed sum in case of others. Demand or acceptance of dowry above the prescribed maximum should be deemed to be "Dowry extortion" and punishable as such under law.

(f)There should be in-built incentives for proper listing of such gifts or presents wherein:

(i)Such presents up to the prescribed maximum limit should be free of any Gift Tax.

(ii)Source of payment in case of such gifts/presents should not be accountable. A provision for Income Tax rebate u/s 88 of Income Tax Act for such gifts may be made. This suggestion may be opposed on the ground that it will encourage 'black money' as parents could settle for maximum dowry to lighten their tax accruals and also encourage dowry. To fight the tax evaders the government has however, already, been periodically launching schemes for unearthing 'black' or 'tainted' money by allowing declaration or investment in specified schemes without any penal consequences. Relating voluntary gifts to the bride as permissible under the law to a similar scheme would have the merit of making such gifts, which are being given and taken in any case, at least properly accountable and for the benefit and interest of the daughter, not only in affluent but even amongst middle class families, and help in improving social acceptability of the provision, thus making it easier for law to intervene in case of marriage breakups and reclaim for the woman her *streedhan* or any matter connected to it.

(g)As a reimbursement for her share in parental property the gifts should be deductible from her share. Similarly, to put the sons and daughters on a par in this regard, gifts of jewellery or other costly items to the daughter-in-law should be deductible from the share of the son. For this a proper planning of property has to be done so as to prevent problems in the future.

(h)Cognisance of a complaint u/s 6 of the Act should be registered at a place where the wife has been residing continuously for six months or more as it is not possible in case of marriage breakdown for the women to reside in her matrimonial home any more and therefore make her unable to get the case registered there.

(i)To arrest the spirit of unhealthy competition which has entered society regarding dowry gifts, display of dowry should be totally banned.

(j)A curb should be placed on the ostentatious and wasteful expenditure on marriage which is another source of trouble to the not-so-well-off parents of girls. A limit on such expenditure as well as on the size of marriage party/number of guests and entertainment etc. should be strictly enforced.

To implement the Dowry Prohibition Act effectively a team of Dowry Prohibition Officers and Advisory Boards comprising local social workers already provided under the Act should be appointed with proper rules and powers to regulate the functioning of such officers and constitution of the Advisory Boards. The responsibility for preventing any demand or giving or taking of dowry in violation of the provisions of the Act should basically be fixed on such officers. Police should stay out of enforcement in this regard. This is suggested in order to avoid complaints of malpractices even though they should remain fully responsible for handling cases of dowry-related violence or deaths. Requisite powers of a police officer should be conferred on Dowry Prohibition Officers in terms of section 8-B(3) of the Act. Under Section 7, cognisance of offences under the Act can be taken, inter alia, on a complaint from any 'recognised' Welfare Institution or Organisation. The recognition for the purpose should be accorded by the Central or the State Governments. Proper rules for grant of such recognition should be framed to ensure effective and responsible functioning of such organisations/institutions and provide motivation and incentive to the more active and responsible ones among them.

In sum, 'dowry' as discussed elsewhere in the study, is a complex social problem closely related to the matter of the daughter's share in the parental property. The practice can as such be checked basically through cooperation from society and public education after taking steps to effectively ensure that the daughter actually gets her share. The thrust of criminal law needs to be on curbing 'dowry extortion' through exploitation, harassment and cruelty which is totally indefensible. The above suggestions have been made to facilitate the achieving of this objective. The amendments to the law should be accompanied by an extensive campaign to educate the public, both about the objectives of the law as well as the substance of provisions and punishments provided under the Act, and strict enforcement thereof as part of a well-defined and unambiguous clear public policy. The important role which the media — print and electronic can play in safeguarding and promoting the interests of women is no doubt worth mentioning laws relating to 'Dowry Deaths' and dowry related 'cruelty' by Husband/his Relatives, are discussed below under head 'Domestic Violence'.

**Domestic Violence**

Domestic violence against married women — wife beating and harassment, sometimes even wife murders — arises from various causes. Legislative measures were introduced as late as 1983 and 1986 to bring domestic violence against married women specifically within the ambit of criminal law. Earlier there were no specific legal provisions for dealing with such gender-related violence within the home which was covered only under the general laws relating to murder, homicide, abetment to suicide, hurt, assault, wrongful confinement, etc. In cases of wife harassment or battering, cognisance and action by the police depended on the nature of physical injury caused or the weapon used. Cases not involving grievious injury as defined under Section 320 IPC or use of dangerous weapon or means or poison in terms of Section 324 IPC fell in the category of non-cognisable offences in which no cognisance or action could be taken by the police except with the magistrate's permission.

The main provisions/amendments are discussed below:

*1. Murders of married women by husband/in-laws or suicides as a result of cruelty or harassment by them*

Such cases were earlier dealt with u/s 302 IPC (murder) or 306 IPC (abetment to suicide). The evidence of the standard as required under criminal law (proof beyond doubt) in such crimes which normally occurs within the privacy of the matrimonial home with no witnesses other than the perpetrators of the crime or their associates present is hard to get. It is sometimes difficult even to establish whether it is a case of 'murder' or 'suicide'. Convictions accordingly u/s 302 or 306 IPC in such cases were an exception, if at all. The basic strategy followed in legal amendments to get over this problem and facilitate successful prosecutions in such cases has been to shift the burden of proof on to the accused. The amendments made were as follows:

*(i) Section 304-B, IPC (Dowry Deaths)*

*(enacted under Act No. 43 of 1986)*

The Section, unique to the Indian penal law to deal with a crime typical to Indian society, introduced a new offence in the penal code viz. 'dowry death'. The term covers any death of a married woman which satisfies three basic criteria:

(a)under unnatural circumstances;

(b)within seven years of marriage; and

(c)preceded by cruelty or harassment by the husband or any of his relatives in connection with demand for 'dowry' (as defined under Dowry Prohibition Act).

The Section provides for a presumption of 'guilt' against the husband/his relatives in case of death of a woman in such circumstances and lays down a minimum punishment of seven years, extendable to life imprisonment. The provision for presumption under this Section was further reinforced u/s 113/B introduced in the Evidence Act in 1986 providing specifically for a statutory presumption of 'causing dowry death' against a person subjecting a woman to cruelty or harassment in connection with dowry demand soon before her death. This Section is in addition to the earlier provisions u/s 302 and 306, IPC, covering both homicidal and suicidal deaths and can be invoked where no direct evidence is available to substantiate a charge of murder against the offenders but 'unnatural' death follows dowry — demand — related harassment/cruelty, evidence basically required being about such cruelty. Cases where specific evidence is available are still to be dealt u/s 302 or 306 IPC, depending on the nature and circumstances of death.

*(ii) Section 306 IPC (Abetment to Suicide)/113-A Evidence Act*

While no amendment was made to Section 306 IPC itself which is taken recourse to for prosecuting the offenders for abetment in case of suicide by a married woman as a result of cruelty or harassment by the husband or in-laws, etc., to get over the difficulty in getting evidence to satisfy the essential ingredients of willful, 'instigation', 'conspiracy' or 'intentional aiding' for constituting 'abetment' in terms of Sec. 107 IPC, and to facilitate successful prosecution under the section, a new section (113-A) was introduced in the Evidence Act in 1983 (Act No. 46) providing for presumption of abetment to suicide against the husband/his relatives where the wife commits suicide within seven years of marriage following cruelty by them. Unlike Sec. 304-B IPC, this section is applicable only to cases of suicide but is not confined to dowry related cases and covers suicides by married women following 'cruelty' or 'harassment' for reasons other than dowry demand.

*(iii) Section 174(3) and 176 Cr. P.C. (Inquest Reports)*

These amendments to the existing provisions were made basically to streamline and further tighten the procedure for enquiries into suicides/unnatural deaths of women within seven years of marriage by making examination of the dead body by a doctor (sub-section (3) of Sec. 174 Cr. P.C.) and magisterial enquiry, either instead of or in addition to police investigation (Sec. 176, Cr. P.C.) mandatory. Amendment to Sec. 176, Cr. P.C. also provided for the relatives of the deceased in such cases to be informed and being allowed to remain present at such enquiries by a Magistrate.

The facilitating provisions and shifting of the burden of proof on the accused and streamlining of procedures for investigations/enquiries in such cases have not had any positive results. Due to lack of public support and ooperation and loopholes present, there has been no hange in statistics related to dowry.

*Convictions and Aquittals*

In Delhi, only 4 (0.7%) cases of dowry deaths had ended in conviction with acquittals 20 (4%) and in Mumbai, only in one case (0.3%) there was conviction with 6 (2%) acquittals till the time of collection of information for the study. Bangalore was better with 23 (5%) convictions with 57 (12%) acquittals. In respect of cases under Dowry (Prohibition) Act, and in dowry deaths also, there was heavy pendency — 91 per cent in Delhi, 88 per cent in Mumbai and 76 per cent in Bangalore.

*Causes of Failures*

The reasons for these failures, however, are not caused by the laws themselves but mostly elsewhere. Even though the amended laws presume guilt against the accused in cases of unnatural deaths within seven years of marriage, the basic requirement for raising this presumption, namely, dowry demand and cruelty or harassment in that connection (or for any other reason u/s 306 IPC) soon before the death has itself been difficult to prove. The reason being the extreme reluctance on the part of the women and their parents to report such earlier demands or cruelty/harassment often till the very end (after the death), and gross lack of awareness of legal requirements of such cases among the public. Besides a substantial number of cases where the main witnesses, mostly the parents and other close relatives of the deceased turn hostile during trials under various pressures, as is evident from case studies of acquitted cases. Indifferent, even shoddy, investigation of cases and inconsistent attitude of the courts sometimes further compound the situation, thus the law is not only to be blamed.

These amended and liberalised laws themselves have come under some criticism from the more radical among women activists. The restriction on the period for drawing the statutory presumption against the accused may by far be fair but it should not be forgotten that eventhough majority of such deaths take place within the period of seven years their occurrence afterwards is not unknown, where the violence starts much earlier. These provisions may not, in fact, be of much help if the woman/her parents have continued to bear the violence/harassment without any resistance or action for seven years. Any further relaxation regarding requirements of evidence can only make a mockery of the judicial system and throw the flood-gates open for exploitation and misuse of these provisions. The remedy would lie not in doing away with all evidence but educating women and their parents to recognise the storm signals of violence and be on their toes in time and take timely action, including reports to the police, the National Commission State Commissions for Women, voluntary organisations, panchayats, etc. before it gets too late. Such action may if not save the victim at least help to provide the required evidence for successful action against the guilty.

**Suggestions for Improvement in Laws**

Some suggestions for improvements in laws did, however, emerge during the study which might help in making them more purposeful:

1. To make the provision more rational and avoid any pitfalls arising from the definition of 'dowry' as discussed earlier. It is suggested to substitute the term "any demand for dowry" u/s 304 B(1) IPC by the term "any unlawful demand for any property or valuable security" (b) for "cruelty u/s 498-A IPC and deletion of explanation of the term dowry under the sub-section.

2. A suggestion for representative of the Social Welfare Department or any recognised non-governmental organization of the area, in addition to other respectables of the neighbourhood, in enquiries both u/s 174 and 176, Cr. P.C. was met with resistance from a majority of police officers during the study but is expected to help in improving the credibility of such enquiries and will improve coordination between NGOs and police. Every care should be taken in associating NGOs with a proven track record and enjoying the trust of the community. They should have transparency and full accountability in their functioning.

3. Regarding post-mortem examinations there were statutory provision under sub-section (3) (v) of section 174, Cr.P.C.; or rules made by the state governments under this sub-section, for the examination of the body in such cases to be conducted by a team of at least two doctors, to replace the executive instructions of the Home Ministry on 22 July 1980 addressed to all State Governments and Union Territory Administrations which are not often complied with. The date of marriage should be given in all requests for post-mortem examination or even a separate colour-coding given to forms in such cases to enable the doctors conducting post mortem examination to know about the applicability of this provision.

4. Specific provision under Cr. P.C. or Dowry Prohibition Act on the lines of Section 5A of Prevention of Corruption Act. The Act provides for Investigation of cases of 'dowry deaths' or suicides (u/s 304-B or 302 or 306 IPC) in case of unnatural death or suicide of a married woman within seven years of marriage, to be conducted by an officer not below the rank of Inspector. This should replace the earlier executive instructions of the Ministry of Home Affairs for investigation of such cases by officers not below the rank of Dy. S.P. issued on 22 July 1980 referred to above.

*Wife beating and harassment u/s 498 — A I.P.C. (cruelty by husband or his relatives)*

This Section, introduced in 1983 (Act No. 46), makes such 'cruelty' a specific cognisable offence punishable with imprisonment up to three years and fine. The offence is 'non bailable' under the entry in the First Schedule of Cr. P.C. for this section and 'non compoundable' because of non-inclusion of this section in the list of 'compoundable offences' u/s 320 of the Cr.P.C. Even 'mental cruelty' under specified circumstances has become actionable under this provision.

The definition of 'cruelty' in the 'Explanation' under this section is in two parts, part (i) to cover conduct unconnected with dowry demand but depending on its consequences or likely consequences; and part (ii) to specifically deal with harassment relating to 'any unlawful demand for property or valuable security' — 'dowry demand' in common parlance though the use of the term has been wisely avoided.

*Cognisance of Offences*

Cognisance of offences under this Section by the Court is, however, restricted u/s 198-A Cr.P.C., also introduced by amendments under Act No. 46 of 1983, only upon a police report or a complaint by the aggrieved person or specified relatives (father, mother, brother, sister, father's or mother's brother or sister) or with the leave of the court, any other person related by blood, marriage or adoption. Cognisance by police has also been restricted under Col. 4 of the entry under this section in the First Schedule of Cr.P.C. (amended in 1983) on the basis of report by the aggrieved person or a person related by blood, marriage or adoption, or, in the absence of any such relative by a public servant of the class or category notified by the State Government for the purpose (No such notification had been issued by the concerned State Governments till the time of the study). Neither the Magistrate nor the police can take cognisance of an offence under this section on their own information or report or information from any other source.

*Main Thrust of the Provision*

While the provision would appear to cover all types of domestic violence, dowry-related or from other causes, with the background of public and media concern over increasing incidence of 'bride burnings' and suicides by girls and married women, the main thrust of this provision too is on combating property (dowry) demand related harassment and violence.

*Attitude of Society*

The attitude of ambivalence, both in society and in law towards domestic violence, excepting when it is related to 'dowry demand' or results in serious consequences — death or grievous injury, etc., is the basic reason for efforts and measures to curb such violence remaining ineffective in spite of all the legal amendments. What is required is a clear and unambiguous message that such violence in marital relationship, whatever its nature, extent or causation, is unacceptable. Unless the prevailing social notion of the wife being the husband's property, which can be ill-treated or abused as he likes is removed, there is no chance of ending marital violence against women. The women should ensure proper, timely action and provide ample scope for proof that the crime is being perpetrated only then can be the offender to be punished and discouraged from initiating such violence in future.

*Rape*

The offence of rape is the ultimate violation of the self and the most humiliating event in a woman's life. This is particularly so when the victim happens to be a young girl raped, within or outside her home, molested and beaten she has no option but to cope in silence. The social dimensions of rape have a special relevance and significance in harbouring such crimes in future. The girl is slienced due to social stigma which makes the offender have no fear whatsoever in repeating such an act. It is not only the victim, but her entire family which suffers in one way or the other deprived of any formal support whether financial, social or psychological; police investigations merely add to the trauma. The end result is that whereas the victim cannot conceal her shame a man can successfully hide his sin.

Mere statistics or laws do not explain the dimensions of this problem. There have been various case studies and interviews with police officers, lawyers and women's groups which have helped in understanding and analysing the various dimensions of the problem. On the persistent demand of women's groups and social activists, the Indian Penal Code was amended in 1983, providing for more stringent punishment for rape. However, according to government statistics, incidents of rape have over the years reached menacing proportions thereby demonstrating not just the inefficacy of the partly, changed law but also the warped nature of the machinery designed to implement it. While the social stigma attached to rape is deterrence enough to reporting such crimes, the callous attitude of the police which puts the victim through most gruelling and embarrassing interrogation, also prevents women from seeking the help of the law. Men as law makers and in positions of power have been lenient to such crimes and have further helped in perpetrating the crime. The rape victims hopes of getting any kind of justice have further been stifled. It is because of these circumstances that rape is the most under reported crime, "out of every case that comes to light 20 go unrecorded" says Ms. Pramila Dandavate, of Mahila Dakshata Samiti a well known Delhi based NGO.

The Special Cell to deal with crimes against women set up by the Delhi Police at Nanak Pura has no comprehensive data on rape. If this is the story of New Delhi, then where is the hope for smaller towns and villages. This is because rape cases are dealt with by different police stations and not necessarily referred to them. In Mumbai too the number of rape cases has been rising over the years. The police officers believe it is largely the result of love affairs where the young couple indulge in sex on the sly. Some social workers feel that in a majority of cases the rapist is known to the victims. However, it would be wrong to take a simplistic view and evade such gruesome acts.

The Indian Evidence Act, still permits the character of the victim to be used as a defence, and thereby undercuts the positive amendments to the Indian Penal Code. In any case Section 376 of the IPC, which lays down a minimum punishment of ten years' rigorous punishment and even a life term applies only to custodial rape, of a girl under twelve and gang rape.

*Punishment, Arrests and Convictions*

Shri L.K. Advani, present Union Minister of Home Affairs has suggested capital punishment for rapists. While the National Commission for Women has supported the Minister, several women's organisations and individual activists hold a different view. According to them, if the death penalty is made mandatory, trials will continue for a long time and judges will be reluctant to award the sentence. According to Ms. Indira Jai Singh, a well known lawyer "It is not the severity of the punishment but its certainty that deters a crime. And also the most important view is not how the guilty is punished but to what extent the crimes of rape and other violence against women can be prevented". She is highly critical of the Indian system of administration of justice which is heavily loaded against the victim. Accordingly, to rough estimates, out of an averge of 3,50,000 sexual assault cases filed in courts all over the country the number of accused arrested was less than 2,00,000 and those convicted a mere 33,000.

A review of laws dealing with women has been taken up by the Law Commission and the National Commission for Women with the assistance of lawyers and women's organizations.

A draft is being prepared by the National Commission for Women on the amendments to the obsolete rape laws. The proposals under consideration include public shaming/ostracization of the accused, enhancement of punishment where the accused is also HIV positive and has passed on the infection to the victim. Other suggestions proposed by NCW are insertion of a statutory provision in the rape laws to allow adequate compensation, and provision for counselling for the victims. The exercise is an outcome of years of concerted effort of women activists across the country who have been advocating a complete overhaul of the rape laws. Such suggestions hold weight and have been made after years of research on laws dealing with women. Only if they are kept in mind in future will we have any hope for a change for the better in future.

As many as 20 offences under the Indian Penal Code and Local and special laws are considered broadly to be crimes against women:

*A. Offences Affecting the Human Body*

1.Abetting the commission of suicide (Sec. 306 IPC).

2.Molestation (Sec. 354 IPC).

3.Kidnapping, abduction or inducing a woman to compel her marriage etc. (Sec. 364/366 IPC).

4.Procuration of minor girl (Sec. 366-A IPC).

5.Importation of girls (Sec. 366-B IPC).

6.Selling minor for purposes of prostitution (Sec. 372 IPC).

7.Buying minor for purposes of prostitution (Sec. 373 IPC).

8.Rape (Sec. 376 IPC).

9.Unnatural offence, involving women (Sec. 377 IPC).

*B. Offences Against Property*

10.Chain snatching (Sec. 356 and Sec. 392 IPC).

*C Offences Relating to Marriage*

11.Marrying again during the life time of wife (Sec. 494 IPC).

12.Adultery (Sec. 497 IPC).

13.Enticing or taking away or detaining with criminal intent a married women (Sec. 498 IPC).

*D. Offences Relating to Criminal Intimidation, Insult and Annoyance*

14.Uttering any word, making any gesture or act intended to insult the modesty of women (Sec. 509 IPC).

*E. Suppression of Immoral Traffic of Women and Girls Act*

15.Punishment for keeping a brothel or allowing premises to be used as a brothel (Sec. 3 of Suppression of Immoral Traffic in Women and Girls Act—SITA).

16.Procuring, inducing or taking a woman or girl for the sake of prostitution (Sec. 5 of SIT Act).

17.Detaining woman or girl in premises where prostitution is carried on (Sec. 6 of SIT Act).

18.Seducing a girl for purpose of prostitution (Sec. 8 of SIT Act).

19.Seduction of a woman or girl in custody (Sec. 9 of SIT Act).

*F. Dowry Act*

20.Penalty for demanding dowry (Sec. 4 of Dowry Prohibition Act 1961).

In all, we selected only five important crimes for our study, viz. (i) Rape or Seduction, (ii) Kidnapping and abduction, (iii) Dowry deaths, (iv) Wife battering, and (v) Eve-teasing which take prominent place in media.

# APPENDICES

## INCIDENCE AND RATE OF CRIME COMMITTED AGAINST WOMEN IN STATES AND UTs

| Sl. No. | State/UT | Incidence of Total COG. Crimes | Percentage Contribution To All-India Total | Estimated Mid-Year Population (In Lakhs) | Rate of Total COG. Crimes | Rank* | Rank** |
|---|---|---|---|---|---|---|---|
| (1) | (2) | (3) | (4) | (5) | (6) | (7) | (8) |
| ***States*** | | | | | | | |
| 1. | Andhra Pradesh | 11201 | 8.5 | 741.7 | 15.1 | 9 | 6 |
| 2. | Arunachal Pradesh | 125 | 0.1 | 11.3 | 11.1 | 16 | 21 |
| 3. | Assam | 3388 | 2.6 | 256.5 | 13.2 | 12 | 13 |
| 4. | Bihar & Jharkhand | 7105 | 5.4 | 969.6 | 7.3 | 22 | 7 |
| 5. | Goa | 109 | 0.1 | 15.1 | 7.2 | 23 | 22 |
| 6. | Gujarat | 6658 | 5.1 | 471.0 | 14.1 | 11 | 9 |
| 7. | Haryana | 3002 | 2.3 | 193.4 | 15.5 | 8 | 14 |
| 8. | Himachal Pradesh | 778 | 0.6 | 64.2 | 12.1 | 14 | 18 |
| 9. | Jammu & Kashmir | 1715 | 1.3 | 95.4 | 18.0 | 5 | 16 |
| 10. | Karnataka | 5516 | 4.2 | 509.8 | 10.8 | 17 | 10 |
| 11. | Kerala | 4799 | 3.7 | 317.8 | 15.1 | 10 | 11 |
| 12. | Madhya Pradesh & Chhattisgarh | 15865 | 12.1 | 774.0 | 20.5 | 2 | 2 |
| 13. | Maharashtra | 14266 | 10.9 | 894.1 | 16.0 | 6 | 3 |
| 14. | Manipur | 86 | 0.1 | 23.9 | 3.6 | 28 | 24 |
| 15. | Meghalaya | 71 | 0.1 | 23.1 | 3.1 | 29 | 25 |

(Contd.)

(Annexure Contd.)

| (1) | (2) | (3) | (4) | (5) | (6) | (7) | (8) |
|---|---|---|---|---|---|---|---|
| 16. | Mizoram | 141 | 0.1 | 9.0 | 15.6 | 7 | 20 |
| 17. | Nagaland | 32 | 0.0 | 15.9 | 2.0 | 31 | 28 |
| 18. | Orissa | 4450 | 3.4 | 353.0 | 12.6 | 13 | 12 |
| 19. | Punjab | 1238 | 0.9 | 231.0 | 5.4 | 27 | 17 |
| 20. | Rajasthan | 12159 | 9.3 | 520.1 | 23.4 | 1 | 4 |
| 21. | Sikkim | 37 | 0.0 | 5.3 | 7.0 | 25 | 27 |
| 22. | Tamil Nadu | 11201 | 8.5 | 608.8 | 18.4 | 4 | 6 |
| 23. | Tripura | 319 | 0.2 | 35.8 | 8.9 | 20 | 19 |
| 24. | Uttar Pradesh & Uttaranchal | 17497 | 13.3 | 1640.4 | 10.7 | 18 | 1 |
| 25. | West Bengal | 6811 | 5.2 | 772.5 | 8.8 | 21 | 8 |
| | **Total (States)** | **128569** | **97.9** | **9552.6** | **13.5** | | |
| ***Union Territories*** | | | | | | | |
| 26. | A & N Islands | 26 | 0.0 | 3.7 | 7.1 | 24 | 29 |
| 27. | Chandigarh | 97 | 0.1 | 8.4 | 11.5 | 15 | 23 |
| 28. | D & N Haveli | 17 | 0.0 | 1.8 | 9.4 | 19 | 30 |
| 29. | Daman & Diu | 2 | 0.0 | 1.3 | 1.5 | 32 | 32 |
| 30. | Delhi | 2556 | 1.9 | 130.4 | 19.6 | 3 | 15 |
| 31. | Lakshadweep | 2 | 0.0 | 0.7 | 3.0 | 30 | 32 |
| 32. | Pondicherry | 69 | 0.1 | 10.5 | 6.6 | 26 | 26 |
| | **Total (UTs)** | **2769** | **2.1** | **156.8** | **17.7** | | |
| | **Total (All-India)** | **131338** | **100.0** | **9709.3** | **13.5** | | |

*Note:* 1. *Rank on the basis of Rate of total cognizable crimes (Col. 6).
2. **Rank on the basis of Percentage share (Col. 4).

## INCIDENCE OF CRIMES COMMITTED AGAINST WOMEN

| Sl. No. | State/UT | Est.Mid Year Population | Rape | | | Kidnapping & Abduction | | | Dowry Deaths | | | Cruelty by Husband and Relatives | | |
|---|---|---|---|---|---|---|---|---|---|---|---|---|---|---|
| | | | I | R | P | I | R | P | I | R | P | I | R | P |
| (1) | (2) | (3) | (4) | (5) | (6) | (7) | (8) | (9) | (10) | (11) | (12) | (13) | (14) | (15) |
| **States** | | | | | | | | | | | | | | |
| 1. | Andhra Pradesh | 741.7 | 869 | 1.2 | 5.8 | 738 | 1.0 | 4.5 | 500 | 0.7 | 7.2 | 4310 | 5.8 | 10.4 |
| 2. | Arunachal Pradesh | 11.3 | 32 | 2.8 | 0.2 | 38 | 3.4 | 0.2 | 0 | 0.0 | 0.0 | 8 | 0.7 | 0.0 |
| 3. | Assam | 256.5 | 744 | 2.9 | 4.9 | 1117 | 4.4 | 6.8 | 32 | 0.1 | 0.5 | 739 | 2.9 | 1.8 |
| 4. | Bihar & Jharkhand | 969.6 | 1421 | 1.5 | 9.5 | 1043 | 1.1 | 6.4 | 1039 | 1.1 | 15.0 | 1507 | 1.6 | 3.6 |
| 5. | Goa | 15.1 | 16 | 1.1 | 0.1 | 14 | 0.9 | 0.1 | 3 | 0.2 | 0.0 | 16 | 1.1 | 0.0 |
| 6. | Gujarat | 471.0 | 368 | 0.8 | 2.4 | 1182 | 2.5 | 7.2 | 90 | 0.2 | 1.3 | 3602 | 7.6 | 8.7 |
| 7. | Haryana | 193.4 | 364 | 1.9 | 2.4 | 318 | 1.6 | 1.9 | 309 | 1.6 | 4.5 | 977 | 5.1 | 2.4 |
| 8. | Himachal Pradesh | 64.2 | 128 | 2.0 | 0.9 | 115 | 1.8 | 0.7 | 7 | 0.1 | 0.1 | 228 | 3.5 | 0.6 |
| 9. | Jammu & Kashmir | 95.4 | 178 | 1.9 | 1.2 | 629 | 6.6 | 3.8 | 9 | 0.1 | 0.1 | 18 | 0.2 | 0.0 |
| 10. | Karnataka | 509.8 | 233 | 0.5 | 1.6 | 312 | 0.6 | 1.9 | 200 | 0.4 | 2.9 | 1501 | 2.9 | 3.6 |
| 11. | Kerala | 317.8 | 589 | 1.9 | 3.9 | 130 | 0.4 | 0.8 | 21 | 0.1 | 0.3 | 2125 | 6.7 | 5.1 |
| 12. | Madhya Pradesh & Chhattisgarh | 774.0 | 3354 | 4.3 | 22.3 | 925 | 1.2 | 5.6 | 598 | 0.8 | 8.6 | 2765 | 3.6 | 6.7 |
| 13. | Maharashtra | 894.1 | 1154 | 1.3 | 7.7 | 772 | 0.9 | 4.7 | 420 | 0.5 | 6.1 | 7728 | 8.6 | 18.7 |
| 14. | Manipur | 23.9 | 13 | 0.5 | 0.1 | 60 | 2.5 | 0.4 | 0 | 0.0 | 0.0 | 0 | 0.0 | 0.0 |
| 15. | Meghalaya | 23.1 | 42 | 1.8 | 0.3 | 16 | 0.7 | 0.1 | 1 | 0.0 | 0.0 | 0 | 0.0 | 0.0 |

*(Contd.)*

*(Annexure Contd.)*

| (1) | (2) | (3) | (4) | (5) | (6) | (7) | (8) | (9) | (10) | (11) | (12) | (13) | (14) | (15) |
|---|---|---|---|---|---|---|---|---|---|---|---|---|---|---|
| 16. | Mizoram | 9.0 | 84 | 9.3 | 0.6 | 4 | 0.4 | 0.0 | 0 | 0.0 | 0.0 | 0 | 0.0 | 0.0 |
| 17. | Nagaland | 15.9 | 13 | 0.8 | 0.1 | 14 | 0.9 | 0.1 | 0 | 0.0 | 0.0 | 0 | 0.0 | 0.0 |
| 18. | Orissa | 353.0 | 679 | 1.9 | 4.5 | 514 | 1.5 | 3.1 | 240 | 0.7 | 3.5 | 935 | 2.6 | 2.3 |
| 19. | Punjab | 231.0 | 219 | 0.9 | 1.5 | 222 | 1.0 | 1.4 | 219 | 0.9 | 3.2 | 397 | 1.7 | 1.0 |
| 20. | Rajasthan | 520.1 | 1266 | 2.4 | 8.4 | 2499 | 4.8 | 15.3 | 433 | 0.8 | 6.3 | 4947 | 9.5 | 12.0 |
| 21. | Sikkim | 5.3 | 7 | 1.3 | 0.0 | 4 | 0.8 | 0.0 | 0 | 0.0 | 0.0 | 2 | 0.4 | 0.0 |
| 22. | Tamil Nadu | 608.8 | 362 | 0.6 | 2.4 | 993 | 1.6 | 6.1 | 176 | 0.3 | 2.5 | 440 | 0.7 | 1.1 |
| 23. | Tripura | 35.8 | 73 | 2.0 | 0.5 | 39 | 1.1 | 0.2 | 10 | 0.3 | 0.1 | 115 | 3.2 | 0.3 |
| 24. | Uttar Pradesh & Uttaranchal | 1640.4 | 1605 | 1.0 | 10.7 | 2882 | 1.8 | 17.6 | 2229 | 1.4 | 32.2 | 5113 | 3.1 | 12.4 |
| 25. | West Bengal | 772.5 | 757 | 1.0 | 5.0 | 783 | 1.0 | 4.8 | 249 | 0.3 | 3.6 | 3704 | 4.8 | 9.0 |
| | **Total States** | **9552.6** | **14570** | **1.5** | **96.9** | **15363** | **1.6** | **93.8** | **6785** | **0.7** | **98.1** | **41177** | **4.3** | **99.7** |
| ***Union Territories*** | | | | | | | | | | | | | | |
| 26. | A & N Islands | 3.7 | 4 | 1.1 | 0.0 | 2 | 0.5 | 0.0 | 0 | 0.0 | 0.0 | 3 | 0.8 | 0.0 |
| 27. | Chandigarh | 8.4 | 11 | 1.3 | 0.1 | 31 | 3.7 | 0.2 | 5 | 0.6 | 0.1 | 25 | 3.0 | 0.1 |
| 28. | D & N Haveli | 1.8 | 7 | 3.9 | 0.0 | 2 | 1.1 | 0.0 | 0 | 0.0 | 0.0 | 7 | 3.9 | 0.0 |
| 29. | Daman & Diu | 1.3 | 0 | 0.0 | 0.0 | 0 | 0.0 | 0.0 | 0 | 0.0 | 0.0 | 1 | 0.8 | 0.0 |
| 30. | Delhi | 130.4 | 438 | 3.4 | 2.9 | 978 | 7.5 | 6.0 | 126 | 1.0 | 1.8 | 103 | 0.8 | 0.2 |
| 31. | Lakshadweep | 0.7 | 0 | 0.0 | 0.0 | 0 | 0.0 | 0.0 | 0 | 0.0 | 0.0 | 1 | 1.5 | 0.0 |
| 32. | Pondicherry | 10.5 | 1 | 0.1 | 0.0 | 5 | 0.5 | 0.0 | 1 | 0.1 | 0.0 | 1 | 0.1 | 0.0 |
| | **Total (UTs)** | **156.8** | **461** | **2.9** | **3.1** | **1018** | **6.5** | **6.2** | **132** | **0.8** | **1.9** | **141** | **0.9** | **0.3** |
| | **Total (All-India)** | **9709.3** | **15031** | **1.5** | **100.0** | **16381** | **1.7** | **100.0** | **6917** | **0.7** | **100.0** | **41318** | **4.3** | **100.0** |

*(Contd.)*

*(Annexure Contd.)*

| Sl. No. | State/UT | Molestation | | | Eve-Teasing | | | Importing of Girls | | | Sati Pre. Act | | |
|---|---|---|---|---|---|---|---|---|---|---|---|---|---|
| | | I | R | P | I | R | P | I | R | P | I | R | P |
| (1) | (2) | (16) | (17) | (18) | (19) | (20) | (21) | (22) | (23) | (24) | (25) | (26) | (27) |
| **States** | | | | | | | | | | | | | |
| 1. | Andhra Pradesh | 2967 | 4.0 | 9.6 | 1050 | 1.4 | 12.9 | 8 | 0.0 | 5.5 | 0 | 0.0 | - |
| 2. | Arunachal Pradesh | 46 | 4.1 | 0.1 | 1 | 0.1 | 0.0 | 0 | 0.0 | 0.0 | 0 | 0.0 | - |
| 3. | Assam | 648 | 2.5 | 2.1 | 12 | 0.0 | 0.1 | 0 | 0.0 | 0.0 | 0 | 0.0 | - |
| 4. | Bihar & Jharkhand | 432 | 0.4 | 1.4 | 89 | 0.1 | 1.1 | 1 | 0.0 | 0.7 | 0 | 0.0 | - |
| 5. | Goa | 22 | 1.5 | 0.1 | 8 | 0.5 | 0.1 | 0 | 0.0 | 0.0 | 0 | 0.0 | - |
| 6. | Gujarat | 1210 | 2.6 | 3.9 | 139 | 0.3 | 1.7 | 57 | 0.1 | 39.0 | 0 | 0.0 | - |
| 7. | Haryana | 611 | 3.2 | 2.0 | 385 | 2.0 | 4.7 | 25 | 0.1 | 17.1 | 0 | 0.0 | - |
| 8. | Himachal Pradesh | 283 | 4.4 | 0.9 | 15 | 0.2 | 0.2 | 0 | 0.0 | 0.0 | 0 | 0.0 | - |
| 9. | Jammu & Kashmir | 516 | 5.4 | 1.7 | 361 | 3.8 | 4.4 | 0 | 0.0 | 0.0 | 0 | 0.0 | - |
| 10. | Karnataka | 1340 | 2.6 | 4.3 | 139 | 0.3 | 1.7 | 0 | 0.0 | 0.0 | 0 | 0.0 | - |
| 11. | Kerala | 1773 | 5.6 | 5.7 | 96 | 0.3 | 1.2 | 0 | 0.0 | 0.0 | 0 | 0.0 | - |
| 12. | Madhya Pradesh & Chhattisgarh | 7310 | 9.4 | 23.5 | 741 | 1.0 | 9.1 | 26 | 0.0 | 17.8 | 0 | 0.0 | - |
| 13. | Maharashtra | 2923 | 3.3 | 9.4 | 765 | 0.9 | 9.4 | 0 | 0.0 | 0.0 | 0 | 0.0 | - |
| 14. | Manipur | 13 | 0.5 | 0.0 | 0 | 0.0 | 0.0 | 0 | 0.0 | 0.0 | 0 | 0.0 | - |
| 15. | Meghalaya | 12 | 0.5 | 0.0 | 0 | 0.0 | 0.0 | 0 | 0.0 | 0.0 | 0 | 0.0 | - |
| 16. | Mizoram | 53 | 5.9 | 0.2 | 0 | 0.0 | 0.0 | 0 | 0.0 | 0.0 | 0 | 0.0 | - |

*(Contd.)*

*(Annexure Contd.)*

| (1) | (2) | (16) | (17) | (18) | (19) | (20) | (21) | (22) | (23) | (24) | (25) | (26) | (27) |
|---|---|---|---|---|---|---|---|---|---|---|---|---|---|
| 17. | Nagaland | 4 | 0.3 | 0.0 | 0 | 0.0 | 0.0 | 0 | 0.0 | 0.0 | 0 | 0.0 | - |
| 18. | Orissa | 1586 | 4.5 | 5.1 | 234 | 0.7 | 2.9 | 0 | 0.0 | 0.0 | 0 | 0.0 | - |
| 19. | Punjab | 150 | 0.6 | 0.5 | 10 | 0.0 | 0.1 | 7 | 0.0 | 4.8 | 0 | 0.0 | - |
| 20. | Rajasthan | 2908 | 5.6 | 9.4 | 54 | 0.1 | 0.7 | 3 | 0.0 | 2.1 | 0 | 0.0 | - |
| 21. | Sikkim | 22 | 4.3 | 0.1 | 2 | 0.4 | 0.0 | 0 | 0.0 | 0.0 | 0 | 0.0 | - |
| 22. | Tamil Nadu | 1779 | 2.9 | 5.7 | 1230 | 2.0 | 15.1 | 5 | 0.0 | 3.4 | 0 | 0.0 | - |
| 23. | Tripura | 73 | 2.0 | 0.2 | 0 | 0.0 | 0.0 | 9 | 0.3 | 6.2 | 0 | 0.0 | - |
| 24. | Uttar Pradesh & Uttaranchal | 2423 | 1.5 | 7.8 | 2571 | 1.6 | 31.7 | 3 | 0.0 | 2.1 | 0 | 0.0 | - |
| 25. | West Bengal | 1243 | 1.6 | 4.0 | 27 | 0.0 | 0.3 | 2 | 0.0 | 1.4 | 0 | 0.0 | - |
| | **Total States** | **30347** | **3.2** | **97.7** | **7929** | **0.8** | **97.6** | **146** | **0.0** | **100.0** | **0** | **0.0** | **-** |
| ***Union Territories*** | | | | | | | | | | | | | |
| 26. | A & N Islands | 15 | 4.1 | 0.0 | 2 | 0.5 | 0.0 | 0 | 0.0 | 0.0 | 0 | 0.0 | - |
| 27. | Chandigarh | 10 | 1.2 | 0.0 | 10 | 1.2 | 0.1 | 0 | 0.0 | 0.0 | 0 | 0.0 | - |
| 28. | D & N Haveli | 1 | 0.6 | 0.0 | 0 | 0.0 | 0.0 | 0 | 0.0 | 0.0 | 0 | 0.0 | - |
| 29. | Daman & Diu | 0 | 0.0 | 0.0 | 1 | 0.8 | 0.0 | 0 | 0.0 | 0.0 | 0 | 0.0 | - |
| 30. | Delhi | 653 | 5.0 | 2.1 | 172 | 1.3 | 2.1 | 0 | 0.0 | 0.0 | 0 | 0.0 | - |
| 31. | Lakshadweep | 1 | 1.5 | 0.0 | 0 | 0.0 | 0.0 | 0 | 0.0 | 0.0 | 0 | 0.0 | - |
| 32. | Pondicherry | 19 | 1.8 | 0.1 | 9 | 0.9 | 0.1 | 0 | 0.0 | 0.0 | 0 | 0.0 | - |
| | **Total (UTs)** | **699** | **4.5** | **2.3** | **194** | **1.2** | **2.4** | **0** | **0.0** | **0.0** | **0** | **0.0** | **-** |
| | **Total (All-India)** | **31046** | **3.2** | **100.0** | **8123** | **0.8** | **100.0** | **146** | **0.0** | **100.0** | **0** | **0.0** | **-** |

*(Contd.)*

(Annexure Contd.)

| Sl. No. | State/UT | ITP Act | | | Ind. Rep. of Women (P) Act | | | Dowry Proh. Act | | | Total | | |
|---|---|---|---|---|---|---|---|---|---|---|---|---|---|
| | | I | R | P | I | R | P | I | R | P | I | R | P |
| (1) | (2) | (23) | (29) | (30) | (31) | (32) | (33) | (34) | (35) | (36) | (37) | (38) | (39) |
| **States** | | | | | | | | | | | | | |
| 1. | Andhra Pradesh | 507 | 0.7 | 5.8 | 40 | 0.1 | 20.8 | 212 | 0.3 | 6.1 | 11201 | 15.1 | 8.5 |
| 2. | Arunachal Pradesh | 0 | 0.0 | 0.0 | 0 | 0.0 | 0.0 | 0 | 0.0 | 0.0 | 125 | 11.1 | 0.1 |
| 3. | Assam | 34 | 0.1 | 0.4 | 0 | 0.0 | 0.0 | 62 | 0.2 | 1.8 | 3388 | 13.2 | 2.6 |
| 4. | Bihar & Jharkhand | 37 | 0.0 | 0.4 | 48 | 0.0 | 25.0 | 1488 | 1.5 | 42.6 | 7105 | 7.3 | 5.4 |
| 5. | Goa | 30 | 2.0 | 0.3 | 0 | 0.0 | 0.0 | 0 | 0.0 | 0.0 | 109 | 7.2 | 0.1 |
| 6. | Gujarat | 8 | 0.0 | 0.1 | 2 | 0.0 | 1.0 | 0 | 0.0 | 0.0 | 6658 | 14.1 | 5.1 |
| 7. | Haryana | 4 | 0.0 | 0.0 | 1 | 0.0 | 0.5 | 8 | 0.0 | 0.2 | 3002 | 15.5 | 2.3 |
| 8. | Himachal Pradesh | [illegible] | 0.0 | 0.0 | 0 | 0.0 | 0.0 | 1 | 0.0 | 0.0 | 778 | 12.1 | 0.6 |
| 9. | Jammu & Kashmir | 1 | 0.0 | 0.0 | 0 | 0.0 | 0.0 | 3 | 0.0 | 0.1 | 1715 | 18.0 | 1.3 |
| 10. | Karnataka | 1403 | 2.8 | 16.1 | 4 | 0.0 | 2.1 | 384 | 0.8 | 11.0 | 5516 | 10.8 | 4.2 |
| 11. | Kerala | 27 | 0.1 | 0.3 | 30 | 0.1 | 15.6 | 8 | 0.0 | 0.2 | 4799 | 15.1 | 3.7 |
| 12. | Madhya Pradesh & Chhattisgarh | 16 | 0.0 | 0.2 | 2 | 0.0 | 1.0 | 128 | 0.2 | 3.7 | 15865 | 20.5 | 12.1 |
| 13. | Maharashtra | 444 | 0.5 | 5.1 | 36 | 0.0 | 18.8 | 24 | 0.0 | 0.7 | 14266 | 16.0 | 10.9 |
| 14. | Manipur | 0 | 0.0 | 0.0 | 0 | 0.0 | 0.0 | 0 | 0.0 | 0.0 | 86 | 3.6 | 0.1 |
| 15. | Meghalaya | 0 | 0.0 | 0.0 | 0 | 0.0 | 0.0 | 0 | 0.0 | 0.0 | 71 | 3.1 | 0.1 |
| 16. | Mizoram | 0 | 0.0 | 0.0 | 0 | 0.0 | 0.0 | 0 | 0.0 | 0.0 | 141 | 15.6 | 0.1 |

(Contd.)

*(Annexure Contd.)*

| *(1)* | *(2)* | *(28)* | *(29)* | *(30)* | *(31)* | *(32)* | *(33)* | *(34)* | *(35)* | *(36)* | *(37)* | *(38)* | *(39)* |
|---|---|---|---|---|---|---|---|---|---|---|---|---|---|
| 17. | Nagaland | 0 | 0.0 | 0.0 | 1 | 0.1 | 0.5 | 0 | 0.0 | 0.0 | 32 | 2.0 | 0.0 |
| 18. | Orissa | 11 | 0.0 | 0.1 | 2 | 0.0 | 1.0 | 249 | 0.7 | 7.1 | 4450 | 12.6 | 3.4 |
| 19. | Punjab | 5 | 0.0 | 0.1 | 7 | 0.0 | 3.6 | 2 | 0.0 | 0.1 | 1238 | 5.4 | 0.9 |
| 20. | Rajasthan | 47 | 0.1 | 0.5 | 1 | 0.0 | 0.5 | 1 | 0.0 | 0.0 | 12159 | 23.4 | 9.3 |
| 21. | Sikkim | 0 | 0.0 | 0.0 | 0 | 0.0 | 0.0 | 0 | 0.0 | 0.0 | 37 | 7.0 | 0.0 |
| 22. | Tamil Nadu | 5937 | 9.8 | 68.3 | 10 | 0.0 | 5.2 | 269 | 0.4 | 7.7 | 11201 | 18.4 | 8.5 |
| 23. | Tripura | 0 | 0.0 | 0.0 | 0 | 0.0 | 0.0 | 0 | 0.0 | 0.0 | 319 | 8.9 | 0.2 |
| 24. | Uttar Pradesh & Uttaranchal | 31 | 0.0 | 0.4 | 7 | 0..0 | 3.6 | 633 | 0.4 | 18.1 | 17497 | 10.7 | 13.3 |
| 25. | West Bengal | 43 | 0.1 | 0.5 | 0 | 0.0 | 0.0 | 3 | 0.0 | 0.1 | 6811 | 8.8 | 5.2 |
| | **Total (States)** | **8586** | **0.9** | **98.7** | **191** | **0.0** | **99.5** | **3475** | **0.4** | **99.6** | **128569** | **13.5** | **97.9** |
| ***Union Territories*** | | | | | | | | | | | | | |
| 26. | A & N Islands | 0 | 0.0 | 0.0 | 0 | 0.0 | 0.0 | 0 | 0.0 | 0.0 | 26 | 7.1 | 0.0 |
| 27. | Chandigarh | 5 | 0.6 | 0.1 | 0 | 0.0 | 0.0 | 0 | 0.0 | 0.0 | 97 | 11.5 | 0.1 |
| 28. | D & N Haveli | 0 | 0.0 | 0.0 | 0 | 0.0 | 0.0 | 0 | 0.0 | 0.0 | 17 | 9.4 | 0.0 |
| 29. | Daman & Diu | 0 | 0.0 | 0.0 | 0 | 0.0 | 0.0 | 0 | 0.0 | 0.0 | 2 | 1.5 | 0.0 |
| 30. | Delhi | 75 | 0.6 | 0.9 | 1 | 0.0 | 0.5 | 10 | 0.1 | 0.3 | 2556 | 19.6 | 1.9 |
| 31. | Lakshadweep | 0 | 0.0 | 0.0 | 0 | 0.0 | 0.0 | 0 | 0.0 | 0.0 | 2 | 3.0 | 0.0 |
| 32. | Pondicherry | 29 | 2.8 | 0.3 | 0 | 0.0 | 0.0 | 4 | 0.4 | 0.1 | 69 | 6.6 | 0.1 |
| | **Total (UTs)** | **109** | **0.7** | **1.3** | **1** | **0.0** | **0.5** | **14** | **0.1** | **0.4** | **2769** | **17.7** | **2.1** |
| | **Total (All-India)** | **8695** | **0.9** | **100.0** | **192** | **0.0** | **100.0** | **3489** | **0.4** | **100.0** | **131338** | **13.5** | **100.0** |

* In absence of data for newly created crime heads in crime in India data. Figures of monthly crime statistics have been used against Daman & Diu UT.

*Source:* Crime in India data except col. 21 which is based on Monthly crime statistics.
I: Incidence; R: Rate; P: Percentage.

## DISPOSAL OF CRIMES AGAINST WOMEN CASES BY POLICE

| Sl. No. | Crime Head | Total No. of cases for investigation including pending cases | | Percentage of cases investigated | | Percentage of cases charge-sheeted | | No. of cases pending investigation | | Percentage of cases pending investigation | |
|---|---|---|---|---|---|---|---|---|---|---|---|
| | | 1997 | 1998 | 1997 | 1998 | 1997 | 1998 | 1997 | 1998 | 1997 | 1998 |
| 1. | Rape | 20736 | 20864 | 71.7 | 72.1 | 62.4 | 62.1 | 5828 | 5793 | 28.1 | 27.8 |
| 2. | Kidnapping and Abduction | 23448 | 24966 | 62.8 | 61.3 | 36.1 | 35.9 | 8586 | 9565 | 36.6 | 38.3 |
| 3. | Dowry Deaths | 7543 | 8938 | 72.3 | 72.7 | 63.5 | 63.8 | 2048 | 2393 | 21.2 | 26.8 |
| 4. | Molestation | 34937 | 35594 | 86.8 | 85.0 | 79.1 | 77.0 | 4528 | 5306 | 13.0 | 14.9 |
| 5. | Sexual Harassment | 6131 | 8578 | 92.4 | 92.1 | 89.3 | 88.3 | 461 | 668 | 7.5 | 7.8 |
| 6. | Cruelty by Husband and Relatives | 43130 | 49532 | 80.5 | 79.1 | 67.9 | 65.9 | 8268 | 10248 | 19.2 | 20.7 |
| 7. | Immoral Traffic (Prevention) Act | 9076 | 9895 | 86.8 | 89.3 | 86.5 | 89.1 | 1198 | 1062 | 13.2 | 10.7 |
| 8. | Dowry Prohibition Act | 3853 | 4649 | 70.8 | 75.3 | 59.3 | 62.4 | 1100 | 1142 | 28.6 | 24.6 |
| 9. | Indecent Rep. of Women (P) Act | 96 | 206 | 85.4 | 80.1 | 81.3 | 62.1 | 14 | 41 | 14.6 | 19.9 |
| 10. | Sati Prevention Act | 1 | 0 | 100.0 | | 100.0 | | 0 | 0 | 0.0 | - |

*Note:* Similar details for importation of girls (upto 21 years of age) are not available.

## DISPOSAL OF CRIME AGAINST WOMEN CASES BY COURTS

| *Sl. No.* | *Crime Head* | *Total No. of Cases for Trial Including Pending Cases* | | *Percentage of Cases Tried* | | *Percentage of of Cases Convicted* | | *No. of Cases Pending Trial* | | *Percentage of Cases PendingTrial* | |
|---|---|---|---|---|---|---|---|---|---|---|---|
| | | *1997* | *1998* | *1997* | *1998* | *1997* | *1998* | *1997* | *1998* | *1997* | *1998* |
| 1. | Rape | 55863 | 58655 | 17.4 | 16.6 | 4.9 | 4.4 | 45955 | 48685 | 82.3 | 83.0 |
| 2. | Kidnapping and Abduction | 44262 | 46165 | 14.7 | 14.5 | 3.9 | 4.0 | 37254 | 39103 | 84.2 | 84.7 |
| 3. | Dowry Deaths | 19435 | 22055 | 14.8 | 15.2 | 5.2 | 4.9 | 16455 | 18523 | 84.7 | 84.0 |
| 4. | Molestation | 100654 | 105204 | 17.1 | 14.1 | 6.3 | 4.3 | 78200 | 84869 | 77.7 | 80.7 |
| 5. | Sexual Harassment | 14130 | 16945 | 29.5 | 23.9 | 18.0 | 14.4 | 9437 | 12407 | 66.8 | 73.2 |
| 6. | Cruelty by Husband and Relatives | 13181 | 127691 | 13.0 | 13.2 | 3.1 | 2.6 | 95409 | 107192 | 84.3 | 84.0 |
| 7. | Immoral Traffic (Prevention) Act | 12660 | 14302 | 54.1 | 56.8 | 49.4 | 53.1 | 5505 | 6134 | 43.5 | 42.9 |
| 8. | Dowry Prohibition Act | 8295 | 8974 | 22.7 | 17.8 | 8.3 | 5.7 | 6186 | 7223 | 74.6 | 80.5 |
| 9. | Indecent Rep of Women (P) Act | 578 | 625 | 13.3 | 13.4 | 6.2 | 7.4 | 499 | 538 | 86.3 | 86.1 |
| 10. | Sati Prevention Act | 4 | 1 | 0.0 | 100.0 | 0.0 | 0.0 | 1 | 0 | 25.0 | 0.0 |

## VICTIMS OF RAPE UNDER DIFFERENT AGE GROUPS

| Sl. No. | State/UT/City | No. of Cases Reported | Number of Victims | | | |
|---|---|---|---|---|---|---|
| | | | Below 10 Years | 10-16 Years | 16-30 Years | 30 Years & Above |
| (1) | (2) | (3) | (4) | (5) | (6) | (7) |
| | **States** | | | | | |
| 1. | Andhra Pradesh | 869 | 57 | 231 | 427 | 154 |
| 2. | Arunachal Pradesh | 32 | 3 | 7 | 20 | 2 |
| 3. | Assam | 744 | 25 | 184 | 460 | 75 |
| 4. | Bihar & Jharkhand | 1421 | 4 | 193 | 919 | 305 |
| 5. | Goa | 16 | 1 | 5 | 9 | 1 |
| 6. | Gujarat | 368 | 27 | 108 | 193 | 40 |
| 7. | Haryana | 364 | 25 | 106 | 177 | 56 |
| 8. | Himachal Pradesh | 128 | 5 | 28 | 81 | 14 |
| 9. | Jammu & Kashmir | 178 | 0 | 15 | 135 | 28 |
| 10. | Karnataka | 233 | 15 | 64 | 119 | 35 |
| 11. | Kerala | 589 | 25 | 146 | 352 | 66 |
| 12. | Madhya Pradesh & Chhattisgarh | 3354 | 81 | 725 | 1882 | 666 |
| 13. | Maharashtra | 1154 | 79 | 373 | 522 | 180 |
| 14. | Manipur | 13 | 2 | 5 | 4 | 2 |
| 15. | Meghalaya | 42 | 4 | 7 | 29 | 2 |
| 16. | Mizoram | 84 | 20 | 29 | 28 | 7 |
| 17. | Nagaland | 13 | 1 | 3 | 9 | 0 |
| 18. | Orissa | 679 | 11 | 111 | 437 | 120 |
| 19. | Punjab | 219 | 13 | 78 | 104 | 24 |
| 20. | Rajasthan | 1266 | 25 | 132 | 755 | 354 |
| 21. | Sikkim | 7 | 2 | 0 | 3 | 2 |
| 22. | Tamil Nadu | 362 | 16 | 75 | 233 | 38 |
| 23. | Tripura | 73 | 2 | 14 | 57 | 0 |
| 24. | Uttar Pradesh & Uttaranchal | 1605 | 98 | 418 | 845 | 244 |
| 25. | West Bengal | 757 | 15 | 199 | 455 | 88 |
| | **Total States** | **14570** | **556** | **3256** | **8255** | **2503** |

*(Contd.)*

*(Contd.)*

| (1) | (2) | (3) | (4) | (5) | (6) | (7) |
|---|---|---|---|---|---|---|
| ***Union Territories*** | | | | | | |
| 26. | A & N Islands | 4 | 0 | 2 | 2 | 0 |
| 27. | Chandigarh | 11 | 2 | 2 | 4 | 3 |
| 28. | D & N Haveli | 7 | 1 | 1 | 5 | 0 |
| 29. | Daman & Diu | 0 | 0 | 0 | 0 | 0 |
| 30. | Delhi | 438 | 67 | 172 | 147 | 54 |
| 31. | Lakshadweep | 0 | 0 | 0 | 0 | 0 |
| 32. | Pondicherry | 1 | 0 | 0 | 1 | 0 |
| | **Total UTs** | **461** | **70** | **177** | **159** | **57** |
| | **Total (ALL-INDIA)** | **15031** | **626** | **3433** | **8414** | **2560** |
| ***Cities*** | | | | | | |
| 33. | | 20 | 3 | 9 | 7 | 1 |
| 34. | Bangalore | 41 | 4 | 13 | 20 | 4 |
| 35. | Bhopal | 39 | 0 | 8 | 17 | 14 |
| 36. | Calcutta | 27 | 7 | 4 | 15 | 1 |
| 37. | Chennai | 24 | 0 | 6 | 18 | 0 |
| 38. | Coimbatore | 2 | 1 | 1 | 0 | 0 |
| 39. | Delhi* | 365 | 56 | 143 | 122 | 46 |
| 40. | Hyderabad | 36 | 7 | 16 | 7 | 6 |
| 41. | Indore | 30 | 1 | 2 | 25 | 2 |
| 42. | Jaipur | 38 | 1 | 7 | 23 | 7 |
| 43. | Kanpur | 41 | 4 | 5 | 25 | 7 |
| 44. | Kochi | 10 | 0 | 5 | 3 | 2 |
| 45. | Lucknow | 23 | 0 | 4 | 17 | 2 |
| 46. | Ludhiana | 17 | 3 | 12 | 2 | 0 |
| 47. | Madurai | 3 | 0 | 3 | 0 | 0 |
| 48. | Mumbai | 118 | 9 | 56 | 48 | 5 |
| 49. | Nagpur | 53 | 8 | 15 | 28 | 2 |
| 50. | Patna | 16 | 0 | 0 | 13 | 3 |
| 51. | Pune | 56 | 4 | 21 | 27 | 4 |
| 52. | Surat | 31 | 2 | 10 | 15 | 4 |
| 53. | Vadodara | 9 | 0 | 3 | 6 | 0 |
| 54. | Varanasi | 8 | 0 | 3 | 5 | 0 |
| 55. | Vishakhapatnam | 11 | 0 | 3 | 8 | 0 |

*Note:* *Victims were more than the cases reported.

# Bibliography


Albari, K.M., *Women, a Vulnerable Lot*, Mumbai, 1985.

Altekar, A.S., *The Position of Women in Hindu Civilization*, Varanasi: Motilal Banarsidas, 1962.

Anshen, R.N., (ed.), *The Family: Its Functions and Destiny*, New York: Harper & Row, 1959.

Asthana, P., *Women's Movement in India*, Delhi: Vikas Publishing House, 1974.

Baig, T.A., *India's Women Power*, New Delhi: S. Chand & Co., 1976.

Bhasin, K. (ed.), *The Position of Women in India*, Bombay: Leslie Sawny, 1971.

Blalock, H.M. and Blalock, A.B., *Methodology in Social Research*, New York: McGraw-Hill, 1969.

Blau, P. (ed.), *Focus on Social Structure*, and Introduction to the Programme of the ASA meeting in Montreal, 1974.

Blau, P.M., A Macrosociological Theory of Social Structure, *American Journal of Sociology*, 1977.

Brayfield, A.H. and Crockatt, W.H., Employee attitude and employee performance, *Psychological Bulletin*, 1955.

Burke, P.J. and Reitzes, D.C., An Identity Theory Approach to Commitment, *Social Psychological Quarterly*, 1991.

Caplow, T., *Sociology of Work*, Mc-Graw-Hill, New York, 1954.

Chaturvedi, Geeta., *Women Administration in India: A study of the socio-economic background*, Jaipur, RBSA Publication, 1985.

Cofer, C.N. and Appley, M.N., *Motivation Theory and Research,* A Wiley International Edition, John Wiley and Sons Inc., 1964.

Deckard, B.S, *The Women's Movement*, Harper and Row, New York, 1979.

Drucker, P.F., *An Introductory View of Management*, Harper College Press, New York, 1977.

Evan, M. William, *Organizational Theory Structure, Systems and Environments*, Wiley Interscience Publications, John Wiley and Sons Inc, London: 1976.

Fleishman, E.A., A Relationship Between Incentive, Motivation and Ability Level in Psychomotor, *J. Exp. Psychol.*

French, Elizabeth, G., Effects of Interaction of Achievement Motivation and Intelligence on Problem Solving Success, *American Psychologist*, 1951.

Giri Mohini, *Kanya,* Gyan Publishing House, New Delhi, 1998.

Good, W.J., *World Revolution and Family Patterns*, London: CollierMacMillan, 1963.

Gorwaney, N., *Self Image and Social Change: A Study of Female Students*, Delhi: Sterling Publishers, 1977.

Hate, C.A., *Changing Status of Women in Post-Independence India*, Bombay: Allied Publications, 1969.

Inkeles, A. and Smith, D., *Becoming Modern*, London: Heinmann Educational Books Ltd., 1974.

Kuppuswamy, B., *Social Change in India*, Delhi: Vikas Publishing House, 1972.

Mead, M., Adolescence Issue, *UNICEF News*, 1974.

Marshall, Katherine, Employed Parents and Division of Housework, *Perspectives*, Autumn, 1993.

Mies, M., *Indian Women and Patriarchy: Conflicts and Dilemmas of Students and Working Women.* Concept Publishers, New Delhi, 1980.

Myrdal, A. and Klien, V., *Woman's Two Roles*, Routledge & K. Paul, London, 1968.

Noditch, Murray, P. and Demaw, T., Locus of Control and Competence. *Journal of Personality*. Dec. 1975.

Prakash, G., *After Colonialism: Imperial Histories and Post Colonial Displacements*, Princeton University Press, Princeton, 1995.

Rajawat Mamta, *Human Rights: Burning Issues,* Gyan Publishing House, New Delhi, 2002.

Rani, K., *Role Conflict in Working Wives*, Chetana Publications, New Delhi, 1976.

Roby, Pamela, *Women in the Work Place*, MA. Schenkrnan, Cambridge, 1981.

Rotter, J.B., Generalized expectancies for internal versus external control or reinforcement. Psychological Monographs. General Applied, 1966.

Safilios-Rothschild, C., The Influence of the Wife's Degree of Work Commitment upon Some Aspects of Family Organization and Dynamics, *Journal of Marriage and the Family*, 1970.

Taylor, Ronald, N., Age and experience as determinants of managerial information processing and decision making performance. *Academy of Management, Journal*, 1975.

Tolman, E.C., Principles of Purposive Behavior. In S. Koch (ed.)

Vitels, M.S., *Motivation and Morale in Industry*. New York: Morton 1953.

Watson, T., *Management Organization and Employment Strategy*, Routledge and Kegan Paul, London, 1986.

Whyte, F.W., *Money and Motivation*, Harper and Row. Inc., New York: 1955.

Zaheer M, *The Myth of Protection,* Nile Publications, Cairo, 2001.

# References


Gender Indicators of Developing Asian and Pacific Countries, 1993, Asian Development Bank.

Human Development Report, UNDP, New York: Oxford University Press, 1996.

Report of the Committee on Status of Women in India (1974), *Towards Equality*. Department of Social Welfare, Government of India, New Delhi.

# Index